MW01199072

The Political Philosophy
of George Washington

THE POLITICAL PHILOSOPHY OF THE
AMERICAN FOUNDERS

Garrett Ward Sheldon, Series Editor

PATRIÆ PATER

Washington.

From the Original Portrait Painted by Rembrandt Peale.

THE

POLITICAL PHILOSOPHY

OF

George Washington

JEFFRY H. MORRISON

The Johns Hopkins University Press
Baltimore

© 2009 The Johns Hopkins University Press
All rights reserved. Published 2009
Printed in the United States of America on acid-free paper
2 4 6 8 9 7 5 3 1

The Johns Hopkins University Press
2715 North Charles Street
Baltimore, Maryland 21218-4363
www.press.jhu.edu

Library of Congress Cataloging-in-Publication Data

Morrison, Jeffry H., 1961–
The political philosophy of George Washington / Jeffry H. Morrison.
p.   cm. — (The political philosophy of the American founders)
Includes bibliographical references and index.
ISBN-13: 978-0-8018-9109-0 (hardcover : alk. paper)
ISBN-10: 0-8018-9109-4 (hardcover : alk. paper)
1. Washington, George, 1732–1799—Political and social views.   2. Political
science—Philosophy.   I. Title.
JC211.W37M67 2008
320.5092—dc22
2008021239

A catalog record for this book
is available from the British Library.

Frontispiece: Portrait by Rembrandt Peale c. 1827.
Courtesy of National Portrait Gallery,
Smithsonian Institution, Washington, D.C.

Special discounts are available for bulk purchases of this book.
For more information, please contact Special Sales at 410-516-6936
or specialsales@press.jhu.edu.

The Johns Hopkins University Press uses environmentally friendly book
materials, including recycled text paper that is composed of at least 30 percent
post-consumer waste, whenever possible. All of our book papers are acid-free,
and our jackets and covers are printed on paper with recycled content.

FOR
Alex

In all Causes of Passion admit Reason to Govern.
—George Washington's "Rules of Civility,"
Number 58, 1747

CONTENTS

PREFACE

EVEN DURING THE genteel eighteenth century, George Washington managed to earn a reputation for standoffishness. Rather than shake hands, he preferred to bow from the waist; this habit caused his critics to suspect monarchical tendencies in the first president. The children who lived in Washington's home were cowed into silence when he entered the room. In our own age, when presidents are expected to "feel our pain," the Father of His Country continues to hold us at arm's length; after all, it is hard to embrace a secular god. So attempts to humanize Washington abound. As they recently completed the new interpretive museum at Mount Vernon, the historians and staff there undertook what Director James Rees called a "search for the real George Washington," one partly inspired by efforts to create a three-dimensional image of Jesus of Nazareth from the Shroud of Turin.[1] The Mount Vernon project has produced lifelike figures of Washington at various ages, not only as we think of him today (old) but also as a young man of nineteen, and in his prime as the forty-five-year-old commander of the Continental Army. Because he was deified in the nineteenth century, and remains a popular icon in the twenty-first, Americans feel the need to make Washington approachable, to bring him down to earth from our patriotic heaven. Above all we want to know Washington as he really was: no longer content with a myth, we want the real man.

One way to approach the real Washington, and a relatively untried one, is to recreate him as a political thinker and actor. That is the aim of this book, as well as to provide a brief readable introduction to Washington's political thought and the ideologies of his day.[2] But although books about him tumble off the presses—four biographies a year for the last quarter-century—almost none treat George Washington as a political thinker.[3] Perhaps that is because earlier myths about him, like the story of the cherry tree in Mason Weems's imaginative biography, have been replaced by others.

One of the more misleading myths about Washington is that he was simple and transparent. John C. Fitzpatrick, editor of *The Writings of George Washington*, declared in 1933 that it "is easy to understand George Washington. It is easy to understand any thoroughly sincere, honest, simple soul."[4] But it turns out that the real George Washington was not simple in the least. New studies of Washington reveal that he was far more complicated than we have thought—that he was, in fact, a "singularly complex human being," according to Robert and Lee Dalzell.[5] (Washington was also clever and, more like Machiavelli's cunning prince than Fitzpatrick's simple saint, knew when to be dishonest: in the early days of the Revolution, he almost singlehandedly devised America's first successful covert operations.)[6] To John Adams, Washington's mind was, like Jefferson's, shadowy; he was "like the great rivers, whose bottoms we cannot see and make no noise."[7] Washington was, and remains, an enigma.

Yet if his mind or personality are enigmatic, his political philosophy is not necessarily so. A patient and systematic analysis of Washington's writing—and he left behind an enormous paper trail, including as many letters as Thomas Jefferson—reveals a coherent theory of American constitutionalism. This book attempts to lay out that political theory, triangulated among the ideologies of classical republicanism, British liberalism, and Protestant Christianity.[8] As Garrett Sheldon has pointed out in the prior volumes in this series on the political philosophies of Thomas Jefferson and James Madison, those three ideologies, and their permutations, were dominant during the American founding.[9]

The book begins with a chronology of his political career, for no man of his day was more active in the business of American nation-building than Washington. It is followed by an introduction to Washington's political mind that places him in the context of his intellectual and historical peers. Chapter 1 recounts his political life. It concentrates on formative experiences that made an impact on Washington's later political thought and career and highlights often-overlooked aspects of Washington's role as a kind of public intellectual. Above all, this chapter attempts to convey the sense of Washington's mind in motion. His complex though untutored brain was constantly at work on America's political problems; his proposed solutions comprise the remaining substantive chapters of the book.

Chapter 2 deals with Washington as a classical republican, both in his embodiment of Roman political virtues, and in his classical political theorizing, particularly as it was related to Aristotle, Cicero, and Seneca the Younger. Chapter 3 reveals Washington as a British Enlightenment liberal who turned British constitutional theories (especially those of John Locke) back on King George III and Parliament to justify the American Revolution, and who then promoted a new American empire of liberty based on British theories of natural rights in the domestic and foreign realms. Chapter 4 examines Washington's use of what he called the "indispensable supports" of religion and morality in America through the creation of a civil religion with strong Protestant undercurrents flowing from his upbringing and lifelong membership in the Anglican Church and so deals with him in the role of nominally Protestant Christian. It pays special attention to Washington's use of political rhetoric derived from the Bible and the *Book of Common Prayer*. An epilogue reiterates Washington's political principles through his final statements to the American people, his Farewell Address of 1796, and his Last Will and Testament of 1799, which itself was laced with subtle political lessons. An appendix with a selected inventory of Washington's surprisingly substantial library of political philosophy and related subjects rounds out the book.

Because he was uniquely the incarnation of early American political thought, each substantive chapter begins with a prologue—a vignette from Washington's career in which he put into play what he called his political "principles" and in which he embodied the three major ideologies of the founding. Throughout the chapters are interwoven anecdotes about other thinkers already profiled in this Johns Hopkins series on the Political Philosophy of the American Founders: Jefferson, Madison, and Franklin. References to John Adams, Alexander Hamilton, and John Marshall, whose volumes are yet to appear, are also included.

Writing a brief book on such an enigmatic and iconic figure

was necessarily daunting. Richard Norton Smith, author of the best study of Washington's presidency, suggests that "of all American lives, George Washington's may be the single most intimidating to write in this antiheroic age."[10] If that is true of a conventional biography of Washington, how much more true must it be of an intellectual biography, especially since the jury is still out on the quality of his intellect and political thought? One of his more perceptive biographers, James Thomas Flexner, concluded that "no American is more completely misunderstood than George Washington."[11] Paul Johnson, in his pithy book on Washington, puts the matter thus: "He puzzled those who knew and worked with him, and who often disagreed violently about his merits and abilities. He puzzles us. No man's mind is so hard to enter and dwell within."[12] Possibly so—but that is all the more reason to try. And a neglected and perhaps significant piece of the puzzle of Washington's mind is his political philosophy.

THE BALTIMORE WIT AND JOURNALIST H. L. Mencken once remarked, "Writing books is certainly a most unpleasant occupation. It is lonesome, unsanitary and maddening. Many authors go crazy." Fortunately for me, many people made the writing of this book less lonesome and kept me sane. Certainly it would have been more flawed than it is without their help.

For the privilege of writing this volume I am chiefly indebted to the executive editor of the Johns Hopkins University Press, Henry Y. K. Tom, and to the father of this series, Garrett Ward Sheldon. Others who shared their time, knowledge, and advice include: William B. Allen of Michigan State University; Herman Belz of the University of Maryland; Susan Borchardt and Kevin Shupe at Gunston Hall Plantation; Philander Chase, Frank Grizzard, and Dorothy Twohig at the *Papers of George Washington,* University of Virginia; Ellen McCallister Clark, Librarian of the Society of the Cincinnati; Daniel Dreisbach of American University; Robert Faulkner of Boston College; Fred Greenstein of Princeton University; Gail Greve, Special Collections Librarian of the Rockefeller Library, Colonial Williamsburg Foundation; Kevin Hardwick of James Madison University; Don Higginbotham of the University of North Carolina at Chapel Hill; Gary Sandling of Monticello; Sue Storey Keeler and Barbara McMillan at Mount Vernon; Stuart Leibiger of LaSalle University; Richard Ryerson of the David Library of the American Revolution; David Skarka and Julie Young, graduate assistants at Regent University; Albert Zambone at the University of Oxford; the historical staff of Sulgrave Manor, Oxfordshire, England; and the faculty and staff of the James Madison Program in the Department of Politics at Princeton University, who provided me with a teaching fellowship during the 2003–2004 academic year, when much of the research for this book was done.

1732   GW born by the Potomac River in Washington Parish, Westmoreland County, Virginia.

1739   Moves with family to Ferry Farm on Rappahannock River near Fredericksburg; begins schooling.

1743   Father dies.

1744–47   Lives with half-brothers Augustine at Westmoreland County plantation and Lawrence at Epsewasson plantation (later renamed Mount Vernon); "adopted" by Fairfax family; studies surveying, geography, mathematics, rudimentary law, and accounting; formal schooling ends.

1748–49   Surveys western frontier of the Shenandoah Valley with George William Fairfax, where he meets settlers and Indians; named surveyor of Culpeper County, surveys nearly two hundred tracts in Shenandoah Valley; buys nearly fifteen hundred acres in Valley.

1751   Sails to Barbados with Lawrence: survives smallpox, becoming immune to greatest killer of the Revolution; sees first play, *George Barnwell,* kindling lifelong love of theater.

1752   Appointed major in Virginia militia, aged nineteen.

1754   Inadvertently triggers French and Indian War between France and England with "assassination" of French officer Ensign de Jumonville; surrender of Fort Necessity in Pennsylvania; retires rather than face demotion.

1755   Disastrous Braddock campaign.

1756   Appointed commander of Virginia militia; befriends British officer Thomas Gage, his future enemy in the Revolutionary War; travels to Boston to meet with Massachusetts governor; experiences first taste of intercolonial squabbling over currency, military rank among various state units.

1758–74   Serves in Virginia House of Burgesses.

1759   Marries Martha Dandridge Custis, reputed to be the wealthiest widow in Virginia.

1768   Appointed Justice in Fairfax County Court.

1769   Helps draft and transmit Virginia's nonimportation Articles of Association protesting Townshend Acts.

1774   Drafts Fairfax Resolves with George Mason; participates in drafting of Virginia Resolutions; serves in First Continental Congress.

1775   Serves in Second Continental Congress.

1775–83   Commander in chief of Continental Army: twice given quasi-dictatorial powers (1775, 1776); quells Newburgh Conspiracy.

1780   Elected to American Philosophical Society.

1781   Victory over British in battle of Yorktown, effectively ending Revolutionary War.

1783   Issues Circular to the States; resigns his commission as commander in chief of the Continental Army at Annapolis before Confederation Congress.

1785   Hosts Mount Vernon Conference, first step toward a stronger national constitution.

1786   Attends Annapolis Convention, precursor to Constitutional Convention.

1787   Presides over Constitutional Convention; sends out Constitution to states for debates on ratification with letter over his signature.

1788	Works behind the scenes for ratification of Constitution; elected Chancellor of College of William and Mary.
1789–96	Serves as first president of the United States, to which he is twice elected unanimously in Electoral College.
1793	"Citizen" Genet affair; proclaims neutrality; suppresses Whiskey Rebellion.
1795	Hamilton resigns as Secretary of the Treasury; Jay Treaty.
1796	Declines to stand for third presidential term and resigns; issues Farewell Address.
1796–99	Corresponds with his successor during Adams presidency; advances career of John Marshall.
1798	Recalled from retirement and appointed commander in chief of the Armies of the United States by President Adams as war looms.
1799	Writes Last Will and Testament disposing of his property, providing for founding a national university, freeing his slaves and establishing a trust fund for their support; dies at Mount Vernon December 14.

The Political Philosophy
of George Washington

INTRODUCTION

THREE IDEOLOGIES IN WASHINGTON'S THOUGHT AND CAREER

[I am] a Philanthropist by character, and . . . a Citizen of the great republic of humanity at large.

Washington to Lafayette, 1786

CLASSICAL REPUBLICANISM, BRITISH LIBERALISM, AND PROTESTANT CHRISTIANITY

WHEN THAT PROTEAN American Benjamin Franklin set about to make himself virtuous, he chose for his motto thoughts from Cicero, from a British liberal poet, and from the biblical Proverbs. "This my little Book [of virtues]," he wrote in his *Autobiography,* "had for its Motto these Lines . . . from Cicero. . . . from the Proverbs of Solomon . . . [and] I us'd also sometimes a little Prayer which I took from Thomson's Poems."[1] The self-educated Franklin had revealingly picked his quotations from classical republican, British liberal, and Judeo-Christian sources. Marcus Tullius Cicero had been the ablest defender of the republic in the Senate of ancient Rome; James Thomson, whose poems were in Washington's library at Mount Vernon, was a product of the Scottish Enlightenment and author of a tribute to British constitutionalism called *Liberty;* and the Proverbs were a major component of Western wisdom literature that appealed to Franklin's moralistic and pragmatic mind.[2]

Franklin was representative of eighteenth-century American

public intellectuals. In a sermon delivered during the late 1760s, the Protestant political preacher Jonathan Mayhew also drew on authorities from the classical past and early modern Britain: "Having been initiated in youth into the doctrines of civil liberty as they were taught by such men as Plato, Demosthenes, and Cicero among the ancients, and such as Sidney, Milton, Locke, and Hoadley among the moderns,—I liked them: they seemed rational."[3] Many years after the Revolution, Thomas Jefferson traced out the intellectual origins of the polyglot political philosophy summed up in his Declaration of Independence. That document was meant to be "an expression of the American mind," whose entire "authority rests then on the harmonizing sentiments of the day" expressed "in the elementary books of public right, as Aristotle, Cicero, Locke, Sidney, etc." Jefferson insisted, "All American Whigs thought alike on these subjects."[4] In other words, they all thought like classical republicans and British liberals.

Unlike many contemporary American scholars, who emphasize one line of influence over the others, Franklin, Mayhew, and Jefferson saw no conflict between these various authorities from the past. In a similar fashion, Benjamin Rush combined three ideologies when he mused that America seemed "destined by heaven to exhibit to the world the perfection which the mind of man is capable of receiving from the combined operation of liberty, learning, and the gospel upon it."[5] Indeed, there is much overlap in the political and ethical theory of the classical, Christian, and modern worlds. The apostle Paul, for example, quoted the Stoics Cleanthes and Aratus when preaching the Christian gospel to Greeks in Athens.[6] Augustine of Hippo took the title of his famous *City of God* not only from the Psalms but also from the Roman emperor Marcus Aurelius.[7] And the medieval humanist Petrarch said of Cicero, "You would fancy sometimes it is not a Pagan philosopher but a Christian apostle who is speaking."[8] Later thinkers like John Locke practiced a similar kind of syncretism, combining classical republican, Protestant Christian, and British Enlightenment ideas. Locke, one of the "British Empiricist" philosophers, is also considered an "heir of Puritan political theorists," and he began his famous *Second Treatise of*

Government by quoting Cicero: *Salus populi suprema lex esto*— "the public good is the supreme law."[9]

George Washington similarly mixed classical republican and British Enlightenment liberal ideas in a single sentence of his 1783 Circular to the States. "We shall be left nearly in a state of Nature," he wrote, invoking the concept of a brutal pre-governmental state of nature employed by Thomas Hobbes, Locke, and other British social contract thinkers, "or we may find . . . that there is a natural and necessary progression, from the extreme of anarchy to the extreme of Tyranny; and that arbitrary power is most easily established on the ruins of Liberty abused to licentiousness," a reference to the classical republican typology of political regimes used by Plato and Aristotle.[10]

Less educated and even illiterate Americans also took their bearings from the classical past, identifying with the classical republican rhetoric of Washington and the founders. Speaking of the influence of classical republicanism, Paul Johnson warns: "Let us not underestimate this [influence]. It was strongly intuited by a great many people who could barely write their names. It was vaguely associated in their minds with the ancient virtue and honor of the Romans."[11] In fact, all three founding ideologies—classical republicanism, British liberalism, and Protestant Christianity—were, as the phrase goes, "in the air" of the eighteenth century. A man like George Washington breathed them in as naturally as he filled his lungs with air. Put differently, Washington and his peers wove those three strands together into the patchwork intellectual fabric of the early republic.

Leading scholars have labeled attempts to unravel those tangled skeins as anachronistic. Writing before the historiographical discovery of classical republicanism, Louis Hartz marked "the alliance of Christian pessimism with liberal thought" in early America, a fusion which he claimed has had "a deep and lasting meaning."[12] More recently, David Hackett Fischer, who won the Pulitzer Prize for his *Washington's Crossing*, cautioned against the "learned anachronisms" of professional historians of American political thought.[13] The political scientist Donald Lutz reminds us that it simply "will no longer do to examine a text from the American founding era without considering the possibility of multiple influences."[14] James Kloppenberg has demonstrated how "liberal ideas could be joined with ideas from the different traditions of Protestant Christianity and classical republicanism" during the founding.[15] And the legal historian John Witte Jr. has noted: "To be sure, Civic Republicans," for whom "George Washington was . . . [among the] principal spokesmen," shared "much common ground with Evangelicals and Enlightenment exponents."[16]

In fact, Washington's ability to personify all of these traditions and his popularity with most Americans helped secure his place as Father of His Country. He shored up his popularity across the spectrum of society—Federalists and Republicans (including Hamilton and Jefferson within his own cabinet), Enlightenment skeptics and evangelical Christians, and everyone in between—by drawing on all three major sources of intellectual and cultural capital that Americans shared. When he totted up the sources and benefits of human progress, Washington paid homage to classical, modern liberal, and Christian resources:

> The researches of the human mind, after social happiness, have been carried to a great extent; the Treasures of knowledge, acquired through a long succession of years, by the labours of Philosophers, Sages and Legislatures, are laid open for our use, and their collected wisdom may be happily applied in the Establishment of our forms of Government; the free cultivation of letters, the unbounded extension of Commerce, the progressive refinement of Manners, the growing liberality of sentiment, and above all, the pure and benign light of Revelation, have had a meliorating influence on mankind and increased the blessings of Society.[17]

The philosophies of the classical past, modern liberalism, and Christian Revelation were all at Americans' disposal and were to be called into service. That sentence from his 1783 Circular to the States comes as close as any to describing the ground of "the harmonizing sentiments of the day" on which he and his colleagues raised a republic. Washington himself combined classical Roman political virtues with the liberal theory of the British Enlightenment and baptized the result in the tepid waters of Anglican Christianity. These are the traditions we will be tracing out in the political thought and career, or what we might even call the political philosophy, of George Washington.

Washington and Historiography

Thanks to President Warren Harding, who in a rare moment of eloquence coined the phrase in his inaugural address, we call the men who conceived the United States the Founding Fathers. Harding managed to capture in the early twentieth century a trope of the eighteenth: nearly every founder had been called by his contemporaries the Father of something. Most of those paternal titles have faded with time—who refers to John Adams as the Father of the U.S. Navy anymore?—but two of them remain in our national vocabulary. We call George Washington the Father of the Country, and we call James Madison the Father of the Constitution.

Even though Washington hosted the Mount Vernon Conference, a preliminary to the Constitutional Convention, and then presided over that gathering at Philadelphia and held it together through the long summer of 1787, we still give the constitutional laurels to Madison. While Madison certainly played a key role in fathering the Constitution, his title and Washington's imply a mental difference between the two patriarchs. It is as though we think to ourselves, "Washington may have had leadership skills, but Madison had *brains.*" After all, Madison left behind our supreme organic law—the Constitution and its Bill of Rights—which is enshrined in our civil-religious reliquary, the National Archives in Washington, D.C. Although the capital city was named for him, no document of Washington's is so enshrined. And the only one he wrote (or co-wrote) that may deserve a place in those Archives—his Farewell Address—is no longer studied as it once was.

Washington was mentally outshone by his founding brothers, many of whom gave, and continue to give, an appearance of brilliance; he can appear dull by contrast. Indeed, Washington was in a sense the least philosophical of the major founders. Nor was he a public intellectual of the caliber of Jefferson or Madison, to name two who have previously been profiled in this series. His only authorized biographer, David Humphreys, noted that "his talents were rather solid than brilliant" (a judgment Washington allowed), and Peter Henriques has recently written in *Realistic Visionary* that "Washington was not a brilliant man in the way

Thomas Jefferson, Alexander Hamilton, and James Madison were brilliant," but he had "remarkably astute judgment on the really important issues of his time."[18] Washington was quick to acknowledge that his mind had been "long employed in public concerns" rather than purely intellectual ones.[19] He was also sensitive to what he called his "defective" formal education—one reason he fobbed off writing his autobiography—and his contemporaries were aware of the perception as well.[20] Washington's vice president, John Adams, who began his career teaching Greek to Massachusetts schoolchildren, declared that the first chief executive was "not a scholar" and too "illiterate" for the job.[21] He agreed with Benjamin Rush that Washington "wrote a great deal, thought constantly, but read (it is said) very little."[22] Washington himself encouraged this view. "My life has been a very busy one," he insisted in the late 1780s while trying to avoid becoming the first president of the United States. "I have had but little leisure to read of late years, and . . . I cannot indeed pretend to be so well acquainted with civil matters, as I was with military affairs."[23] Jefferson paid Washington the left-handed compliment of having sound judgment but a slow mind that lacked "imagination."[24]

But other contemporaries recognized Washington's mental abilities during his lifetime. The electors of the American Philosophical Society, America's version of the British Royal Society, were one such group. His election in 1780 to that body alongside the likes of Jefferson, Franklin, David Rittenhouse, and other scientifically minded Americans flattered Washington, although his note of acknowledgment was characteristically self-deprecating.[25] So did his appointment as Chancellor of the College of William and Mary in 1788. In his acceptance letter, Washington expressed his "heart-felt desire to promote the cause of Science in general" and to place "the system of Education on such a basis, as will render it most beneficial to the Sate and the Republic of letters, as well as to the more extensive interests of humanity and religion."[26] The potential political benefits of religion and education was a theme sounded throughout his career, down to the concluding remarks in his Farewell Address.

Though he had little of it himself, George Washington was an enthusiastic proponent of formal education. He believed that the study of "Philosophy, Moral, [and] Natural" would yield "very desirable knowledge for a Gentleman" and, more importantly, that it would yield political dividends for the young nation. As he wrote to the former headmaster of a Virginia grammar school, "The best means of forming a manly, virtuous and happy people, will be found in the right education of youth. Without *this* foundation, every other means, in my opinion, must fail."[27] There is ample evidence that Washington quietly worked to gain that sort of knowledge for himself.

However, scholars in the early twentieth century treated Washington with less than filial piety when it came to his education and understanding. Perhaps this was an overreaction to the nineteenth-century tendency toward hagiography represented by Parson Weems, but it resulted in rough handling of Washington for decades.[28] Particularly in the first half of the twentieth century, it was fashionable to portray Washington as crafty in an economically self-interested way but no contemplative. Typical of this attitude is the essay by Samuel Eliot Morison, *The Young Man Washington* (1932). "Ideas did not interest him, nor was he interested in himself," Morison wrote. "Washington gained little discipline from book-learning," he continued, "but like all young Virginians of the day he led an active outdoor life which gave him a magnificent physique."[29] Though he did grudgingly give Washington credit for adopting a "great philosophy" (Stoicism), Admiral Morison considered Washington all brawn and no brains. This characterization is reminiscent of Abigail Adams's breathless quotation of Dryden after seeing Washington for the first time: "Mark his Majestick fabrick! he's a temple / Sacred by birth, and built by hands divine / His Souls the deity that lodges there. / Nor is the pile unworthy of the God."[30] In a similar vein, Charles Beard, whose *Economic Interpretation of the Constitution of the United States* (1913) exerted such influence on American historiography, claimed that "it does not appear that in public document or private letter he ever set forth any coherent theory of government."[31] In the 1960s, another historian, Harold Bradley, insisted that "one may search the public papers of Washington without finding a concise statement of political philosophy."[32]

But Morison was demonstrably wrong about Washington's interest in his own reputation, an interest we now know bordered on self-absorption and, as we shall see, about the religious roots of Washington's political rhetoric.[33] And the statements of Beard and Bradley, particularly the latter's assertion that Washington gave no concise statement of his political philosophy in his public papers, are particularly curious, for two reasons. First, the Farewell Address, Washington's most famous public document, was manifestly a statement of political principles and therefore of political philosophy. Thomas Jefferson certainly thought it such a statement. To the Board of Visitors of the new University of Virginia, he wrote that Washington's "valedictory address" was to be assigned in the Law School as one of a handful of "the best guides" to "the distinctive principles of the government . . . of the United States."[34] Moreover, in 1996 Matthew Spalding and Patrick Garrity published a sustained analysis of the Farewell Address to favorable reviews, one of which described the Address as "the supreme expression of the American political community until it was surpassed by Abraham Lincoln's Gettysburg Address."[35] Second, with the possible exception of Jefferson himself, it is hard to think of any founder who ever did provide a "concise" statement of his political philosophy.

Assertions like those of Beard, Morison, and Bradley, made with regularity by past Washington scholars for decades, now have an air of unreality about them. In recent decades scholars have shown a newfound appreciation for Washington's intellectual qualities. Though they are no longer willing, like Abigail Adams, to call him a god—even an "imperfect" one, as Henry Wiencek recently has—they have at least upgraded their evaluations of Washington's mental capacity.[36] One historian suggested in 2001 that "the best Washington scholarship of the last fifteen years or so has dealt with the intellectual dimensions of Washington's public image, including his part in creating it."[37] The new Gilder-Lehrman Gallery at Mount Vernon pays tribute to what it calls Washington's "insatiable hunger for knowledge, his keen curiosity, and his life-long desire to better understand the world around him," which was especially "shown through manuscripts, maps, prints, and books." So it seems that the days are past when scholars can cavalierly dismiss Washington as a non-intellect or repeat the old non sequitur that because he wrote no systematic political treatise he had no coherent political philosophy.

It is true that as a political thinker Washington was no groundbreaker. But perhaps none of the founders, even the best-educated, was an entirely original political philosopher in his own right. Jefferson, fending off a charge that he had cribbed the Declaration of Independence from John Locke, admitted fifty years later to heavy borrowing, though he denied consulting any particular book during the composition of his draft. That eclectic draftsman of the Declaration was typical of the founders as a group. The contemporary philosopher Morton White assures us that "we may repeat what scholars have always known, and what the most candid rebels always admitted, namely, that they did not invent a single idea that may be called philosophical in the philosopher's sense of the word."[38]

Though he may have been unoriginal, there is evidence of a strong intelligence behind Washington's inscrutable forehead: curiosity, an autodidactic streak, an excellent memory (despite his protestations), and, *pace* Jefferson, an ability to imagine on a large scale. In fact, Madison insisted to Jefferson that Washington's efforts to open the west proved that "a mind like his, capable of great views, and which has long been occupied by them, cannot bear a vacancy, and surely he could not have chosen an occupation more worthy of succeeding to that of establishing the political rights of his country."[39] Perhaps the most intriguing question that presents itself to the historian is how Washington was able to raise his mind's eye so quickly above the narrow provincialism of his Virginia neighbors and conjure up a continental vision of America, a vision that guided him from his late teens to the end of his life. Washington was farsighted throughout his career (this meant that he was a better strategist than tactician during the Revolution, for example) and sometimes unusually prescient. He perceived earlier than many of his contemporaries the need for a strong union of colonies, and later states, to protect and build a distinct American nation. John C. Fitzpatrick noted that Washington's suggestion to Virginia Governor Francis Fauquier in 1758 for "commissioners from each of the colonies" to manage the Native American trade "contains the same germ of political union which later was to develop as a dominant principle of Washington's life."[40]

Literate if not literary, Washington maintained a lifelong relationship with the written word that until recent decades had been relatively neglected. This is especially true of printed material and even the classics of political philosophy. He kept his boyhood lesson books and letters including a childish note to Richard Henry Lee (future author of the resolution of American independence) and lovesick adolescent poems for girlfriends ("From your bright sparkling Eyes, I was undone . . .") and fastidiously conserved every scrap of paper from his adult life that he could.[41] After his marriage to Martha, Washington refused to allow his stepson John Parke Custis to go on the Grand Tour of Europe until he had sufficient book learning. Washington wrote to Jack's tutor, "I conceive a knowledge of books is the basis upon which all other knowledge is to be built."[42] Around that time he also systematically built a large first-rate library, including works of political philosophy, theology, and economy; poetry by John Milton and Alexander Pope; hundreds of bound political pamphlets; histories of England and Rome—even a *Life of Mohamad*. He kept all of his Revolutionary papers and made sure they survived the war intact. Because of his voluminous and international correspondence during the years between the Revolution and his presidency, David Humphreys described Washington in his study as "the focus of political intelligence in the New World."[43]

But at this point the intellectual historian is confronted with a dilemma. How are we to know which of these weighty books Washington read, from which he derived his political ideas? He almost never wrote in them; one exception is his copy of Adam Smith's *Wealth of Nations,* which contains a single marginal note in Washington's hand. Other founders did so more often, and historians can use those notes as evidence to make arguments about intellectual pedigree. The personal books of John Adams, for instance, are well-worn and contain extensive handwritten diatribes on history and politics in the margins. We know that Washington read Joseph Addison's *Spectator* essays as an adolescent because he noted the fact, as he claimed to have read every polemical essay he could obtain during the ratification debates over the new constitution. But as a general rule, Washington's extant diaries (some are missing) are narratives of his military, political, and farming activities, not transcripts of his mental processes. Starting in their school days, more pedantic founders like Adams and Jefferson kept "commonplace books" in which they copied out and evaluated passages from works they were reading for later citation. These records, along with their college curricula, have become guides to their reading habits. By contrast, no commonplace book of Washington's has survived, and he never went to college. Nor did he have the learning or temperament of a pedant. Except for the Bible and Addison's *Cato,* he rarely quoted from literary or philosophical works. Rarely, but not never: for example, in a letter to Annis Boudinot Stockton, whom he called "the Muse of Morven," Washington referred to Cicero and the ethics of the Greek philosopher Epicurus. "But, with Cicero in speaking respecting his belief of the immortality of the Soul, I will say, if I am in a grateful delusion, it is an innocent one," he wrote, alluding to a line from Cicero's dialogue *On Old Age* (*De Senectute*), and then declared himself inclined "to dispute your Epicurean position concerning the economy of pleasures."[44] But as a rule Washington did not show off what learning he had acquired, nor did he engage in the sort of literary one-upmanship typical of the Adams-Jefferson correspondence, for example. So with a few exceptions, we must be content with making suggestions rather than assertions about the literary sources of Washington's thinking and actions and try to avoid arbitrary and anachronistic historical arguments about influence. More important to this study is how Washington reflected and contributed to the dominant political ideas of his time. After all, it was part of Washington's genius and a source of his charisma that he was able to embody so completely the political thought of the American founding, including its classical republican, British Enlightenment liberal, and Protestant Christian sources.

Washington considered himself a member of the eighteenth-century "republic of letters." This concept of a transnational country of intellectuals was variously expressed by Europeans and Americans, and by none better than that European-cum-American farmer, J. Hector St. John de Crèvecoeur. "There is, no doubt, a secret communion among good men throughout the world," Crèvecoeur wrote, "a mental affinity connecting them by a similitude of sentiments . . . [and] extensive intellectual consanguinity."[45] Washington occasionally harbored ambitions in the intellectual line and allowed them to peek through in his private correspondence. He wrote to Lafayette that he considered himself "a Philanthropist by character, and . . . a Citizen of the great republic of humanity at large" and hoped to contribute to advances so that "mankind may be connected like one great family in fraternal ties."[46]

Despite such ambitions, Washington distrusted (or played at distrusting) his own mental abilities and so gave his critics fodder. Some of his habitual diffidence was doubtless genuine, as when he confessed to relying on "much abler heads than my own" to school him in the niceties of British law, or when he protested that he lacked the "political skill, abilities and inclination which is necessary to manage the helm" of the new federal government.[47] (Of course it turned out that Washington had consummate political skill, which is recognized by modern presidential historians.) But a becoming modesty was also part of the Stoic code to which he adhered throughout his adult life, and it reflected the Christian virtue of humility as well. His own diffidence, even his slowness to speak, did much to perpetuate the myth of Washington as intellectually under-endowed. But although Washington's mind, like the proverbial mill of the gods, may have ground slowly, it ground exceedingly fine.

Scholarship in the latter twentieth century and now into the twenty-first has shown an increasing appreciation for Washington's political sagacity and intelligence. The editors of *Patriot Sage*, a collection of revisionist essays published in 1999, regretted that Washington is "too often seen simply as a man of action; as a doer, not a thinker. His words are often overlooked or simply dismissed by scholars interested in those founders considered to be intellectually more sophisticated. But Washington's letters and speeches deserve much more of our attention."[48] Washington surely was a "doer," and he was, above all others, the "embodiment" of early American political thought, as Michael Kammen and many others have noted.[49] Richard Stevens has called Washington the "very embodiment of the Constitution."[50]

Scholar-turned-president Woodrow Wilson pointed out that during the final years of the Revolution, in "the absence of any real government, Washington proved almost the only prop of authority and law."[51] Joseph Ellis, in his Pulitzer Prize–winning *Founding Brothers,* called Washington "the closest approximation to a self-evident truth in American politics."[52] All of these assessments are fair and accurate so far as they go. Indeed, Washington was the flesh-and-blood exemplar of the constitutional principles that lay behind the American Revolution and the early republic. But he was also a thinker. Washington did not enjoy the leisure for study that Jefferson or Madison had, but his mind was always at work, and the ideas he snatched from books and pamphlets were hammered out on what in another context he called "the anvil of necessity."[53] Paul Longmore noted in his study of Washington's reputation that ironically, "precisely because of his skillful embodiment of contemporary ideals, this is perhaps his least recognized and least appreciated gift," a gift Longmore suggests amounted to "genius."[54]

Washington was unique among public intellectuals and politicians of his day for the neutrality of his political ideas. Indeed, Washington was able to play the critical role of embodiment of the Constitution only by being nonpartisan. Jefferson noted with grudging admiration that Washington was the "only man in the United States, who possessed the confidence of all. There was no other one, who was considered as any thing more than a party leader."[55] To James Thomas Flexner, Washington "resembled the keystone of an arch, holding all upright and in equilibrium, while the Hamiltonians curved off to the right and the Jeffersonians to the left."[56] Indeed, as first president Washington was the first national symbol, and Flexner noted how the roles Washington played were necessarily complicated by the fact that in "each citizen's preference concerning Presidential behavior, political theory was entangled . . . with nationalistic, aesthetic, and moral considerations."[57]

Washington confirmed these centrist assessments of himself. Writing to the secretary of war in 1795, he spoke of the "difficulty to one, who is of no party, and whose sole wish is to pursue, with undeviating steps a path which would lead this Country to respectability, wealth and happiness" of watching the ethic of victory at any cost increasingly infect party politics in the new nation.[58] Washington was, in other words, America's first political Independent. Being the nonpartisan embodiment of the new republic was part of what it meant to be the unique Father of His Country.

The new school of Washington scholarship emphasizes Washington's political intelligence and denies that he was merely a man of action or a political actor. It takes exception to John Adams's jealous assessment that if Washington "was not the greatest President, he was the best actor of [the] presidency we have ever had."[59] A close cousin of this criticism charges Washington with being a passive conduit through which his cleverer advisors poured their thoughts—that he was, in effect, a shill for Madison or Hamilton, especially toward the end of his career. This charge was first made by contemporary characters as opposite as Adams and Jefferson. According to James McHenry, Adams accused him of being "subservient to Hamilton, who ruled Washington and would still rule if he could."[60] Writing in 1818, Jefferson recalled that from "the moment . . . of my retiring from the administration, the federalists got unchecked hold of Genl. Washington," who finally exhibited "a willingness to let others act and even think for him."[61] At best, so this line of thinking goes, Washington was merely "a clockwork figure programmed to do wisely."[62] This thinking resurfaced recently, along with a newly discovered letter of Washington's, written during the Constitutional Convention in the summer of 1787. Commenting on the discovery, a historian was quoted in *The New York Times* as saying that the letter reveals that Washington's "position was sympathetic to the strong, nationalist implications of Alexander Hamilton and James Madison," as though the Hamiltons and Madisons supplied the important theories of the founding while Washington silently nodded in agreement.[63]

Such conventional wisdom, however, is as mythical as Parson Weems's tale of the cherry tree. That Washington himself contributed to the myth through his diffidence and complaints about his "defective" formal education makes it all the harder to dispel. But during the Revolution Washington had to think and act not only as military commander, quartermaster, chief of intelligence, and recruiter but also as "something of a de facto president" in the words of Ron Chernow.[64] In the post-Revolutionary period, Washington thought more deeply about constitutional matters. Political scientist Glenn Phelps published a volume in 1993 devoted entirely to Washington's constitutionalism, and historian Don Higginbotham has claimed that Washington "displayed, in his own unique way, the creativity of an intellectual giant."[65] Edmund Morgan, in the *Genius of George Washington,* wrote of "the quick perception of political realities that lay behind Washington's understanding of power."[66] Paul Longmore, introducing his meticulous appendix on Washington's library and reading habits, noted that "a thorough examination of his papers and library discloses that he gave more thought to reading, learning, and ideas than historians have credited. More important, it makes clear the place of reading in his life."[67] That reflective reading, though he was never able to do as much as he wished, helped reinforce Washington's stable and coherent political philosophy.

POLITICAL "PRINCIPLES"

Washington expressed clearly what he called his political "principles" in his Farewell Address of 1796, a joint production by Washington, Madison, Hamilton, and John Jay, the latter three authors of *The Federalist Papers.* (Because of its patrimony, it could be argued that Washington's Farewell Address is the single best summation of the elite political mind of the founding era.) Washington summed up those principles in one stem-winding sentence in the Address:

> Profoundly penetrated with this idea [of support from the American people], I shall carry it with me to my grave, as a strong incitement to unceasing vows that Heaven may continue to you the choicest tokens of its beneficence; that your Union and brotherly affection may be perpetual; that the free constitution, which is the work of your hands, may be sacredly maintained; that its Administration in every department may be stamped with wisdom and Virtue; that, in fine, the happiness of the people of these States, under the auspices of liberty, may be made complete, by so careful a preservation and so prudent a use of this blessing as will acquire

to them the glory of recommending it to the applause, the affection, and adoption of every nation which is yet a stranger to it.[68]

There, within what he might have called a "brief compass," was Washington's core political philosophy as it pertained to the American experiment. That philosophy revolved around the central principles of union, liberty, and self-government under the Constitution, administered with virtue as an example to the world, all under the superintendence of a benevolent Providence. These principles collectively made up the political polestar of his half-century of public service. In a eulogy of Washington in which he (not Richard Henry Lee) penned the famous line "first in war, first in peace, first in the hearts of his countrymen," John Marshall reproduced the "wise principles announced by [Washington] himself, as the basis of his political life." Those principles were "the indissoluble union between virtue and happiness, between duty and advantage, between the genuine maxims of an honest and magnanimous policy and the solid rewards of public prosperity and individual felicity." Washington "laid the foundations of our national policy in the unerring immutable principles of morality, based on religion, exemplifying the pre-eminence of a free government, by all the attributes which win the affections of its citizens, or command the respect of the world." Marshall noted that throughout his career the "finger of an overruling Providence [was] pointing at Washington."[69] Washington expressed similar principles and hopes in a letter to Roman Catholics in 1790, just as he was assuming the presidency. "America, under the smiles of a Divine Providence, the protection of a good government, and the cultivation of manners, morals, and piety, cannot fail of attaining an uncommon degree of eminence, in literature, commerce, agriculture, improvements at home and respectability abroad."[70]

In Washington's mind, religion in general, and Christianity in particular, formed an "indispensable support" of the young republic. He claimed that from the time of the Revolution, Heaven had granted its favor to America, and that favor would have to continue if the American experiment were to succeed. Churches, synagogues, religious bodies of all kinds would have to continue their good work of saving souls and, perhaps just as important to

Washington, producing moral citizens. The union—which had hardly been a union at all under the Confederation Congress—needed to be perpetual, and the friendship of the states that made union possible had to be nurtured. The Constitution that solidified and codified the union would have to be maintained with something like religious awe. The branches of the government had to be administered with wisdom and, as if that were not difficult enough, with virtue. And it all had to be done in an atmosphere of liberty as an example to foreign nations, as though America were to be an extension of the New England Puritans' "city on a hill."

Most of these political principles marked Washington's thinking and career from his earliest days in the Virginia House of Burgesses, and a few, from even earlier. Some, like his high regard for the federal Constitution, of course unfolded as historical events themselves unfolded—indeed, as he helped them to unfold—but none of them was inconsistent with the others, and none was a novelty. Washington claimed to have steered by them throughout his career. At the beginning of his first presidential term he wrote to Madison that since "the first of everything, *in our situation* will serve to establish a Precedent, it is devoutly wished on my part, that these precedents may be fixed on true principles."[71] At the end of his second term he told the American people: "How far in the discharge of my official duties, I have been guided by the principles which have been delineated, the public Records and other evidences of my conduct must witness to You and to the world. To myself, the assurance of my own conscience is, that I have at least believed myself to be guided by them."[72]

Although not systematic, Washington's political philosophy was remarkably consistent throughout his long public life. Once it was formed as a young man, its essentials never changed, and all of his reading and actions were guided by a small constellation of fixed political stars. Of course, on some important issues—most notably slavery—Washington's thinking did change over time, and his journey from provincial Virginian to continental American was an intellectual odyssey of incalculable importance to the success of the American experiment. But unlike Jefferson, a man of massive contradictions, or Madison, who reversed course on a number of issues, including even separation of church and state, the core of Washington's political thought remained steady and constant during his career. The solid republican theory and architectural metaphors of his Farewell Address, composed in 1796 after two unprecedented terms as president, could easily be transposed into his first farewell, the Circular to the States of 1783, which he wrote before there was even a United States government properly speaking.

All of this bespeaks a fully formed political philosophy. Again, this is not to suggest that Washington was a political thinker in the same class with his contemporaries like Jefferson, Madison, Hamilton, and Adams. But Washington was a better theorist than he let on, and more comprehensive than some of his own contemporaries and our own have been aware. One measure of the comprehensiveness of Washington's political thought is his reflection of the three dominant ideologies present at the American founding throughout nearly five decades of public life.

CHAPTER 1

A POLITICAL LIFE OF WASHINGTON

A mind that has been constantly on the stretch since the year
1753, with but short intervals, and little relaxation, requires rest,
and composure.

Washington to Gov. Jonathan Trumbull, 1799

As the year 1799 expired, the eighteenth-century American Enlightenment was dying—and so, coincidentally,
was George Washington. On the evening of Friday, December 13, though he suspected the sore throat he had
was "mortal," Washington insisted on staying up to read
the newspaper aloud to his secretary and family. Had
news traveled faster in that era, he would have read of the
new French constitution promulgated that very day, one
that set up a "republic" to be headed by a young civil-
military leader called Napoleon Bonaparte, who was
already being compared to Washington himself. Instead,
his reading that night consisted mainly of local and national items of interest. A voracious consumer of newspapers (even in retirement he had ten of them delivered
to Mount Vernon), Washington refused to go to bed
until he had read out the latest political news to the
household. Firelight played on the broadsheet; outside,
the snow had stopped, but a cold wind still blew against
the windows, the damp chill of the Virginia winter in-
truded itself into Mansion House, and the old man's
voice grew hoarse. After Martha retired, Washington
had his secretary Tobias Lear read him a report of the

19

debates in the Virginia Assembly while the former burgess croaked out a running commentary as best he could. Late in the evening, Lear urged Washington to take some medicine and then wished him goodnight. Washington moved to the study, where he scratched out a few lines in his journal, as was his nightly custom.

That study was Washington's most private and thoughtful space at Mount Vernon, a room that few visitors ever saw—indeed, "none entered" except by invitation, according to his step-grandson. He spent early mornings and late evenings there, often beginning before dawn and working into the night at a rolltop desk opposite the bookcases covering the room's east wall. Those shelves held nearly a thousand books, plus several hundred volumes of bound political pamphlets, making it one of the finest collections of its kind in early America. It contained many works of political theory and history, including works by classical republicans such as Cicero and Seneca, various editions of the Bible and the Anglican *Book of Common Prayer,* and works by British liberals such as John Locke, Adam Smith, and Joseph Addison. But his was no mere showcase library built to impress his grandee houseguests. Washington bought books to use them, and his entire life was a campaign in self-improvement, from his systematic reading of British history and Addison's *Spectator* as a schoolboy and his purposeful study of military manuals as a young militia officer to his mature study of agricultural books, political pamphlets, and classics of political philosophy and economy such as Smith's *Wealth of Nations.*

Finally finished with the newspapers, reports from the General Assembly, and his journal, Washington put out the light and climbed the back stairs from his study up to bed, possibly aware that he would never rise from it again. Years before, Washington, who enjoyed gambling, had made a playful bet with some friends "not to quit the theatre of this world before the year 1800." But that was one wager he was destined to lose; by the next night, December 14, 1799, the Father of His Country was dead.

Even in his final illness, Washington had been determined to end his life as he had always lived it, with his mind on the political state of his country.[1]

"A Life Nearly Consumed in Public Cares"

The United States had many founding fathers (and a few founding mothers), but only one Father of the Country. George Washington had no children in the flesh, but he sired a baker's dozen of political offspring, the thirteen original United States of America. No individual was more involved, or involved for a longer time—nearly fifty years—in the political life and founding of the nation than Washington. Yet he always claimed to be a reluctant politician. On learning of his election to the presidency, Washington wrote to Henry Knox, "My movements to the chair of Government will be accompanied by feelings not unlike those of a culprit who is going to the place of his execution: so unwilling am I, in the evening of a life nearly consumed in public cares, to quit a peaceful abode for an Ocean of difficulties, without the competency of political skill, abilities and inclination."[2] Whatever his true feelings, Washington sublimated his expressed desires to live a private life and answered the calls to preserve the ordered liberty of his country, as the codes of classical republicanism, British liberalism, and Protestant Christianity demanded. Indeed, Washington became the most visible representative of Jefferson's "harmonizing sentiments" of the American founding.[3]

Though he was not the sophisticated thinker Jefferson was, Washington lived out the political philosophy of the American founding more than his Virginia colleague, coming to stand for its principles in a way that no other founder, not even the ubiquitous Benjamin Franklin, ever quite did. He was, as Paul Johnson has pointed out, "Eighteenth-Century Man writ large."[4] The lone *Pater Patriae,* Washington played by turns the role of Roman Stoic, British Enlightenment Liberal, and Protestant Christian in the full glare of history. He was conscious that every action, every gesture, every word would be construed—or misconstrued—by watching Americans and a watching world, especially during his presidency. As he put it to his nephew Bushrod in 1789, "The eyes of Argus are upon me." (Argus was a many-eyed monster from Greek mythology as well as the name of a contemporary newspaper.)[5] Sometimes those eyes were hostile, and during the 1780s and 1790s Washington was accused of betraying American principles, and even the Revolution itself. Once, in a meeting during his first presidential term with his department heads, each of whom had impeccable revolutionary credentials, Washington was shown a cartoon from Philip Freneau's *National Gazette* of himself dressed as a king laid out on the guillotine. The implication, of course, was that Washington had betrayed the Revolution and desecrated the Spirit of '76. He was furious. According to Jefferson (who actually had Freneau on the federal payroll), the "Presidt. was much inflamed," ran on "much on the personal abuse which had been bestowed on him" and swore "he had rather be on his farm than to be made *emperor of the world* and yet that they were charging him with wanting to be a king."[6] Washington meant exactly what he said in these self-righteous outbursts. Even in his first administration he had already grown weary of public scrutiny and longed for the private domestic ease of Mount Vernon. The many tumultuous decades in the public eye had cooled the passion for celebrity that burned in him as a young militia officer and Virginia burgess. By the 1790s Washington the president had come a long way from the fame-hungry days of his youth in tidewater Virginia.

Fame came quickly enough to the young George Washington, and it remained with him to the end of his life, when he was the most famous man in America and quite possibly in the western world. That notoriety came at a high price—the loss of privacy and leisure the whole of his adult life. As he put it in 1799, Washington's public responsibilities had forced his mind to be "constantly on the stretch since the year 1753, with but short intervals, and little relaxation."[7] His public career began in earnest in 1754, when as a twenty-two-year-old officer in the Virginia militia he unwittingly touched off the French and Indian War between England and France, thus setting in train events that would eventually lead to the American Revolution. His career ended with his death in 1799, by which time the stumble-footed colonial major had become the first elected head of state in western history and one of its most celebrated characters. It was a remarkable transformation and a remarkable rise to power. How did that transformation come about, and what circumstances and events combined to make Washington into the political actor and thinker he became?

YOUTH, 1732–1753

Nathaniel Hawthorne once quipped that judging by Washington's nineteenth-century reputation, the Father of His Country must have been born fully clothed and with his hair powdered.[8] But of course Washington came, like Job, naked from his mother's womb, into his family's small home on the Potomac in Washington Parish of Westmoreland County, Virginia.[9] By the Julian calendar then in use, it was February 11, 1732. Two months later Washington's parents had him baptized into the Anglican church, a denomination in which he remained for the rest of his life.[10] His mother was the former Mary Ball, second wife of Augustine Washington. Financially, the baby boy and his family were not particularly well off. One of the many myths about Washington is that he was born, like Jefferson (whose first memory was of being carried on a pillow by a slave), with a silver spoon in his mouth. But despite owning some ten thousand acres, Washington's father was only a modest farmer and perennially cash-poor. This is borne out by the inventory of Augustine Washington's home, which indicates comfort but no luxury: some furniture and bedding, a little plate and china, and seven able-bodied slaves.[11] In 1732 the Washingtons were not even proper gentry, much less members of the First Families of Virginia, like Jefferson, whose mother was a blue-blooded Randolph. Until his marriage to Martha Custis, Washington himself was only a minor planter.[12]

Had he bothered to investigate his lineage, George Washington would have discovered that his branch of the Washington family had been lower gentry in England prior to relocating to the New World. But Washington never concerned himself with such matters; indeed, we know more about his ancestry than he himself did. The Washington family seat, Sulgrave Manor in Oxfordshire, England, was already nearly three centuries old by the time George was born in America.[13] Washington was possibly related to King Edward III on his father's side; his great-great-grandfather, Lawrence Washington, had been a don at Brasenose College, Oxford.[14] If the means had been available, George might have attended Oxford himself, or at least been sent to England's Appleby School like his father and older half-brothers.

It turned out that the means were not available, and despite his wishes, Washington never set foot in England or continental Europe. Except for one trip to Barbados in his teens, Washington's entire life was played out on North American soil. He was a fourth-generation colonial: his great-grandfather John Washington was the first of his line to come to the New World, which he did in 1657, settling on a stretch of the Potomac River in Virginia, not far from where George was born.

Washington was the eldest child of his father's second marriage, and the third son overall, which, according to the primogeniture laws in Virginia, meant that his inheritance would be relatively small. Of Washington's boyhood we know little, hardly more than we know of the boyhood of Abraham Lincoln, who summed up his own youth with a line from Thomas Gray's "Elegy": "The short and simple annals of the poor."[15] The young Washington was not poor in an absolute sense, though James Flexner says that Washington was, "for the environment in which he moved, poor during his young manhood."[16] But his father died suddenly when George was eleven, and this altered the family fortunes and the trajectory of his life. Unlike his half-brothers, young George got comparatively little schooling, some of it at home and all of it in Virginia, and was perpetually embarrassed by what he called his "defective education."[17]

According to Woodrow Wilson, the last Virginia-born president, "a boy never gets over his boyhood, and never can change those subtle influences which have become a part of him, that were bred in him when was a child."[18] This was particularly true of Wilson, whose relationship with his loving but stern minister father probably contributed to the somewhat brittle character traits manifested during his presidency.[19] Washington, the first Virginian president, lost his father before he could be much influenced by him for good or for ill, and unlike Wilson, who left the Old Dominion for New Jersey, he remained a lifelong Virginian. Powerful influences from his Virginia upbringing early insinuated themselves into Washington's character; they conditioned, though they did not determine, the thoughts and actions of the mature public figure he became.

George Washington's earliest memories were of Epsewasson, the small house and surrounding farm in northern Virginia with the Indian name that would later be rechristened Mount Vernon. Small wonder that Mount Vernon exercised such sway over Washington throughout his life: his first as well as his last memories were made there, and the home provided the bookends to his eventful life. In 1735, Augustine Washington moved the family to the juncture of Little Hunting Creek and the Potomac. There, over an ancient foundation Augustine constructed the sturdy story-and-a-half farmhouse that forms the core of Mount Vernon to this day. It was the first home George Washington knew in conscious memory.

In 1739 Augustine moved the Washingtons again, this time to Ferry Farm, across the Rappahannock River from Fredericksburg. There the seven-year-old George got his first taste of the wider world as he watched transatlantic ships ply the nearby river and listened to travelers talk with his parents when they boarded in the family's home. About this age George began to receive lessons from "a domestic tutor."[20] His formal education would never progress much beyond the rudimentary, though the rudiments in the mid–eighteenth century were far more demanding than those of today. In addition to his tutoring at home, some of young Washington's education took place in a schoolhouse proper.[21] He also took dancing and fencing lessons and performed certain "military exercises" in an effort to prepare himself to be a "gentleman," as that term was understood by Virginians of his era.[22] Over the next eight or so years, Washington learned to read and write a clear, elegant hand; he also learned to value the knowledge that came from books and other printed matter. Though he later claimed to lack the time to read as much as he was inclined, Washington early developed the habit of self-improvement through the careful study of written materials.[23] As Lord Fairfax predicted of the sixteen-year-old George Washington, he was a young man who would "go to school all his life."[24] His studies included "the highest branches of mathematics," history and the humanities, rhetoric, geography, astronomy, basic law and accounting, and surveying.[25] The last subject was to furnish him the skills for his first vocation and, more broadly, to provide the platform for his later work as a planter, military commander, and even geopolitical strategist.

Before he became a surveyor, however, the youthful George Washington wanted to ship aboard His Majesty's royal navy. His "mental acquisitions & exterior accomplishments were calculated to give him distinction in that profession," according to David Humphreys.[26] His mother, however, ruled that career out, which diverted George into the army; history turns on such small contingencies as these. Thereafter he put to sea only once in his life. In 1751 George, then nineteen years old, accompanied his half-brother Lawrence to the island of Barbados, where the older man hoped to recover from tuberculosis. Unfortunately the trip did nothing for Lawrence's condition, and he sent George back to Virginia without him. But while on Barbados the younger Washington encountered two significant things. One was the theater, the other the smallpox.

The Washington brothers attended a play called *George Barnwell*, and George was instantly captivated by the drama, the costumes, and the delivery of the lines. His love and appreciation of theatrics were to stay with him all his life, and Washington was to put that appreciation to political effect on numerous occasions. He himself became a political thespian of no mean ability, and the theater developed Washington's eye for the trappings and costumes of military and political office. He designed his own army uniforms and was careful about appearances of all sorts, from clothing to carriages to the furnishings of the presidential residence. Washington wanted to strike the proper balance between the dignity of office and republican simplicity, and no detail was too small to be overlooked.

The second event of significance in Barbados was a bout of smallpox George suffered and survived. The disease killed large numbers of people throughout the eighteenth century, but Washington was left with only minor scarring on his face. While it was unpleasant to endure, the disease inoculated Washington against what would be the principal killer of soldiers during the Revolution.

After his return to America, Washington spent more time at

Belvoir, the plantation of his neighbors, the land-rich and aristocratic Fairfaxes, who became his sponsors and informal teachers of the social graces lacking in his own more plebeian home.
The Fairfax clan, including George's older friend George William
Fairfax and his charming and beautiful wife Sarah (called "Sally"),
were models not only of taste but of Anglophile culture. Of
course part of that culture included respect for an established
Church of England; the Fairfax Anglophilia probably contributed to Washington's lifelong belief in the social utility of a
public religion. The Fairfax males were also enthusiastic out-
doorsmen, and on Belvoir's wooded acres Washington honed
his skills at foxhunting, and more significantly, by demonstrating
his athleticism and hardiness, got himself invited on a surveying
expedition in 1748, laying off boundaries of the Fairfax land over
the Blue Ridge into the Shenandoah Valley.

Accompanying the Fairfaxes onto the frontier gave young
Washington his first real adventure; more than that, it impressed
him with the seemingly limitless potential of the American west.
As he journeyed deeper into the interior, Washington began
to record his impressions in a diary he labeled "Journey Over
the Mountains." He wrote with increasing admiration of the
"most beautiful Groves of Sugar [Maple] Trees" and "the Land
[which] exceeding Rich and Fertile all the way produces abun-
dance of Grain Hemp Tobacco &ca."[27] To the young Washington, it was a land flowing with milk and honey—or at least it
could be made so with proper cultivation. It was also a land that
was flourishing under the hand of independent British-American
farmers, reaping the benefits of what Edmund Burke would later
call the "salutary neglect" of Parliament.[28]

Ten days into the journey, Washington also had his first close
look at a Native American war party. After traveling "I believe
the worst Road that ever was trod by Man or Beast," Washington recorded: "We were agreeably surpris'd at the sight of thirty
odd Indians coming from War with only one Scalp." According to Washington, the Indians, induced by liquor, "had a War
Daunce" around the fire after dark. The teenager was fascinated;
he put down his detailed impressions at length late that night in
his journal.[29] In this first recorded impression of Native Americans, one gets a sense of slight bemusement and even conde-

scension on Washington's part, as though he considered them an utterly foreign and perhaps inferior people. Washington was to have more dealings with Native Americans during the French and Indian War and, many years later, as president of the United States. His appreciation for them and their natural rights would grow over the years, but Washington seemed always to retain the sense of Indian foreignness evident in his early journal record.

After 1748 Washington instinctively turned to the western territories in his mind's eye. Recalling his first experience with substandard roads, to the end of his life Washington promoted projects to improve America's infrastructure and link the west with the east. He hoped such linkage would encourage settlement, agriculture, and commerce, for such benefits might one day make America a power to be reckoned with. And internal improvements would also knit different areas of the continent together, breaking down geographical and cultural barriers and promoting fellow-feeling among colonials, later United States citizens. Many of the adult Washington's geopolitical assumptions and pet projects, such as the Potomac Navigation Company, had their origins in that first surveying trip he took into the interior with the Fairfaxes as a stripling sixteen-year-old.

The following year, 1749, Washington parlayed the experience gained on that trip into his first paying job as official surveyor for Culpeper County, Virginia. He was seventeen years old. Earlier that spring, Washington had been complaining, not unlike today's teenager who lacks money for a "road trip," that he could not supply his horse with enough corn to make a trip to meet with his brother Lawrence.[30] Now, as county surveyor, he was in a position to do something about his cash poverty. Over the next year and a half, Washington performed nearly two hundred surveys, most of them on the western frontier of the Shenandoah Valley. For the first time in his life, hard cash jingled in his pockets; "a Dubleloon is my constant gain every Day that the Weather will permit my going out and sometime Six Pistoles," he wrote.[31] He used it to acquire land, some fifteen hundred acres of rich bottom land in the frontier valley he had surveyed. Thus began his many land acquisitions, and thereafter Washington valued land and agriculture, both for himself and for his countrymen, almost to the point of reverence.

The young Washington was beginning to appreciate agrarianism with a classical republican fervor. He was also embracing the British liberal concept, popularized by John Locke, of the importance of improving fallow land and the benefits to civilization that resulted from such cultivation. In the American context he noted the vast potential that lay in the continent's interior. He likewise appreciated what hard money could do for a young man on the rise, and in that appreciation one can see the beginnings of his commitment to putting American interests on a solid financial footing. That commitment ultimately resulted in several important actions while president: his appointment of Alexander Hamilton as first secretary of the Treasury, his sanction of a national bank, and his general endorsement of Hamilton's financial plans, including national assumption of state debts from the Revolution.

It is easy to underestimate the effect that Washington's early travels in North America had on his political imagination. Jefferson may have cited his lack of "imagination," but Washington had foresight, and what is foresight but imagination? By exploring the frontier and by traveling widely among the existing colonies while still a youth—he met with the governor of Massachusetts in Boston in his early twenties—the young Washington became personally acquainted with realities that later gave him his grasp of American geopolitics. (By contrast, Jefferson, though he oversaw the purchase of the Louisiana Territory and sent Lewis and Clark to explore it, was never west of Virginia's Appalachian Mountains in his long life; he was content to travel to the frontier territory vicariously, while Washington knew it firsthand.) From his late teens onward, George Washington began to think ahead, both for himself and for America as a whole. He showed an unusual appreciation for American "unity" from the beginning of his public service, first suggesting the concept to Virginia's governor in 1756 while still a jejune militia officer.[32]

Indeed, one of the interesting puzzles of Washington's life is how he was able to move so quickly beyond the narrow provincialism of his Virginia colleagues. Prior commentators on Washington have tied his development to the hard lessons he learned as commander in chief of the Continental Army and to the disabilities of the Confederation government.[33] To be sure, his often frustrating service in the Continental Army had a great deal to do with it; but it was Washington's thoughts and actions as an adolescent that first started him down the long unswerving road to a continental mindset. By age twenty-two Washington had penetrated deep into the Ohio Territory to the west, been north to Lake Erie, the present-day border between the United States and Canada, and been as far south as North Carolina. This knowledge by acquaintance of his country and countrymen served to break down the young Washington's sectional prejudices and later furnished him with the ability to think on a national scale, especially as commander in chief of a continental army, as a prime mover toward a federal government, and as the first president of the United States.

"The Juvenal Period of Life": Young Manhood, 1753–1761

At the end of his second presidential term, a sixty-four-year-old Washington, wearied by the administrative burdens of office, revisited his earlier work on a farewell address to put the capstone on his public career. With that special nostalgia in which the old indulge themselves, Washington thought back to his own youth and his practical apprenticeship in local and national politics. Generalizing from his own experience and considering how young Americans could best be educated and prepared for political leadership, Washington implored Alexander Hamilton to help him draft language about a national university. He wrote,

> That which would render it of the highest importance, in my opinion, is, that the Juvenal period of life, when friendships are formed, and habits established that will stick by one; the youth, or young men from different parts of the United States would be assembled together, and would by degrees discover that there was not that cause for those jealousies and prejudices which one part of the Union had imbibed against another part . . . prejudices are beginning to revive again, and never will be eradicated so effectually by any other means as the intimate intercourse of characters in early life, who, in all probability, will be at the head of the councils of this country in a more advanced stage of it.[34]

Washington quite likely had his own juvenile years in mind. He always regretted that he had never gone to college, although his twenties were filled with lasting friendships, the intentional formation of habits, the gradual diminution of sectional prejudices, and experiences that he filed away in his orderly brain for later use. Beginning in the 1750s Washington forged a durable friendship with Dr. James Craik as well as his relationship with his future wife, Martha Custis, both of whom would attend him at his deathbed, and one with a young British officer named Thomas Gage, who would become his adversary in the New England theater of the Revolution. He also came face-to-face with prejudices between British and Americans and between individual colonies and experienced the first of many "interpositions of Providence," as he styled it, on behalf of him and his aborning country.

His brother Lawrence's death from tuberculosis in 1752 left vacant the position of adjutant general of the Virginia militia. So George set about obtaining a commission in the Virginia militia himself and, with help from the Fairfaxes, got himself appointed adjutant general of the militia for the Southern District of Virginia. The twenty-year-old Major Washington immediately volunteered for a mission into the Ohio Valley to deliver an ultimatum on behalf of Lieutenant Governor Robert Dinwiddie to the French and Iroquois. The intentions of the French and their allies in the Six Nations were uncertain, and the British wanted it understood that the valley belonged to England. Washington led an expedition into the region in the fall of 1753. He found the French civil but insistent; they denied the British claim to the western lands and announced their intention to continue building and occupying forts there. On Washington's return to Tidewater, his account of the journey and meetings was ordered printed by Dinwiddie, and it was received with praise not only in the colonies but in England. Washington's international star seemed to be on the rise.

It fell soon enough. Later in 1754 Washington headed another expedition into the wilderness, this time to expel the French from Fort Duquesne, at present-day Pittsburgh. On their way there, Washington's corps stumbled onto a party of French, and he ordered them to open fire. What happened next is unclear.

American muskets and tomahawks killed ten Frenchmen, including their commander, Ensign Joseph Coulon de Jumonville, who was carrying diplomatic papers. (Jumonville himself was probably tomahawked after the French surrendered.) Washington, who could not read French, was gulled into signing a paper admitting the "assassination" of Jumonville, and the episode became known to the outraged French as *L'affaire Jumonville*. The French military response was swift and severe, and it led directly to the French and Indian War, also called the Seven Years War, of 1756–63.

The Jumonville affair was followed by an unmitigated military disaster for Washington and the Anglo-American force at his command. After cutting a wilderness road that "opened, for the first time in the history of the world, the Ohio Valley to wheeled vehicles," Washington selected a site at Fort Necessity for an encampment and dug his forces in during the first week of July 1754.[35] Thinking his position impregnable, Washington, quickly disabused of that notion, was forced to surrender his position, a rude fortification whose location in the middle of a meadow could hardly have been worse from a military perspective. Surrounded, outnumbered, and mired in standing water from a torrential downpour, Washington and his troops capitulated. On the portentous date of July 4th, Washington led his defeated forces back toward the Virginia capitol, where his bravery was commended by the House of Burgesses at the same time that private questions about his judgment were being raised.

This fiasco was followed by a second defeat a year later, in the company of troops led by General Edward Braddock against the French Fort Duquesne. Ignoring tactical advice from Washington and his colonials, Braddock's Anglo-American force was surprised in the deep woods near the Forks of the Ohio River by the French and their Indian allies en route to Duquesne. The slaughter was horrific, and Washington wrote to his brother afterward, "By the miraculous care of Providence, that protected me beyond all human expectation; I had 4 Bullets through my Coat, and two Horses shot under me, and yet escaped unhurt."[36] Braddock died of his wounds a few days after the encounter, and Washington was again commended for bravery and coolness under fire in seeing to an orderly retreat. Washington was underwhelmed by the judgment and behavior of British regulars when faced with the forest tactics of their French and Indian enemies.

On balance, Washington's military career had gotten off to an ignominious start. His "victory" against Jumonville's small force was outweighed by the public relations furor it caused with the French, and two disastrous defeats followed, at the ill-chosen Fort Necessity and at the Forks, with General Braddock. As Washington himself complained to Sally Fairfax, the coquettish neighbor's wife with whom he was especially close, "Surely no man ever made a worse beginning, than I have."[37] Yet his reputation would eventually recover. In his *Sketches of Eighteenth-Century America,* written during the Revolution, Crèvecoeur marveled how this "very Major Washington, the murderer of Captain Jumonville, is the idol of the French. . . . Success in the conclusion always eclipses the infamy, the perfidy of beginnings."[38] And from his experiences during the French and Indian War, Washington learned lessons that would have profound military and political consequences in the years to come.

Perhaps most important, Washington had his first tastes of intercolonial squabbling during a war that was supposed to be against the French. On at least two separate occasions there were disputes about rank, the first with Captain James Mackay of North Carolina, the second with Captain John Dagworthy of Maryland. In both cases Washington outranked the officers in question—at least on paper. But Mackay and Dagworthy, both holding regular commissions from the British army, claimed to outrank colonial militia officers like Washington, regardless of rank. This both infuriated Washington, still hungry for the glories of command, and made cooperation among the units from the different colonies extremely difficult. More important to his burgeoning political philosophy, Washington was given the distinct impression that for the British, colonials had a smaller stock of the rights of Englishmen than their counterparts across the ocean.

These concerns prompted Washington to write to Virginia Governor Robert Hunter Morris in 1756: "Nothing I more sincerely wish than a union of the colonies in this time of eminent danger; and that you may find your assembly in a temper of mind to act consistently with their preservation."[39] Pride in his own rank also prompted Washington to travel north, eventually to Boston, to plead his case. His journey took him through most of the major cities in the colonies: through Baltimore, Philadelphia, New York, and finally to Boston. There he met with Massachusetts Governor William Shirley, the commander of British forces in North America. Shirley listened with apparent interest to Washington's complaints, agreed that Dagworthy's royal commission did not entitle him to give orders to colonial officers of higher rank, but did not offer Washington a commission as a British regular. Washington was disappointed and disaffected; these emotions he had felt before, but he also rode away from Boston with a new attitude toward his limited role in the British empire. For the first time in his life, George Washington thought of himself first and foremost as an American.

From his early military service, Washington had learned that British commissions were worth more in English eyes than superior rank in American militias and that intercolonial disputes were harmful to all concerned. His experiences with Captains Mackay and Dagworthy taught him that lesson. He had learned that American militia troops would be sacrificed to British interests whenever a choice had to be made and, especially in the Braddock campaign, that opinion from afar was no substitute for knowledge up close. Washington was beginning to appreciate how impractical it could be for an island to rule a vast continent three thousand miles distant. And he was finding it difficult to adjust to the notion that simply being an American had somehow deprived him of the rights and benefits of a British subject. As events in the 1760s and 1770s were later to prove, Washington's convictions about his colonial rights would only be strengthened, and those early convictions would have an extraordinary effect on global politics.

During this phase of his life, Washington also began his assault on the upper echelons of Virginia society. He had already joined the Masons in 1752 at age twenty, a common and useful step for a young man with ambitions in colonial society. Beginning in 1758, Washington was elected to the lower house of Virginia's legislature, the House of Burgesses, a position he would hold off and on for the next sixteen years, until he was appointed to the

First Continental Congress in 1774. The following year, 1759, Washington married Martha Dandridge Custis, the mother of two young children from a prior marriage and reputed to be one of the wealthiest widows in Virginia. His marriage to Martha brought Washington domestic stability and happiness, management of a large estate, and a sizeable increase in means. All of these factors, along with his role in the House of Burgesses, resulted in a jump in social status for the young Washington. He was now in a position to assume the role of a substantial planter and "gentleman freeholder" as well as the civic responsibilities that went along with such a role in colonial Virginia society.

"A USEFUL MEMBER OF SOCIETY": BURGESS AND PLANTER, 1759–1775

During his years as a burgess, Washington learned the craft of a legislator, and much about the give-and-take of politics. He witnessed firsthand the deliberate and often willful nature of legislative bodies; his early participation in colonial lawmaking helped him understand the legislatures with whom he would later deal. It built up a reservoir of political experience and enabled him to have a measure of patience with the inefficiencies of the Continental Congress during the eight years of the Revolution and, later, with the Congress of the United States. It also gave him a grudging respect for the important place of constituent legislatures in imperial and federal politics. Even under the constitutional monarchy operating in the British empire of the late eighteenth century, colonial legislatures were the principal lawmaking bodies for British Americans in the minds of most Americans and in actual fact. This was true even of Virginia, which of all the colonies came closest to being a direct transplantation of British political culture and manners. From Virginia politics Washington learned the importance of local legislatures and to respect the work they did. He had an insider's appreciation for their role in political society, their limitations, and the importance of preserving their goodwill. That is one reason Washington took care not to offend or even to appear to ride roughshod over the state legislatures during the Revolution.

His work as a burgess in the late 1760s also radicalized Washington in significant ways. Though his political theory was always conservative—he consistently maintained that property-owning British Americans had a full stock of both natural rights and rights under the British constitution—in 1769 Washington took part in drafting and transmitting Virginia's articles of association and nonimportation, the first of several defiant steps he took during the runup to the Revolution. Those articles were a reaction to Parliament's Townshend Acts of 1767, which taxed various colonial imports in unprecedented ways. By the spring of 1769, merchants in several American colonies were protesting the import duties and forming nonimportation associations. Washington saw the value in such associations and proposed one in Virginia, working with George Mason to draft the agreement creating the association and transmitting it to the burgesses. Arguing in the best British liberal tradition, Washington and Mason catalogued the violations of British-American liberties, and Washington even hinted privately that he might consider force as a legitimate remedy to British excesses. Biographers have made much of Washington's wearing his militia uniform to the Second Continental Congress in 1774 as a signal that he was finally prepared to use force to defend American liberties and even that he was available to lead an army if necessary. But in reality Washington's contemplation of the use of military force, or "arms" as he called it, dates back to his letters to Mason in the spring of 1769. Washington wrote, somewhat cryptically, "that no man shou'd scruple, or hesitate a moment to use a-ms [*sic*] in defence of so valuable a blessing [as liberty] . . . is clearly my opinion; yet A-ms I wou'd beg leave to add, should be the last resource; the denier [*sic*] resort."[40]

Having signaled his own commitment to Mason, Washington helped his Fairfax County neighbor draft the language for the Virginia association and later carried that document to Williamsburg, where he saw that it was adopted by a legislative committee of which he was a member. Through his work on these articles of association, Washington helped to foment resistance to British policies in Virginia, to articulate a case for such resistance, and to encourage solidarity among all the American colonies.

In the summer of 1774, Washington once again aided George

Mason in drawing up the noteworthy Fairfax County Resolves, a further step in continental resistance and cooperation and a giant step in the radicalization of George Washington. On July 17 Mason visited Washington at Mount Vernon, where they conferred about the escalating crisis in Virginia and, by extension, in all the colonies. What emerged was a document not unlike Washington and Mason's earlier collaboration on the Virginia nonimportation association, though it was somewhat broader in scope and more theoretical in its reasoning. The Resolves marshaled classic British liberal arguments against parliamentary policies and signaled a new willingness on the part of the leading southern colony to make common cause with Massachusetts.

During these years Washington also began serving in Truro Parish as an Anglican vestryman, another activity intended to make him what in another context he called "a useful member of society."[41] As an office, the vestry was as civil as it was ecclesiastical; even Jefferson served on one in his own parish. As vestryman, Washington was responsible for some aspects of taxation, poor relief (the eighteenth-century equivalent of welfare), and education in the community, along with ministers' salaries and the repair and maintenance of church buildings and property. This civil-religious vestry work conditioned Washington to appreciate Protestant Christianity as a valuable aid to social and political stability.

The experiences through 1775 amounted to a long tutorial in practical politics for Washington. In particular, his travels and travails as a youthful military officer helped set the course of his later life and contributed greatly to the Americanization of George Washington. They also fixed his mental habits in ways that have seldom been acknowledged by historians. As Fitzpatrick wrote in the 1930s, it still "is not generally realized that before George Washington was twenty-eight years old he had been longer in the saddle and had traveled on horseback over a greater part of America than any other man in the colonies."[42] Nor is it generally realized that the geopolitical lessons he learned in that period—about intercolonial disputes, about bad or nonexistent arteries of travel and communication, about inefficient decentralization—conditioned the political thinking of the mature Washington when he became a national military and political figure. Much as the young Alexander Hamilton learned the value of uniform currency through his international business dealings as a precocious teenager in the West Indies and thus became better prepared for his role as Washington's first secretary of the Treasury, certain of Washington's youthful experiences fitted him out for his own political career in the nation he helped liberate.

"IN THE SERVICE OF MY COUNTRY": REVOLUTION, 1775–1783

Like a number of later presidents (Jackson, Grant, and Eisenhower, for example), George Washington was raised to national prominence, and even celebrity, by a war. Had the Revolution ended with a British victory, Washington might have found himself swinging from an English gibbet, and perhaps he would be portrayed today as a sort of American William Wallace—an intrepid but feckless patriot. Of course the British were denied the pleasure of hanging Washington from a gallows or even from a tree, as they did Nathan Hale, and by the Revolution's end even George III was calling Washington the "greatest character of the age" for returning his commission to the Continental Congress.[43]

Many of the political skills that Washington took with him into the presidency in 1789 were acquired or developed during the eight trying years of the Revolution, years spent in "the service of my country," as he said when he resigned from the army in 1783.[44] As commander in chief of the continental army, Washington was not only a military leader but effectively a chief executive officer and liaison with civil government, including the various state governments and the Confederation Congress at Philadelphia. His civil-military connections and appointments would have lasting significance for the United States. Many of the men who served under him in the army, including the likes of Alexander Hamilton, John Marshall, James Monroe, and Aaron Burr, went on to notable careers on both sides of the political divide in the early republic. Thus, as Ron Chernow has pointed out, in "many respects, the political alignments of 1789 were first forged in the appointment lists of the Revolution."[45]

Furthermore, several of the tenets of Washington's political philosophy, including his conviction of the need for American unity, were strengthened by his often frustrating experiences with the Confederation during the war for independence.

Scholars have long noted the effect the Revolution had on Washington's view of continental America and on his conviction that greater political centralization was needed in the new nation. The war had this effect on other future leaders. John Marshall, who as "the Great Chief Justice" did more than any other individual to consolidate national power in the early republic, wrote that "I was confirmed in the habit of considering America as my country and Congress as my government" during his service under Washington in the Revolution.[46] The same can be said of Washington himself—that is, so long as the emphasis remains on the word "confirmed." For Washington was already in the habit of considering America as his country by the time the war began, more so than the average state-proud Virginian of his day. When Washington corresponded with other Virginians during the war he usually referred to "their" state, not "our" state. In a pleading letter to his neighbor George Mason, Washington wrote, "It would afford me very singular pleasure to be favoured at all times with your sentiments . . . upon public matters of general [i.e., American] concernment as well as those which more immediately respect your own State." Washington went on to chide Mason subtly for his inactivity and provinciality, suggesting that "no man who wishes well to the liberties of his Country and desires to see its rights established, can avoid crying out where are our men of abilities? Why do they not come forth to save their Country?"[47]

To be sure, Washington's relations with his largely New England army beginning in 1775 were not all cloudless glory, and his criticism of northern troops led to one of the few public relations blunders of the war. His attitude also showed that some residue of southern provinciality remained in his mind. To his cousin Lund Washington, he wrote that the "People of this government [New England] have obtained a Character which they by no means deserved; their officers generally speaking are the most indifferent kind of People I ever saw . . . in short they are by no means such Troops, in any respect, as you are led to believe of them from the accts. which are published, but I need not make myself Enemies among them, by this declaration, although it is consistent with truth."[48] But his indiscretion did make him enemies, or at least incensed friends. Unknown to Washington, the contents of his private correspondence were being leaked to prominent New Englanders like John Adams, who had recently recommended Washington for the top post in the Army. Thanks to Virginian Richard Henry Lee, who had formed a friendship with Adams, Washington's private grousings about the New Englanders were making the rounds in Philadelphia. A letter from his friend Joseph Reed warning Washington of the trouble his letters were causing drew the general's thanks and a promise that he would "endeavor at a reformation."[49] (He made good on that promise, so much so that by the time of the ratification debates thirteen years later, Washington was pointing out how it was "a little strange, that the men of large property in the *South*, should be more afraid that the Constitution will produce an Aristocracy or a Monarchy, than the genuine democratical people of the *East* [i.e., New England].")[50]

Washington was under no illusion that soldiers from any geographical region would remain in the field during a long, costly war simply out of principle; their "interest" had to be engaged as well. "Men may speculate as they will; they may talk of patriotism," Washington wrote in 1778, "but whoever builds upon it, as a sufficient Basis for conducting a long and [bloody] War, will find themselves deceived in the end. We must take the passions of Men as Nature has given them." Patriotism "must be aided by a prospect of Interest or some reward. For a time, it may, of itself push Men to Action; to bear much, to encounter difficulties; but it will not endure unassisted by Interest."[51]

The Revolution reinforced Washington's appreciation of financial interest and the profit motive and, indeed, the powerful incentive of all kinds of self-interest, which was one of the key phrases of British Enlightenment liberalism. In 1776 Adam Smith had published his *Inquiry into the Nature and Causes of the Wealth of Nations,* a study of the effects of individual and national pursuit of "self-interest." Smith insisted that altruistic motives were a thin reed on which to hang hopes of good behavior from men. "It is not from the benevolence of the butcher, the brewer, or the baker that we expect our dinner, but from their regard to their self-interest. We address ourselves, not to their humanity, but to their self-love, and never talk to them of our necessities, but of their advantages."[52] As Robert Heilbroner noted in his classic study *The Worldly Philosophers,* "The book took hold only slowly. It was to be almost eight years before it was quoted in Parliament, the first to do so being Charles James Fox, the most powerful member of Commons (who later admitted that he had never actually *read* the book.)"[53] Washington was later to buy and—unlike Fox—study Smith's work carefully, but by 1778 his experience had already taught him a hard lesson about economic "self-interest."

Washington's conviction of the need for more government efficiency and personnel was only reinforced during his long and often frustrating service as commander in chief. He was forced to rely on bright young aides, principally Alexander Hamilton, to help him with administrative and logistical brainwork. In 1776 Washington wrote Joseph Reed in exasperation that "at present, my time is so much taken up at my desk, that I am obliged to neglect many other essential parts of my duty. It is absolutely necessary, therefore, for me to have persons that can think for me, as well as execute orders."[54] Critics would later use this admission against Washington. Benjamin Rush claimed that during the war Washington had been "governed by General Greene, General Knox, and Colonel Hamilton, one of his aides, a young man of twenty-one years."[55] Working in circumstances where no bureaucracy or even routinized procedures existed forced Washington to rely on advisors, an administrative habit that he carried into the presidency, where he faced similar challenges in public administration due to the uniqueness of his position. As president Washington relied heavily on his department heads for advice, just as he had on his councils of general officers during the war, almost to a paralyzing extent.

We need not describe in detail the strategic and tactical moves made by Washington and his commanders during the war itself, which on the whole consisted of a series of delaying actions and fighting retreats. Two incidents in particular deserve our attention, though neither was, strictly speaking, a military engagement. Both concerned supposed plots by the officer corps to subvert the republican form of government Washington had helped to establish and to whose control he had submitted his army. (For example, after the fighting at Kips Bay he had wanted to burn New York and abandon it to the British, but Congress forbade him, and Washington deferred even that military matter to their judgment.) But in May 1782 one Col. Lewis Nicola had written to Washington that "this war must have shewn to all, but to military men in particular the weakness of republicks" and went on to suggest an elected monarchy in its stead, with Washington as king. Claiming to represent the views of other officers, he hoped that Washington would not be one of those "Republican bigots" who "have so connected the ideas of tyranny and monarchy as to find it very difficult to separate them." Unfortunately for Nicola, Washington had great difficulty separating such ideas, and he sent back a frosty reply—sealed and under armed guard—in which he rejected them as unconstitutional and warned Nicola "to banish these thoughts from your Mind, and never communicate, as from yourself, or any one else, a sentiment of the like Nature."[56]

A year later Washington faced down a similar conspiracy among his disgruntled officer corps. Known to history as "the Newburgh conspiracy," to Washington it represented a threat to republican principles nearly as great as the British army, and more pernicious because it came from within his own officers. The Confederation Congress had withheld its promised payments to the army, who considered those monies part of the terms of their enlistment and "a debt of honour," as Washington put it.[57] A group of officers had gathered at Newburgh, New York—on the Ides of March, 1783, in a building they called, in classically lofty tones, the "Temple of Virtue"—to discuss threatening or forcing Congress to pay. In an exquisite piece of political theater, Washington entered unannounced and read prepared remarks after fumbling for his glasses and begging the pardon of the officers, saying "for I have not only grown gray, but almost blind, in the service of my country." According to an eyewitness, many of the officers were in tears by the time Washington finished.[58] The first and last military coup in American history was thus avoided by Washington's gift for theatrical politics and his evident embodiment of classical republican virtue.

During the course of a long and potentially demoralizing war,

Washington sought and received counsel and aid from various quarters, including divine Providence, or so he repeatedly thought and wrote. "The hand of Providence has been so conspicuous in all this, that he must be worse than an infidel that lacks faith, and more wicked, that has not gratitude enough to acknowledge his obligations, but, it will be time enough for me to turn preacher, when my present appointment ceases," he wrote in 1778.[59] By the war's end and the successful conclusion of the Treaty of Paris, Washington was more than ever convinced of the guiding and protecting hand of Providence on the Revolution. In his Circular Address to the States of June 1783, he held forth on the blessings given to American society by Providence, including "above all, the pure and benign light of Revelation." But sounding a note more reminiscent of the Hebrew Jeremiad than of Christian triumphalism, Washington cautioned Americans that at "this auspicious period, the United States came into existence as a Nation, and if their Citizens should not be completely free and happy, the fault will be intirely their own."[60]

The opportunity for his farewell Circular Letter to the States had been a long time coming. Though the decisive battle of Yorktown had been won in 1781, for two more years Washington had to maintain an army in the field until the Treaty of Paris was negotiated and signed in 1783 and he could issue what came to be known as his "Legacy." After circulating it in June, Washington oversaw the disbanding of the army, watched for British compliance with the terms of the treaty, and, in an another affecting piece of political theater, resigned his commission at Annapolis on December 23, 1783, and rode hard to Mount Vernon, where he arrived as dusk was falling on Christmas Eve. Having fought a war with the British over British liberal principles, like the classical republican Cincinnatus, he had eagerly returned to his farm, thinking he had put public life behind him forever.

"A LITTLE REPOSE AND RETIREMENT": 1783–1789

By becoming the first leader of a successful colonial revolution in history, George Washington was vaulted onto the international stage in a far grander way than his unwitting entrance to the Seven Years War. The moment he resigned his command at Annapolis in 1783, Washington took the place in the "great republic of humanity" he so obviously coveted. But citizenship in that republic had costs of its own. As Humphreys described it, "Many official & literary persons, on both sides of the Ocean, [are] ambitious of a correspondence with him. These correspondencies unavoidably engross a great portion of his time; and the communications contained in them, combined with the numerous periodical Publications & News Papers which he peruses, render him, as it were, the focus of political Intelligence for the New World." Meetings with foreign and domestic dignitaries occupied his time as well. "Every foreigner, of distinction, who visits America, makes it a point to see him. Members of Congress & other dignified Personages do not pass his house without calling to pay their respects."[61]

In the seven years prior to the Revolution, the Washingtons had entertained roughly two thousand house guests, and the flow only increased after the war's end.[62] Indeed, the Washingtons received so many visitors at Mount Vernon that Congress considered voting them a stipend to reimburse their entertainment costs. With a characteristic show of republican disinterestedness, Washington refused to accept any subsidy. In addition to correspondence and visitors, books poured into Mount Vernon. Many European and American authors sent him copies of their works, as did Americans. As Humphreys wrote, "There is scarcely one work written in America on any art, science, or subject" that did not find its way into Washington's study.[63] In his first retirement Washington became a clearinghouse of political intelligence not only in America but throughout the western world. Some of what he learned about the international scene was troubling and would come back to haunt Washington during his presidential administrations. In 1788, more than a year before the fall of the Bastille, he penned a concerned note to Lafayette: "I like not much the situation of affairs in France. The bold demands of the parliaments, and the decisive tone of the King, shew that but little more irritation would be necessary to blow up the spark of discontent into a flame, that might not easily be quenched."[64] Washington kept up with domestic political events and ideas by poring over all of those newspapers from around the country in the evenings, as he did literally to his dying day.

In the years immediately following the Revolution, Washington needed information regarding his western land holdings as well. Having only laid eyes on Mount Vernon once, briefly, during the previous eight years, he returned home to find a plantation and unfinished "mansion house" going to seed. He had lost nearly half his net worth through inattention and inefficient absentee management and his refusal to accept a salary; he needed to get his affairs in order during what he hoped would be "a little repose and retirement."[65] Washington was, like so many Virginia planters of his day, perpetually land-rich and cash-poor. He also found to his dismay that he owed unanticipated back taxes on his lands because of changes in jurisdiction during the war. To see what rental income could be generated from his frontier lands, Washington took an extended trip back into the interior. He found squatters who not only owed him back rent but claimed ownership by possession. This so piqued Washington that he broke his longstanding rule of avoiding legal disputes and successfully sued some of the more recalcitrant squatters, though he negotiated terms with them after his judgment was awarded. During those travels Washington also kept his surveyor's eyes open, imagining an improved transportation network by land and water, especially one that improved natural waterways with canals, to connect the American interior to the east.

Travel, correspondence, and reading material of all kinds helped Washington keep his finger on the political pulse of America, which in some important respects seemed to him dangerously weak. As the years following the Revolution went by, he became increasingly convinced of the inefficiency of the Confederation government and of the need to strengthen the existing union. This was accentuated by the controversy between Virginia and Maryland over navigation of the Potomac. Upon return from his inspection of his western lands, Washington became president of the Potomac Navigation Company, and it was his involvement in the company that led him to convene a conference at an enlarged Mount Vernon in 1785, bringing together Virginians and Marylanders to settle their differences over and improve navigation on the Potomac River. Washington handled this skillfully, and the delegates left the conference with Washington's larger vision for internal improvement of all kinds. Plans were made for a national conference on trade, which resulted in the Annapolis Convention in 1786, whose stated purpose had expanded from undertaking internal improvements to rendering "the constitution of the Federal Government adequate to the exigencies of the Union."[66] In that convention, two of Washington's younger protégés, his former wartime aide Alexander Hamilton and fellow Virginian James Madison, played prominent roles and joined the call at meeting's end for a constitutional convention to remedy the "important defects in the system of the Federal Government."

In the intervening months, the rebellion in Massachusetts led by Captain Daniel Shays, late of the American army, conjured up images of peasants with pitchforks shutting down courthouses and caused Washington to lament to Henry Lee, "I am mortified beyond expression when I view the clouds that have spread over the brightest morn that ever dawned upon any Country."[67] To James Madison he wrote, "We are fast verging to anarchy and confusion! . . . Thirteen Sovereignties pulling against each other, and all tugging at the foederal head, will soon bring ruin on the whole; whereas a liberal, and energetic Constitution . . . might restore us to that degree of respectability & consequence, to which we had a fair claim, & the brightest prospect of attaining."[68]

Six months later, in May 1787, Washington was drafted president of the Constitutional Convention, where he got the chance to work on forming "the foederal head" anew. It was a position he had to be coaxed into taking; he was extremely reluctant to leave Mount Vernon, more still to appear hypocritical, having promised in Annapolis in 1783 to retire from public life for good. And having already begged off a concurrent meeting of the Society of the Cincinnati, a fraternal organization of former Revolutionary War officers that was to bedevil him during his presidency, Washington was doubly aware of appearing the hypocrite. But friends and colleagues prevailed upon him, and Washington packed off to Philadelphia and the Federal Convention, where he was promptly and unanimously elected president.

During his time in the chair throughout that intolerably hot summer, Washington learned further lessons about compromise in nation-making and law-making that were important to the future of the republic. He heard Benjamin Franklin expostulate on the virtues of compromise in June, when he addressed the nettlesome problem of congressional representation. "When a broad table is to be made, and the edges of planks do not fit," Franklin said, "the artist takes a little from both, and makes a good joint. In like manner, here, both sides must part from some of their demands, in order that they may join in some accommodating proposition."[69] Washington himself had helped those compromises along by insisting on civil forms of discourse during the Convention debates. His presence lent an aura not only of dignity over the Convention but also of legality, at a time when it was sorely needed. For the delegates knew they could be accused of what Martin Van Buren later called a "heroic" but "lawless act" when they decided to scrap, rather than revise, the Articles of Confederation.[70] Their meeting had been convened by the Confederation Congress's resolution of February 21, 1787, authorizing a federal convention for the "sole and express purpose" of "revising" the Articles of Confederation and the reporting of "such alterations and provisions therein [i.e., in the Articles]" as in their "opinion" should be made. Of course the delegates could later claim they had acted according to the spirit of the congressional resolution, namely to "render the federal constitution adequate to the exigencies of Government and the preservation of the Union."[71] But according to the letter of the law, they had acted *ultra vires.*

Washington quickly realized that his presence was of vast symbolic importance; indeed, it was the principal reason he decided to attend the Convention in the first place. If Washington, so scrupulous in his adherence to the rule of law and to the instructions of Congress during the war for independence, was in attendance, surely the Convention must be legitimate? From the start of the debates, Washington remained nearly mute, so his role was necessarily a symbolic one, both inside and outside the Convention. After the Constitution was ratified, James Monroe, an Antifederalist of sorts, wrote glumly to Thomas Jefferson in Paris, "Be assured, his [Washington's] influence carried this government."[72] Washington's sense of the theater of politics was put to use and reinforced as he sat, day after day, on the raised dais above the delegates, which he left only to sit with the Virginia delegation when the Convention resolved itself into a committee of the whole. His votes from the floor almost invariably favored a stronger, more energetic general government and executive. According to Glenn Phelps, there were apparently nine occasions on which Washington voted during the Convention as a Virginia delegate, and his side won only three of those. He voted for a single executive, for a term of "good behavior" for that executive, and against a two-thirds congressional majority to override a presidential veto.[73] Thus Washington the delegate favored a strong executive, which, as we will see, was in keeping with British liberal political theory and with his eventual practice as president of the United States.

Washington's presence at the Convention also lent an air of civility to the proceedings that they might not have had if a delegate with less gravitas had been in the chair. His stoical deportment helped reinforce the rules of the Convention, rules to guarantee professional courtesies, to force the delegates to act like gentlemen, and to create an environment of unity and reasoned debate. If nothing else, Washington was a gentleman; he was civil, even courtly, a word that forms the root of *courtesy*. Abigail Adams, who had been to court in England, said that Washington's presidential manner "leaves Royal George [III] far behind him."[74] The type of political courtesy Washington exuded and encouraged and the rules he silently enforced fostered reasoned debate among the delegates rather than mere posturing. There was some occasional grandstanding—delegates had to endure what one of them called a two-day "harangue" from Luther Martin, and Hamilton went on for nearly six hours during one stretch—but for the most part delegates spoke their minds and then sat down.[75]

Washington only broke his silence on the Convention's final day, September 17, 1787. The issue that drew him out was the proper ratio of representatives to population. Washington argued in favor of more congressional representatives per thousand inhabitants—in effect, a democratizing or classical republican feature. According to Madison's notes, Washington demurred that although his office as president of the convention "might be thought . . . to impose silence on him, yet he could not forbear expressing his wish that the alteration proposed might take place." Though "the objections to the plan recommended might be made as few as possible," still the "smallness of the proportion of Representatives had been considered," he said, by himself and "by many members of the Convention an insufficient security for the rights and interests of the people." Thus it would "give him much satisfaction" to see it increased.[76] Washington's argument, which combined practical politics with principle, was accepted by the delegates and passed in the affirmative. His stress on the people's rights and interests softens the common picture of Washington as a "high federalist" along Hamiltonian lines.

Washington did, however, want a high-toned executive power, and his hovering genius apparently encouraged the delegates to create a strong unified presidency. Most presidential historians assume that the force of Washington's classical republican character calmed fears of monarchy or the arbitrary exercise of executive power by a single executive. As Clinton Rossiter put it in his seminal study of the American presidency, the "big if silent gun in the arsenal of those who insisted upon the essential republicanism of the proposed Presidency was the universal assumption that George Washington, the Cincinnatus of the West, would be chosen as first occupant of the office, and chosen and chosen again until claimed by the grave."[77] The authoritative source adduced for this belief on the part of the delegates is an ill-humored remark made by Pierce Butler of South Carolina. "Entre nous," Butler wrote to an English relative, "I do [not] believe they [i.e., the executive powers] would have been so great, had not many of the members cast their eyes toward General Washington as President; and shaped their ideas of the Powers to be given a President, by their opinions of his Virtue."[78] A minority of delegates had their doubts. Washington's friend Edmund Randolph complained that the presidency appeared to him "the fetus of monarchy."[79] Benjamin Franklin was optimistic in the short run and pessimistic in the long run. "The first man put at the helm will be a good one," he said on June 4, 1787. "Nobody knows what sort may come afterwards. The Executive will be always increasing here, as elsewhere, till it ends in a monarchy."[80] Yet the delegates voted, with Washington in their peripheral vision, for a strong single executive who was also, concurrently, commander in chief of the army and navy.

Having affected the powers of the presidency both by voting as a Virginia delegate and by projecting classically republican political virtues of his own, Washington conditioned the modern liberal office of president of the United States. It was and is an office that exists to enforce the will of the people, expressed through their representative legislature, in the service of a federal government created to secure their rights to life, liberty, and property. It was also an office he himself would reluctantly assume two years later.

"To the Chair of Government": Presidency, 1789–1796

At the end of the Revolutionary War, Washington passed up the chance to become another King George for America. Instead, he retired to his farm until he became the first popularly elected head of state in western history, a position arguably more powerful than the English king. Yet it was a position he did not want. Cincinnatus-like, Washington had to be called back from his plow into service of his country, and the Roman imagery was not lost on his contemporaries. In republican fashion, the general protested that he did not want the responsibility and was unsuited to the task; in private he said he felt like a criminal who had received his death sentence.[81] But George Washington was not simply a classical republican, he was also a British liberal, and he laid aside his republican desire for a farmer's life in order to become chief executive of the first liberal government explicitly established to secure natural rights. Washington saw the chance to perfect an immature union through a strong executive, a mainstay of Lockean political theory, as one he could ill afford to pass up. So in 1789 he left Mount Vernon for New York, where he was to be invested, not as king or consul over an American version of the Roman republic or even "His High Mightiness," as John Adams suggested, but merely as president of the United States.

Washington and his advisors took particular care in crafting his inaugural ceremony. He wanted to strike a balance between classical republican simplicity, the dignity of a liberal protector of the people's rights, and Judeo-Christian piety. He wove elements of all three traditions into his inauguration. For example, for republican simplicity he wore a specially made plain brown suit of American homespun. Though the inauguration was as solemn as a British coronation at Westminster, Washington substituted for the king's scepter a dress sword as a fitting symbol of executive power. And he swore his constitutionally prescribed oath of office on, and then kissed, a Bible open to Psalm 121: "I will lift up mine eyes unto the hills, from whence cometh my help."[82]

As it turned out, Washington would need a great deal of help during his ground-breaking terms as president. His first crisis was a near-fatal illness, which he endured in June 1789 with stoical resolve, claiming that whether he died then "or twenty years hence" was a matter of complete indifference to him.[83] (Indeed, he feared that the reputation he had worked so hard to cultivate would be squandered during his presidency; his concerns were not unlike those of Virginia's Henry Lee, who said, "I believe that the people of America have been guilty of idolatry, by making a man their god; and that the god will convince them he is only man.")[84] After recovering, Washington set about the important business of establishing proper precedents of public administration. In early 1790, he explained to Catherine Macaulay Graham, "My station is new; and, if I may use the expression, I walk on untrodden ground. There is scarcely any part of my conduct wch. may not hereafter be drawn into precedent."[85]

The president had to walk carefully, and this was true both literally and figuratively. As Leonard White showed in his classic study of American public administration, *The Federalists*, conditions during the first presidential administration were staggeringly primitive.[86] Major thoroughfares were impassable at times; the mail, including all government correspondence and even newly promulgated laws, was often heavily delayed or lost altogether. On one occasion a letter from Washington to the governor of Virginia took fifty-eight days to be delivered. On another, the president was nearly drowned during a ferry crossing at Colchester, Virginia, in the summer of 1791 and had to help rescue horses and baggage from the river himself.[87] Bureaucracies and government infrastructures were nonexistent, and Washington frequently had to improvise procedures, falling back on common devices from earlier in his career such as the circular letter. For example, in the summer of 1789 the First United States Congress, having begun to write federal laws under the Constitution, had forgotten to create a mechanism for distributing them to the states, and Washington had to pick up the slack. In June he wrote a chagrined note "to the Supreme Executives of the Several States" enclosing a congressional resolve and noting that as "Congress have not yet established any Department through which communications can be officially made from the General Government to the Executives of the several States, I do, agreeably to the foregoing Resolution, transmit to your Excellency the enclosed Act."[88] Washington believed the power to raise revenue and put the new national government on a sound financial footing was crucial to creating something more nearly resembling a real, working government.

That task fell to his extraordinarily able secretary of the Treasury, Alexander Hamilton. Washington lent Hamilton his support for an expansive reading of the federal government's constitutional powers, particularly to charter a national bank, that bane of Jefferson's existence. (Jefferson later had Madison take up his pen to answer Hamilton's political "heresies"; the result was a pseudonymous pamphlet war between the two former *Federalist* authors, now calling themselves "Pacificus" and "Helvidius.") Washington had intentionally cobbled together a group of presidential advisors—he did not follow the British custom of calling them a "cabinet"—representative of various regions and interests within the infant United States, including of course Hamilton and Jefferson, who came to embody the political poles of the first Washington administration. He also deliberately chose men with unimpeachable revolutionary credentials, perhaps to convey the impression that the federal government was keeping alive the "Spirit of '76."

That spirit was somewhat divided against itself in the first Washington cabinet, composed of Hamilton, John Jay as secretary of foreign affairs (later shortened to "state") and then first chief justice of the United States, Jefferson as his replacement at

state, Henry Knox as secretary of war, Edmund Randolph as attorney general, and Vice President John Adams. (Madison,
though not head of a department, also acted as a presidential advisor.) The first rift occurred over the Bank and the assumption
of the state debts by the federal treasury. Jefferson, as a strict
constitutional constructionist and Virginian, could find no power
to create a national bank in the Constitution and thought assumption of state debts left over from the Revolution was unfair
to Virginia and other states that had made efforts to pay theirs
off. Hamilton, as a loose constructionist and New Yorker, found
broad inherent powers in the Constitution and believed a national bank and assumption were crucial to establishing the
United States on a firm financial base. President Washington
scrupulously solicited opinions from his advisors, just as he had
done during the Revolutionary War with his generals, and eventually threw his weight behind Hamilton.

In the meantime, a compromise was worked out between Jefferson and Hamilton over dinner one evening, according to Jefferson's later account. Jefferson agreed to argue for assumption
of the state debts if Hamilton could deliver the necessary votes
to seat the national capitol permanently in the south. Hamilton
could, and did, deliver the votes, and eventually a location on the
Potomac was agreed to, with President Washington to choose and
lay out the exact site. (Vice President Adams opposed the plan
and, years later, accused Washington of stealing the idea from a
story about a Roman ruler in a popular ancient history book:
"'Such a governor was Numa at Rome. . . . He commanded his
subjects to build a city, marking out himself the place and cir-
cumference of the walls.' . . . I opposed it in every step of its
progress, and voted against it in [the] Senate on all occasions.")[89]
Jefferson, who suffered a severe case of buyer's remorse over assumption, later claimed he had been duped by Hamilton into
making a bad trade of a southern capitol for assumption.[90]

To help solidify the union and to gauge how far the tensions
between Hamilton and Jefferson were reflected in the citizenry
at large, Washington made extensive tours north and south during his administration, to see and be seen. He met with local
officials, attended church services of a variety of denominations,
and generally kept his eyes and ears open. These tours convinced

Washington that on the whole, Americans were satisfied with the bargain they had made between liberty and order, and they reinforced his earlier impressions of the vast potential that lay in the colonies-cum-nation, and his conviction that centralization was still the key to unlocking that potential. His gimlet eye also took note of the poor modes of transportation and communication, especially in the deep South.

Washington's first term was primarily devoted to domestic issues, but beyond precedents, national finances, and the incipient Federalist-Republican feud on the domestic front, several challenges in international relations arose. Tensions with Great Britain that were unresolved by the Treaty of Paris mounted, expressing themselves in a cold war fought over trade. Hardly had the nation gotten on its feet when it was threatened with a foreign war, once again with the most powerful military on earth, and Washington did his level best to avoid it and other unnecessary foreign entanglements, which was to become a refrain of his political philosophy. War with Britain would be averted in his second administration by the much-maligned Jay Treaty, whose terms appeared to be too pro-British for Jefferson and the Francophile contingent. France and her own revolution, which had begun in 1789, were much on the mind of Washington, Jefferson, and their colleagues in the first term. Early hopes that the French Revolution would resolve itself without much wanton bloodshed were disappointed. Despite receiving the key to the Bastille as a gift from Lafayette and his French admirers in 1790—it hangs in the hallway at Mount Vernon to this day—Washington had his doubts about that revolution, which unfortunately were vindicated. To his mind, British notions of liberty were stable and salutary compared to the more radical ideas and impulses of the French Enlightenment that leveled French society and ultimately paved the road for Bonaparte's empire, though he did not live to see it.

But all of that lay in the future. Meanwhile the Bill of Rights, the first ten amendments to the Constitution, took effect *en bloc* in 1791. Although Washington thought a bill of rights was superfluous to a constitution that did not threaten the people's liberties in the first place, as president he recommended that amendments be given the "dispassionate" attention of Congress, provided they were not "incompatible with the fundamental principles of a free and efficient government."[91] Fundamental rights, yes— but not at the expense of "efficient" government. That is undoubtedly why Washington's annual messages to Congress (the equivalents of modern "state of the union" addresses) during the years surrounding the adoption of the Bill of Rights scarcely mentioned that major textual change to the "supreme law of the land."

Rights were at the core of a particularly irksome problem early in Washington's second term. Known to history as the "Whiskey Rebellion," it was occasioned by Hamilton's Excise Act of 1791 taxing "Spirits distilled within the United States." Though there was widespread noncompliance in virtually all states south of the Mason-Dixon line, in 1794 sporadic violence arose to the north, in four counties in western Pennsylvania, ironically including Washington County. There, back-country settlers concluded that their right to scratch out a living on the frontier was being compromised by tax collectors and money men from the eastern capitol. Washington, haunted by the specter of the Shays Rebellion, raised an army of nearly thirteen thousand militia, which he shrewdly called "the army of the constitution," and marched them out from Philadelphia with himself at the head. He turned back at Carlisle while the army continued on without him; by the time it arrived, the rebels had melted away. Only a handful were rounded up and tried, and Washington pardoned the two who were convicted. Jefferson privately mocked the whole venture, and to some opposition congressmen, Washington's constitutional army resembled the "Macedonian phalanx bear[ing] down all before them" they had prophesied during the debate over the Excise Act.[92] In his sixth annual message to Congress, however, Washington put on a good face and even invoked the spirit of the Revolution. Combining classical republican notions of political community and an army of citizen-soldiers with the modern idea of liberty under law, he claimed that the response to the Whiskey Rebellion "demonstrated, that our prosperity rests on solid foundations; by furnishing an additional proof, that my fellow citizens understand the true principles of government and liberty: that they feel their inseparable union." Washington even implied that the Spirit of '76 was alive and well in '93, for Americans were "now as ready to maintain the authority of the laws against licentious invasions, as they were to defend their rights against usurpation. It has been a spectacle, displaying to the highest advantage, the value of Republican Government, to behold the most and least wealthy of our citizens standing in the same ranks as private soldiers; pre-eminently distinguished by being the army of the constitution."[93]

Washington was not insensitive to the plight of cash-poor farmers—in a sense he was one himself, and even during Shays's Rebellion he counseled redressing the rebels' grievances if they were legitimate—but he drew the line at disobedience to the Constitution. It was lamentable, he said, that combustible elements had "interrupted the tranquillity of any part of our community," giving a nod toward the "domestic tranquility" of the union mentioned in the Preamble. But it was intolerable that the true principles of republican government and liberty were to be subverted on his watch as president. Washington also insinuated that the so-called Democratic Societies, early excrescences of Jefferson's Democratic-Republican party, had instigated the rebellion and duped the rebels by playing on their "prejudice" and "passions." Believing they could frustrate the federal government's constitutional ability "'to lay and collect excises,' . . . certain self-created societies assumed the tone of condemnation," Washington said. "Hence, while the greater part of Pennsylvania itself were conforming themselves to the acts of excise, a few counties were resolved to frustrate them."[94] This mention was impolitic on Washington's part, making him appear to discourage the people's rights to free speech and assembly protected in the First Amendment. No great harm came from this slip of Washington's political tongue, but to some it confirmed fears of a repressive federal government.

He may have overreacted to the Whiskey Insurrection, but on the whole Washington was an assertive president without being high-handed. In some ways his administration prefigured that of a later general-president, Dwight Eisenhower, profiled in Fred Greenstein's *Hidden Hand Presidency*: the exercise of power without seeming to exercise it.[95] (Also like Ike, Washington became head of a university in the years between the war and his presidency.) Washington made a show of being apolitical—he was in fact thoroughly nonpartisan—but he had excellent political instincts and relied on them in making appointments and negotiating, as when he hammered out the Treaty of New York with the Creek Nation in 1790. Careful not to appear to upset the balance of power established in the Constitution, Washington nevertheless thought and acted as though he had an equal right with the other branches to interpret it, for example withholding treaty documents from the House when he thought only the Senate had the constitutional right to them.

Foreign affairs, in fact, dominated Washington's largely frustrating second term. He had only stayed on under pressure from advisors including Jefferson and Hamilton, both of whom insisted that only the nonpartisan president could hold the fragile union together. Washington was not so certain; he even had Madison draw up a preliminary farewell address in 1792 but allowed himself to be convinced to stand for a second term. In the end he came to regret it. Jefferson recounted Washington griping in 1793 that "he had never repented but once the having slipped the moment of resigning his office, and that was every moment since. That *by god* he had rather be in his grave than in his present situation."[96] By the end of his second term, Washington was positively frantic to return to Mount Vernon. He was the first president to learn how difficult it is to maintain the popularity of the first inauguration over eight long years in office. The political fissures in his dream cabinet had widened, splitting that body apart; by 1794 Jefferson was gone and Hamilton was on his way out. Edmund Randolph, who moved from attorney general to fill Jefferson's vacant seat as secretary of state, was accused of treason with the French. Washington handled the case clumsily, causing Randolph to resign and write a vindictive account of Washington as inept and doddering. The seeming successes on the domestic front during the first term, including precedents established on what he called "true principles" and Hamilton's economic package, were overshadowed by personnel problems and dangers from abroad during the second.

Despite efforts to keep his eyes focused on North America and domestic issues, Washington's presidential head was jerked in the direction of Europe by an escalating war between England (and her allies) and France. The antics of the French minister to the United States, "Citizen" Edmond Genet, in combination with raids by French privateers off the coast, sparked debate over U.S. foreign policy with regard to its old ally in the Revolution, a nation that was still in the midst of its own revolution and simultaneously waging war with Great Britain and its coalition partners. At that time Washington was also preparing to send troops under the command of General "Mad" Anthony Wayne against several of the Indian nations in the Northwest and Southwest Territories. To the south, apparent intrigues by Spain with hostile Indian nations, known to history as the "Spanish Conspiracy," further exacerbated tensions, raising concerns over U.S. navigation of the Mississippi. Spanish-English conflict over a British beachhead at Nootka Sound, present-day Vancouver Island in British Columbia, made North America appear once again to be caught in an international tussle involving the major powers of France, Great Britain, and Spain, and made it all the harder for Washington to maintain a neutral posture.

Tensions were only heightened by what was perhaps the defining episode of Washington's second term, the controversial Jay Treaty ratified in 1795. Washington had sent Jay, former secretary of foreign affairs and current chief justice of the Supreme Court, to England to iron out issues still unresolved from the Revolutionary settlement and to stabilize trade relations. The Jay Treaty was vigorously opposed by Jefferson, Madison (by that time under Jefferson's political sway), and the Republicans generally. Though ostensibly a diplomatic success for the administration—it extracted some concessions from the British but most importantly maintained U.S. neutrality and kept the peace between the two nations—the ratification process forced Washington to expend needed political capital and further polarized elements in the early republic. Seen by many as unduly pro-British, the Jay Treaty eroded some of Washington's popular support and increased his feelings of isolation and dismay over party factions.

By the following year, 1796, Washington, firmly committed to retirement, dusted off the outline for a farewell address Madison had drawn up four years earlier. Making copious notes and changes himself, Washington circulated drafts among Madison, Hamilton, and Jay, publishing the finished product in the *Amer-*

ican Daily Advertiser of September 19, 1796. (He did not, as is commonly thought, read it aloud.) Six months later Washington oversaw the peaceful transfer of executive power to John Adams, a remarkable occurrence in the history of government. During the inauguration, the second president noted a satisfied gleam in Washington's eye, as if he were saying to Adams, "You are safely in, and I am safely out." After the swearing-in, the presidential party moved outdoors to greet the crowds. President Adams stepped outside; Washington and the new vice president, Jefferson, arrived at the door at the same time, and there was an awkward moment. Washington motioned for Jefferson to precede him. Eyewitness accounts relate that when Jefferson held back, Washington made an emphatic gesture with his hand for Jefferson to step forward. Citizen Washington was giving a mute speech on republicanism: even the Father of His Country was obliged to give place to popular constitutional government.

"AGAIN SEATED UNDER MY VINE AND FIG TREE": FINAL RETIREMENT, 1796–1799

Like many an old man, George Washington was killed by his retirement. It was his stubborn insistence on riding around his Mount Vernon farm on a day of mixed snow, hail, and rain that led to the lethal sore throat he contracted in late December 1799.[97] Had he remained in office for a third presidential term, Washington might have survived well into the nineteenth century and become the first chief executive to live in the presidential mansion in the city that bears his name. It is one of the interesting "what-ifs" of American political history.

But Washington had resigned in 1796 for political as well as personal reasons. To be sure, Washington was homesick for Mount Vernon, but he also wanted his final political precedent to be stepping down before he died in office. By doing so, Washington guaranteed that the presidency would not become a sort of elected monarchy for life, an option for the executive that had been suggested during the Federal Convention debates. His stepping down was a precedent all future presidents would follow until the audacious Franklin Roosevelt, who served four terms during the Great Depression and died in office near the end of World War II, broke it. Washington, however, wanted no part of even a third term, let alone a fourth, and could not have been happier to get back to the "peaceful abode" of his and Martha's home.

He threw himself into the work of the plantation and resumed his agricultural pursuits with particular vigor, though he kept one eye on the political landscape. Washington quietly advanced the career of John Marshall, and bestowed his blessing on his presidential successor, John Adams, who sorely sought it. "I must ask you sometimes for advice," President Adams wrote. "We must have your name. There will be more efficacy in that than in many an army."[98] Washington was even briefly called out of retirement yet again during the Adams administration when he was named commander of the U.S. army as war with France loomed. Washington wrote wistfully to Sally Fairfax in England: "Worn out in a manner by the toils of my past labour, I am again seated under my Vine and Fig tree, and wish I could add that, there are none to make us affraid; but those whom we have been accustomed to call our good friends and Allies, are endeavouring, if not to make us affraid, yet to despoil us of our property; and are provoking us to Acts of self-defence."[99] But Washington did not have to unsheathe his sword again, to employ the language he used in the section of his will bequeathing his military swords to his heirs. Adams managed to maintain Washington's foreign policy of neutrality and keep the United States out of war, while Washington remained at Mount Vernon until his sudden passing in the last month of the eighteenth century.

CONCLUSION

After his death—an excruciating one that displayed all of Washington's stoical fortitude and British gentlemanliness—Washington's body was laid out for three days in the grand dining room at Mount Vernon. His will provided for his burial in a rebuilt family vault to be located in a pastoral setting removed from Mansion House. It was Washington's "express desire that my Corpse may be Interred in a private manner, without parade, or funeral Oration."[100] That is essentially what happened, and a modest, somber procession ended at the family cemetery with a mixture of Anglican and Masonic funeral rites. Afterwards, an effort was made to have his remains moved to a specially-built crypt beneath the U.S. Capitol. Martha initially refused, then relented; but the plan fell through, and Washington still sleeps in the dreary mansions of his fathers at Mount Vernon. A final comparison with Napoleon Bonaparte, whose remains are housed in a gargantuan sarcophagus in the *Hôtel des Invalides* in Paris, is instructive. The two men designed their final resting places: the diminutive Corsican with the outsized ego who died as an exile lies entombed in a monument that overawes onlookers; the giant American civil-military leader who died a hero rests beneath the green fields of his republican farm. Even his mode of burial was an intentional period at the end of Washington's career. Choosing to be buried without pomp beneath his own "vine and fig tree," Washington was silently teaching a final lesson about a government of laws and not of men. Right up to the end, and even beyond the end, George Washington's life was a literal embodiment of early American political thought.

CHAPTER 2

CLASSICAL REPUBLICAN POLITICAL CULTURE AND PHILOSOPHY

Man's business is virtue, not words.

Seneca, *Epistles*

With me, it has always been a maxim, rather to let my designs appear from my works than by my expressions.

Washington to James Anderson, 1797

He made his reputation by leading an army, often outnumbered, to stunning victories. His soldiers came to believe in him so completely that they would do anything he asked of them, exploits that seemed impossible. He published accounts of his campaigns that were read widely in his time and are still read today. At one stage in his career, he was given dictatorial powers by the legislature. At another, he was offered a king's crown, which he refused. After securing fame as a military leader, he paraded into the capital city to take the reins of the civil government. He went to work refashioning the republic. The people on the whole loved him, idolized him; some even considered him godlike (though he was, of course, an imperfect god). They called him *Pater Patriae*, Father of His Country. Then, after less than a decade at the height of political power, Julius Caesar was murdered by his political enemies in 44 B.C.

Nearly two millennia later, Fortune seemed poised to create an American Caesar in the person of George Washington. But in reality Washington more nearly re-

sembled Cincinnatus or Cicero, who was Caesar's nemesis and the most eloquent defender of the Roman republic in its last days. When Washington crossed his own
version of the Rubicon, the Potomac River, in the spring
of 1789, he may have looked like the proverbial man on
horseback riding to take the capital city by force, but unlike his historical antitype Caesar, Washington was going
to lead a government in peace that he had helped make
possible in war. Washington had read Caesar's *Commentaries on the Gallic Wars* and remembered that when the
latter forded the Rubicon in the spring of 49 B.C., he
had taken his legions with him and marched them toward Rome and civil war. As he headed for New York
and his presidential inauguration, Washington, who had
been called the father of his own country since 1778,
kept his military uniform packed away. He meant to
be a different kind of political parent than Caesar had
been—a model of re-publican rather than imperial
fatherhood.

By 1789 Washington had become the most classically
republican American of his generation. His studied classicism was complemented by his natural agrarianism,
stoical character traits, preference for republican government, and seeming indifference to power. Over the eight
years of the Revolutionary War, Americans—indeed,
the world—had watched as Washington was twice given
quasi-dictatorial powers, which he proceeded to wield
with a light hand. They had watched him delay (like Fabius,
another Roman general), harass, and retreat from British
forces before defeating Cornwallis at Yorktown; finally,
they watched him lay his power down. After liberating
the colonies, Washington said a choked-up farewell to his
officers in New York, resigned his commission at Annapolis, and made a beeline for Mount Vernon, arriving
on Christmas Eve of 1783. Like the legendary Roman
dictator-turned-farmer Cincinnatus, he traded his sword
for a plow and retired under his own "vine and fig tree."
By settling back into his rural routine after the Revolution, Washington made himself "first in peace" as well as

"first in war," as John Marshall was later to say. Never mind that Washington may have angled for the commander's job in the first place by wearing his military uniform to the Continental Congress; he had surrendered power when it counted most. It was only with great reluctance that Washington allowed himself to be coaxed out of retirement. At his inaugural as the first elected national leader in western history, Washington did not appear in uniform; he wore a plain suit of homespun American wool.

After two terms as president, Washington stepped aside again, refusing to stand for a third election. In 1797 a commemorative medal was issued bearing Washington's profile, much as Roman coins had borne Caesar's likeness. But rather than celebrating Washington's unprecedented civic leadership, the medallion commemorated his classical republican resignation.[1]

THE FOUNDERS AND CLASSICAL REPUBLICANISM

George Washington was a votary in what historians have called an eighteenth-century "cult of antiquity."[2] For all their stress on modern progress, Washington and his colleagues in the American Enlightenment also looked back to the classical past for inspiration. From north to south, the founders mimicked classical virtues, copied classical architecture, wrote under classical pseudonyms, and named their slaves and farm animals after classical heroes. A northerner, Joseph Warren, delivered an oration commemorating the Boston Massacre in a Roman *toga*.[3] Benjamin Franklin of Pennsylvania, while on a diplomatic mission to France in 1778, struck the Comte de Ségur as antiquity incarnate: "It was as though . . . a republican of the age of Cato or Fabius, had suddenly been brought by magic into our effeminate and slavish age, the 18th century."[4] A southerner, Thomas Jefferson (whose personal slave was called Jupiter), spent half his life tearing down and rebuilding his home atop Charlottesville's version of Mount Olympus on varying classical patterns. When Jefferson finally got the roof on his mansion, the first neoclassical building in North

America, it was a domed Roman roof, copied from plates by the Italian architect Palladio. When George Washington remodeled Mount Vernon in the mid-1770s, he followed Palladian conventions for the two-story dining room in the mansion's north wing, complete with agricultural motifs on the ceiling and a large Venetian window "of the Tuscan Order" that was to be the room's centerpiece.[5]

These ancient forms and trappings were just the surface manifestations of a deeper classicism embraced by the founders. Classical republicanism gave the Antifederalists, for example, a model of political community that they hoped to reconstruct in early America. The decentralized states-rights position expressed during the ratification debates by articulate Antifederalists like "Brutus" and the "Federal Farmer" and, later in the early republic, by Madison in the Virginia Resolutions of 1799, was a vestige of ancient communitarian political life and thought.[6] For both Federalists and Antifederalists, the political virtues and concepts, and to a lesser degree, institutions, of Greco-Roman antiquity served as models. Not that the founders dusted off classical constitutions to use as blueprints for their own state constitutions or the federal Constitution—of the hundred or so ancient constitutions collected by Aristotle, only one, the constitution of Athens, survived into the early modern era. Instead, the founders borrowed what they saw as useful from the ancients and learned from their classical predecessors what mistakes to avoid, especially the kind that led to the downfall of the Athenian and Roman empires. As Jefferson put it, "History, in general, only informs us what bad government is."[7] Publius complained in *Federalist* 9 that it was "impossible to read the history of the petty republics of Greece and Italy without feeling sensations of horror and disgust at the . . . perpetual vibration between the extremes of tyranny and anarchy."[8]

"Horror and disgust": hardly the sensations on which to model a *novus ordo seclorum*, a "new order of the ages." As Tocqueville was later to observe, a "new political science [was] needed for a world itself quite new."[9] What was called for, so Washington and his Federalist colleagues in the late 1780s claimed, was an extended republic on a scale unimagined in the ancient world. During the heat of the ratification debates over the proposed Constitution, John Adams asked ironically, "What would Aristotle and Plato have said, if anyone had talked to them, of a federative republic of thirteen states, inhabiting a country of five hundred leagues in extent?"[10] Nonetheless, classical Greco-Roman political culture and philosophy informed the Federalist experiment in republicanism in a variety of ways.

THE GREEK LEGACY

Ancient Greek political philosophy provided the founders with a limited set of concepts that they could turn to account in early America. To begin with, they inherited the classical conviction that tyranny would inevitably arise out of a state of anarchy brought on by excessive democracy. "There is a natural and necessary progression, from the extreme of anarchy to the extreme of tyranny," General Washington warned the state governors in his 1783 Circular, "and arbitrary power is most easily established, on the ruins of liberty abused to licentiousness."[11] Here he was following a line of thinking sketched out in Plato's *Republic*, a work that was among other things a critique of pure or direct democracy. Socrates says in the *Republic* that "tyranny develops out of no other constitution than democracy—from the height of liberty, I take it, the fiercest extreme of servitude."[12] Aristotle, Plato's most famous and influential student, shared this view of democracy and classed it among the defective governments. In similar fashion Washington lamented to David Humphreys that it "is one of the evils, perhaps not the smallest, of democratical governments that the People must feel before they will see or act."[13] In other words, in democracies the people's feelings, or "passions" as they were called in the eighteenth century, dominated their reason.

In Aristotle's *Politics* and its companion the *Ethics*, the founders discovered an antidote to excessive democracy: a balanced or mixed regime. They also noted Aristotle's doctrine of natural law and his stress on private property, a middle class to provide ballast for a stable society, societal diversity rather than the extreme unity of Plato's imaginary republic, and friendship as the proper bond of a state.[14] They approved of his overarching empiricism and pragmatism; these characteristics harmonized well with their own inclinations. They accepted his classification of "constitutional government" or "polity," a mixture of democracy and oligarchy administered for the sake of the common good, as the best government.

Aristotle also laid considerable emphasis, as Romans like Cicero were later to do, on the common good, or the "common interest." In Book III of the *Politics,* he said that the "true forms of government, therefore, are those in which the one, or the few, or the many, govern with a view to the common interest . . . [and] when the citizens at large administer the state for the common interest, the government is called by the generic name . . . constitutional government [*politeia*]."[15] Aristotle also stressed the communitarian nature of political life and the end (*telos*) of that life, which is happiness. In the *Ethics* he wrote of "happiness . . . the end of human nature," and in the *Politics* he asserted that "the form of government is best in which every man, whoever he is, can act best and live happily."[16] Aristotle's concern with the pursuit of happiness is doubtless one reason that Jefferson cited him as an authority for the political philosophy of the Declaration of Independence, which of course classed the pursuit of happiness among the inalienable rights.

George Washington, who owned a volume of Plato's works and a commentary on Aristotle, was nearly obsessed with his reputation as a champion of the public good, the common interest, and political happiness throughout his entire public life. As early as 1756 he professed his desire for "the advancement of his Majesty's honor and the interest of his governments" rather than his own interests.[17] During the Revolution he complained bitterly about the self-interestedness of others, which showed itself in "venality, corruption, prostitution of office for selfish ends, abuse of trust, perversion of funds from a national to a private use, and speculations upon the necessities of the times [that] pervade all interests."[18] In 1779 he asked James Warren, "Is the paltry consideration of a little dirty pelf to individuals to be placed in competition with the essential rights and liberties of the present generation, and of Millions yet unborn?"[19] Perhaps the most explicit (and self-pitying) expression of Washington's own disinterestedness and devotion to the common interest is a letter to

Benjamin Harrison from 1778, written during one of many low points of the war. Washington emphasized that his pleas were submitted "by a Man who is daily injuring his private Estate without even the smallest earthly advantage not common to all in case of a favourable Issue to the dispute."[20]

Washington's classical-style disinterestedness was recognized by a variety of people over the years. William Ramsay wrote to Washington of "your disinterestedness, your unwearied application and zeal for your country's good."[21] David Humphreys wrote of Washington's "disinterestedness" in not wanting to be made president and quoted Washington as telling him "God knows that I have but one wish myself, which is to live & die on my own plantation."[22] The final verdict on Washington's personal disinterestedness was delivered by Abigail Adams shortly after Washington's death: "Possesst of power, possesst of an extensive influence, he never used it but for the benefit of his Country."[23]

American political happiness and friendship were also concepts that recurred frequently in George Washington's political communications. Washington saw America as a stage for acting out a new drama of human happiness, as he wrote in his Circular to the States in 1783. "The citizens of America," he wrote, "are, from this period to be considered as the Actors on a most conspicuous Theatre, which seems to be peculiarly designated by Providence for the display of human greatness and felicity . . . [and] a fairer oppertunity for political happiness, than any other Nation has ever been favored with."[24] In the Circular, Washington considered a friendly attitude among the constituent parts of the United States a kind of classical column "on which the glorious Fabrick of our Independency and National Character must be supported." He pointed to the necessity of "that pacific and friendly Disposition, among the People of the United States, which will induce them to forget their local prejudices and policies" and make concessions for the "general prosperity" and the "interest of the Community."[25]

A decade later, during his first presidential term, Washington continued to fret about "unfriendly" sentiments held by some factions toward the government, sentiments that threatened to undo the sort of Aristotelian civic friendship Washington hoped for in the young republic. In 1792 he wrote Hamilton that during his travels "I have endeavoured to learn from sensible and moderate men, known friends to the Government, the sentiments which are entertained of public measures. . . . Others, less friendly perhaps to the Government, and more disposed to arraign the conduct of its Officers (among whom may be classed my neigbour, and quandom friend Colo. M [George Mason]) go further, and enumerate a variety of matters."[26] In his Farewell Address of 1796, Washington warned more sternly against shaking American friendliness along geographical fault lines: "In contemplating the causes wch. may disturb our Union, it occurs as matter of serious concern, that any ground should have been furnished for characterizing parties by *Geographical* discriminations. . . . They tend to render Alien to each other those who ought to be bound together by fraternal affection."[27] According to Washington, it was the duty of every American, native or naturalized, to stir up his feelings of friendliness, his "affections," toward his fellows. "Citizens by birth or choice, of a common country, that country has a right to concentrate your affections. The name of AMERICAN which belongs to you, in your national capacity, must always exalt the just pride of Patriotism."[28]

The kind of nonpartisanship that Washington followed so assiduously in his own career and tried to encourage in his "friends and fellow citizens" was Ciceronian as well as Aristotelian. In his *On Obligations,* which Washington owned, Marcus Tullius Cicero insisted that those "who propose to take charge of the affairs of government should not fail to remember . . . [that] those who are for the interests of a part of the citizens and neglect another part, introduce into the civil service a dangerous element— dissension and party strife. The result is that some are found to be loyal supporters of the democratic, others of the aristocratic party, and few of the nation as a whole."[29] It was also akin to the classical notion of the patriot king, later resuscitated in the eighteenth century by Viscount Bolingbroke.[30] Failure to follow Washington's Ciceronian advice in the Farewell Address and the example he tried to set throughout his career gave rise to the partisan spirit that pitted the seemingly democratic Republicans against the seemingly aristocratic Federalists in the bitter presidential contest of 1800, a spirit that has haunted American politics ever since.

The Greek philosophy of Stoicism was yet another philosophical influence that found its way into early American political culture, primarily by way of Roman adaptations of Greek thought and life. Greek Stoics emphasized ethics and politics above all else, so their thought was tailor-made for use by pragmatic Romans such as Cicero and Marcus Aurelius. The average eighteenth-century American probably never heard of Greeks like Zeno of Citium, the purported founder of Stoicism, or Cleanthes of Assos, the Stoic quoted by St. Paul in the book of Acts, but their Roman counterparts Cicero and Marcus were known and admired as political models. Thus the Stoic desire "to make the personal and political lives of men as orderly as the cosmos" lived on in ancient Rome and early America.[31] So too did the Stoic emphasis on natural law and the obligation of all men to follow it, especially in their public lives. A code of Stoic ethics subsequently evolved, "which was manly, rational, and temperate, a code which insisted on just and virtuous dealing, self-discipline, unflinching fortitude, and complete freedom from the storms of passions [and] was admirably suited to the Roman character."[32] That is also an apt description of the Stoic code by which George Washington tried to live his life.

THE ROMAN LEGACY

Whereas the Roman empire presented an example of political vices to avoid, the Roman republic presented an example of virtues for Washington and his colleagues to emulate. For their national symbol they chose the eagle, which had adorned the standards of the Roman legions from the earliest days of its republic. Of the most frequently cited political authorities during the American founding, five were ancient thinkers, and four of the five were Romans: Plutarch, Cicero, Livy, and Tacitus.[33] The Rome of first-century B.C., with Cicero, Cato the Younger, and the other "noble Romans" profiled by Plutarch, was hardly a "petty republic" of the sort that so disgusted Publius in *Feder-*

alist 9. And though it ended in a decadent empire, Rome had started well, by throwing off a foreign king and maintaining an extended republic over a vast territory for centuries.

The Romans themselves realized that their peculiar talent was for government administration and action; theirs was a practical, derivative genius rather than a purely speculative and inventive one. Virgil put it best in his *Aeneid*: "Some shall plead more eloquently . . ./But yours, my Roman, is the gift of government,/That is your bent—to impose upon the nations/ The code of peace."[34] The Roman historian Sallust wrote that the "best preferred doing to talking" during the glory years of the republic.[35] So did that American Roman, George Washington. Shortly after leaving the presidency, Washington wrote, "With me, it has always been a maxim, rather to let my designs appear from my works than by my expressions."[36]

In addition to its pragmatism, Rome bequeathed the modern world a legacy of morals, law, administration, and even infrastructure like the aqueducts and the great Appian Way, a paved road stretching from Rome down the length of the Italian peninsula that is still serviceable to this day. From Roman histories, especially the character studies portrayed in Plutarch's ubiquitous *Lives,* Washington and his contemporaries became familiar with the features of Roman political life and culture, features that must have struck them as familiar, despite the span of centuries. (They must also have struck them as congenial—Plutarch was among the five most-quoted authorities by the founders during the period 1760 to 1805.)[37]

Indeed, Washington's world was in many respects more like ancient Rome than the United States of today. When he had to travel, General Washington was faced with the same options that the Roman general Cincinnatus, to whom he was endlessly compared, had more than two thousand years earlier: he could go by foot, by horse, or by ship.[38] The same was true when he had to send communications. A pregnant woman in his family who needed a caesarian section was no better off than the mother of Julius Caesar, for whom the procedure was named, and for the first twenty years of his life George Washington marked time by the Julian calendar that had been in place since the days of Caesar's consulship.

But beneath these superficialities there were aspects of Roman political life and thought that resonated more deeply with Americans. Underlying the classical play-acting of the James Warrens among them was a serious commitment to the classical republican practices and principles they thought were best embodied in Rome in the century before the life of Christ. For one thing, their republic (from *res publica*, "public thing") was characterized by Cicero as the *res populi*, the "people's affair," and bottomed on a kind of popular sovereignty.[39] For another, the Roman constitution separated powers among its different governing bodies. The Senate was made up of senior "great men" who had held prior public offices; its virtue was dignity. The tribunate represented the people; the tribunes embodied and protected the liberty of the people. The executive was composed of a pair of consuls, magistrates who embodied Rome's power. Over the centuries a kind of equilibrium or balance was established that kept any one governmental body from overawing the others and in fact blended them together. Cicero considered "the best constitution for a State to be that which is a balanced combination of the three forms [of] kingship, aristocracy, and democracy."[40]

George Washington saw the value of mixed or balanced government. Shortly before the Constitutional Convention, he created a précis of John Jay's recommendations for a revised federal government, and noted approvingly that the New Yorker wanted a "Governor General, limited in his prerogatives and duration; that Congress should be divided into an upper and lower house, the former appointed for life, the latter annually; that the Governor General (to preserve the balance) with the advice of a council, formed, for that only purpose, of the great judicial officers, have a negative on their acts."[41]

Two other notable features of the Roman constitution were collegiality and frequent elections. The reason that there were always two Roman consuls, those highest-ranking executive officers to the Senate, was to keep them in check through the power of the negative. One consul could negate the policies of his colleague with a single word—"*veto*"—which the Americans took directly into their language from the Latin. The consuls, and indeed nearly all Roman officials except the censors, were elected

annually by popular elections of the citizens. This feature was designed to rotate leadership and prevent any one man or party
from becoming entrenched in power. The Americans embraced
this Roman characteristic, as illustrated in John Adams's remark
that "there not being in the whole circle of the sciences a maxim
more infallible than this, 'where annual elections end, there slavery begins.'"[42]

Such political institutions and habits were summed up in the
Latin word *Romanitas,* meaning "all that a Roman takes for
granted, the Roman point of view and habit of thought."[43] Various concepts and characteristics of *Romanitas,* especially agrarianism, civil-military relations, natural law, mixed or balanced government, and political pragmatism, were adopted and adapted
by eighteenth-century Americans. Ancient Rome thus served as
one avenue of political culture for early America—a kind of Appian Way of the mind, down which the founders, especially
George Washington, traveled.

WASHINGTON AND ROMAN POLITICAL MORALITY

According to Elkins and McKitrick, during the age of American federalism, "everyone . . . was more or less Roman. George
Washington ranked first, and John Adams was the next Roman
below him."[44] It helped that Washington looked the part, and
he learned to use his appearance and bearing for political effect.
This was especially true as Washington aged and acquired the
additional dignity of an older man. At fifty he was described as
having a "Roman" face that was "expressive of Sagacity, of
Prudence, and of Moderation . . . in his dress he was perfectly
plain . . . he always wears Boots, & never uses a Carriage, but
when Mrs Washington is with him."[45] This description, by
George Bennet, an English visitor to Mount Vernon, was of the
typical throwback classical republican of the eighteenth century:
the rustic citizen-soldier returned from the wars to his rural
estate. Sagacity and prudence (i.e., wisdom), along with moderation, courage, and justice, were the classical or "cardinal" virtues extolled by Plato, Aristotle, and Cicero in his *On Obligations.* In that work Cicero wrote that what is honorable "is found

in the perception and intelligent awareness of what is true [wisdom]; or in safeguarding the community by assigning to each individual his due, and by keeping faith with compacts made [justice]; or in the greatness and strength of a lofty and unconquered spirit [courage]; or in the order and due measure by which all words and deeds reflect an underlying moderation and self-control." "Wisdom and prudence," he went on, embrace "the search and scrutiny into the truth."[46]

Throughout his life Washington was compared to various noble Romans. Lord Byron called him the "Western Cincinnatus"; to others he was Fabius, Marcellus (John Marshall made this obscure comparison), and even—when he was winning battles—Caesar.[47] During the French and Indian War in 1756, Colonel William Fairfax wrote to Washington that the House of Burgesses was depending on his success. "Your good health and fortune are the toast at every table. Among the Romans, such a general acclamation and public regard, shown to any of their chieftains, were always esteemed a high honor, and gratefully accepted."[48] Later, during the Revolution, Abigail Adams made this comparison when recording her impressions of Washington: "Cato is stern, and *awful as a god*."[49] In particular, Washington embodied the characteristics of agrarianism, civil-militarism, and republican political rhetoric that were such fixtures in classical republican political culture.

Agrarianism

The ancient Romans were "above all, peasants, racy of the soil."[50] This keenness for farming colored much of Roman life, including its political life and thought. As Meyer Reinhold has observed, classical agrarianism was "politico-ethical in nature."[51] Roman farming encouraged virtues such as frugality, rustic simplicity, close adherence to duty, and self-sacrifice, all of which could be put to political purpose in America. Farming required private property, self-sufficiency (or the illusion of self-sufficiency), and, as any farmer then or now knows, hard work.[52] In many cases, it also required slaves. The great Romans, renowned for their republican virtue, had rural villas outside the city, farms where they could retreat from the seamier side of urban life. Cicero often left his home on the Capitoline Hill to escape to his rural villas, one of which was in Tusculum, birthplace of Cato the Elder.

In Washington's day, more than nine of ten Americans lived on a farm, and particularly in Virginia, farming was a way of life time out of mind. Many a Southern planter, including Washington, fancied himself a cross between a Roman *pater familias* and a patriarch in ancient Israel. Jefferson always claimed that he would rather be on his plantation in the Blue Ridge than anywhere on earth; in 1796, only months before his first run for the presidency, he wrote an acquaintance that he had "returned, with infinite appetite, to the enjoyment of my farm, my family & my books, and had determined to meddle in nothing beyond their limits."[53] Jefferson was also extremely skeptical of urban centers, where people would become piled upon one another and where disease and vice would multiply. He wrote to the physician Benjamin Rush that the Yellow Fever came from "close built cities in warm climes near the water," and he emphasized that "I view great cities as pestilential to the morals, the health and the liberties of man."[54] To Jefferson, "those who labor in the earth are the chosen people of god, if ever he had a chosen people."[55] Washington's other Virginian counselor, James Madison, wrote that in "all confined situations, from the dungeon to the crowded work-house, and from these to the compact population of over-grown cities, the atmosphere becomes, in corresponding degrees, unfitted by reiterated use, for sustaining human life and health."[56]

George Washington had an equally jaundiced view of big cities. In the rush to portray him as the booster of a Hamiltonian commercial republic, it has frequently been overlooked that Washington was, in his own way, racy of the American soil. Of course he loved his own ancestral land as only a multigenerational farmer can. His earliest memories were of Epsewasson farm, later named Mount Vernon by his half-brother Lawrence. Once he inherited the farm from Lawrence's widow, he enlarged the house several times and went to work increasing the productivity of the four surrounding farms. Over the years Washington sank his emotional roots as deep in the muddy Potomac soil as Jefferson did in the red clay of the Piedmont. In early 1787, only months before he left for the Philadelphia Convention, Washington wrote his old revolutionary friend Henry Knox that "for scarcely ever going off my own farms I see few people who do not call upon me; and am very little acquainted with the Sentiments of the great world."[57] That last bit may have been somewhat disingenuous—Washington was always an avid reader of political pamphlets and newspapers—but it illustrates his deep sense of place and fundamentally agrarian cast of mind. A year later Washington wrote Lafayette that he did not "entertain a wish beyond that of living and dying an honest man on my own farm."[58]

Washington was naturally and spontaneously agrarian. Especially during his hiatus between the Revolution and the presidency, Washington exulted in his occupation as a planter. "Agriculture has ever been amongst the most favorite amusements of my life," he wrote to Arthur Young in 1786.[59] Two years later Washington again wrote to Young, the world's leading authority on scientific agriculture, that he was "led to reflect how much more delightful to an undebauched mind is the task of making improvements on the earth, than all the vain glory which can be acquired from ravaging it, by the most uninterrupted career of conquests." He was "obliged by your labours to render respectable and advantageous an employment, which is more congenial to the natural dispositions of mankind than any other."[60]

Washington projected his own love of farming in general and of Mount Vernon in particular onto the rest of the continent, and he thought farming ought to play an essential part in American political life for the foreseeable future. To Washington, farming and agricultural life were natural and "honest"; by extension, cities were artificial and harbored the danger of corruption. Washington reminded Native Americans that just as whites would try to cheat them out of their lands, there are "among the Indians as among the Whites, Individuals who will steal their Neighbour's property, when they find the opportunity, in preference to acquiring property to themselves by honest means."[61] Toward the end of his second presidential term, when he was pining for Mount Vernon, Washington wrote to his farm manager that "in politics, as in religion my tenets are few and simple: the leading one of which, and indeed that which embraces most others, is to be honest and just ourselves, and to exact it from others. . . . If this maxim was generally adopted Wars would cease, and our swords would soon be converted into reap-hooks, and our harvests be more abundant, peaceful, and happy. 'Tis wonderful it should be otherwise and the earth should be moistened with human gore, instead of the refreshing streams, wch. the shedders of it might become, instruments to lead over its plains, to delight and render profitable our labours. But alas! the millenium will not I fear appear in our days."[62]

Washington brooded over the image of an urban Atlantic seaboard that would inevitably decay in virtue. He turned his mind's eye, and those of his fellow Americans, westward—away from the vicious cities of the east. In his fragmentary First Inaugural Address, Washington predicted that in the future, the west would become the repository of rural republican virtue. Americans' "extent of territory and gradual settlement, will enable them to maintain something like a war of posts, against the invasion of luxury, dissipation, and corruption. For after the larger cities and old establishments on the borders of the Atlantic, shall, in the progress of time, have fallen a prey to those Invaders; the Western States will probably long retain their primaeval simplicity of manners and incorruptible love of liberty."[63] He likewise warned Lafeyette that the "tumultuous populace of large cities are ever to be dreaded. Their indiscriminate violence prostrates for the time all public authority, and its consequences are sometimes extensive and terrible."[64]

The farming life was the antidote to the vitiating influence of cities, and, for a variety of reasons, the improvement of the land was more important than piling up buildings. In his final annual message to Congress, President Washington charged the legislature that it "will not be doubted, that, with reference either to individual or national welfare, Agriculture is of primary importance." In fact, as nations grew in size and population, "this truth becomes more apparent, and renders the cultivation of the soil, more and more an object of *public patronage*."[65] "Nothing," Washington had written in 1786, "would contribute more to the welfare of these States, than the proper management of lands."[66]

This was a universal truth, applicable to political societies everywhere and indeed to the global community. Washington recommended the "manly employment of agriculture" to the Marquis of Chastellux's countrymen in France. "Your young military men, who want to reap the harvest of laurels, don't care (I suppose) how many seeds of war are sown; but for the sake of humanity it is devoutly to be wished, that the manly employment of agriculture and the humanizing benefits of commerce, would supersede the waste of war and the rage of conquest; that the swords might be turned into plough-shares, the spears into pruning hooks, and, as the Scripture expresses it, 'the nations learn war no more.'"[67] In this passage Washington was playing off the language of sowing and reaping, of war and peace. Young military men want to reap a harvest of glory, not of peace, so they are cavalier about sowing the seeds of war. They associate manly virtue (the Latin *virtus* means "manliness") with war, but Washington coupled it with peace. The real man, for the post-Revolutionary Washington, was a farmer first and only reluctantly a soldier. Washington would rather see fruitful seeds sown in the earth and harvested than the seeds of war; farming would sate the blood lust of the young soldier and calm and redirect his passions. Preferring to see the sword beaten into a plowshare, Washington ended his wordplay with a quotation from the prophet Isaiah, chapter two, verse four.

Agriculture had other potential benefits for Washington. The "life of a Husbandman of all others is the most delectable," he wrote to Governor Alexander Spotswood. "It is honorable. It is amusing, and, with judicious management, it is profitable."[68] Yet even here Washington placed the utilitarian element last in his list of benefits. Farming was of course useful, but it was not merely useful—it encouraged rock-ribbed virtues that were "honorable." Washington did eventually learn what Jefferson never did, namely how to manage "judiciously": he made Mount Vernon and its surrounding farms pay in a way that Jefferson never could at Monticello. But despite his praise for farming and its attendant virtues, Washington never made the leap that Jefferson did, to conclude that agriculture and commerce were natural enemies. In fact, for Washington farming and commerce should be allied for the common weal. In 1789 Washington noted that within "our territories there are no mines either of gold or silver; and this young nation, just recovering from the waste and desolation of a long war, has not as yet had time to acquire riches by Agriculture and Commerce. But our soil is bountiful, and our people industrious; and we have reason to flatter ourselves, that we shall gradually become useful to our friends."[69] Washington wanted a rich and influential America, and he saw farming, with commerce based on agricultural production, as a way to get there.

CIVIL-MILITARY RELATIONS

Republican Rome was known as much for its martial virtues and prowess as for its rusticity. Indeed, Rome had not become mistress of the Mediterranean world (and in scarcely over fifty years, as Polybius explained in his famous history) by being a nation of citizen-farmers only. The typical citizen in pre-Caesarian Rome was not only a farmer, he was also a soldier, or at least a potential soldier. "The Roman mind is the mind of the farmer and soldier; not farmer, nor soldier, but farmer-soldier," according to R. H. Barrow.[70] Every Roman magistrate was therefore by definition a man with military experience. Both Cato the Elder and his republican grandson of the same name had successful commands in the army; even the philosophical Marcus Tullius Cicero did his turn and served on campaign. Yet the Romans nevertheless maintained a certain amount of separation between their military and civilian spheres, exemplified in distinct domestic (*domi*) and military (*militiae*) areas within and without the city. So in 49 B.C., the Senate had every right to expect that Caesar would relinquish his command when he was recalled to Rome; his disregard for a legislative body was a flagrant violation of the Roman principle of the separation of civil and military spheres.

Washington, by contrast, was scrupulous never to violate the trust given him by the Continental Congress during the Revolution or to make even veiled threats to do so at any time during the war or his presidency. Yet before 1783 Washington encouraged the martial side of his nature, strongly identified with the soldierly life, and emulated the Roman military heroes like Cincinnatus, Marcellus, and Fabius Maximus Cunctator—"the Delayer." From his copy of Plutarch's *Lives* (probably the so-called Dryden translation), Washington would have read of the Fabian strategy of delay and harassment of a superior force. Plutarch also related how "the Romans called Marcellus their sword, and Fabius their buckler [shield]."[71] Early in his command of the Continental Army, Washington wanted to bring on large-scale pitched battles in the European mold. But after the disastrous loss of New York City, he described to Congress a decidedly Fabian strategy for their Continental Army: "History, our own experience, the advice of our ablest Friends in Europe, the fears of the Enemy, and even the Declarations of Congress demonstrate, that on our Side the War should be defensive." The army and its commander should, Washington continued, "on all Occasions avoid a general Action, or put anything to the Risque, unless compelled by a necessity, into which we ought never to be drawn."[72] In his more aggressive moments, such as the strike across the Delaware on Christmas Eve of 1776, he reminded Americans such as John Marshall of Marcellus, the Roman "sword."[73] But Washington remained committed to the classical republican (and common-law) belief that the military must be subordinate to civil authorities, especially during the War for Independence. George Mason had written this principle into Article 13 of the Virginia Bill of Rights, probably with his colleague Washington in mind, in June 1776: "In all cases the military should be under strict subordination to, and governed by, the civil power."[74]

In 1778 Washington disclaimed any intention of thinking or acting in a civil capacity. He wrote to Henry Laurens, "You will perceive I have only considered [the situation] in a military light; indeed I was not authorised to consider it in any other," even worrying that "I may be thought, in what I have done, to have exceeded the limits intended by Congress."[75] The next year, during a conference with la Luzerne, Washington assured the French minister that he "could give no opinion of the propriety of the cooperation proposed [between France and the Confederation] in a civil or political light; but [considered] it merely as a military question."[76] And although he did push for a permanent army for the duration of the Revolution, Washington acceded to "the common, received Opinion, which under proper limitations is certainly true, that standing Armies are dangerous to a State," and promised "a due subordination of the supreme Civil Authority."[77]

WASHINGTON AND CAESAR

Washington's Roman mirror-image Julius Caesar crossed the Rubicon in the spring of his fiftieth year and marched on Rome, thereby inaugurating a civil war. He disobeyed the senatorial command to disband his army before crossing. Instead, Caesar forded the little river with his legions, reportedly saying "the die is cast" or "toss the dice high." Contemptuous of the constitution, he even marched his soldiers past the Field of Mars into the sacrosanct domestic area of the city of Rome, sending the message that he intended to rule over all of Rome as a civil-military leader. Cicero spoke for all republicans when he complained of the "effrontery of Gaius Caesar," who "to gain that sovereign power . . . trod underfoot all laws of gods and men." To Cicero, it was a perennial problem that "the ambition for civil office, military command, power and glory is usually nursed by men of the greatest and most outstanding talents."[78]

The young George Washington was something of a glory hound himself, and he certainly had his share of military ambition. But the intrigues and devastation of the Revolution chastened Washington, and the political lessons of an overambitious Caesar were not lost on him. Like other thoughtful students of Roman history, Washington realized that by refusing to lay down his sword, Caesar—a general and a father to the Roman people—had in effect used it against his own political children. Washington intended to follow the examples of Cicero, the first-ever *Pater Patriae* of Rome, and of Cincinnatus, rather than the example of the imperially minded Caesar. Washington modeled his own political behavior on what he called "examples from ancient story, of great atchievements performed by its [patriotism's] influence."[79]

Like Caesar, Washington had made his reputation as a general against great odds; had been made a virtual dictator; had even been offered a king's crown, if only clumsily by an overzealous officer, Col. Lewis Nicola, which he promptly refused. (Washington's reply to Nicola of May 22, 1782, embossed with his personal seal, is the only known instance in which a letter from the commander in chief was delivered to an American recipient under armed guard; Washington was taking no chances that his reply would be misunderstood.)[80] Also like Caesar, Washington inspired a kind of religious awe in his fellow citizens and was apotheosized, after a fashion, even in life; was called the Father of His Country; and was, in 1789, about to take over the reins of the civil government and re-form a republic that he and many others believed was in need of reformation.

Washington was roughly the same age as Caesar when he took control of the civil government, and by then his career had run in eerie parallel to the Roman general. But Washington was determined to avoid the political errors that had ruined Caesar and his republic. He was equally determined to prevent his American colleagues from bringing about the moral tailspin chronicled in the six volumes of Edward Gibbon's *Decline and Fall of the Roman Empire,* which he owned. He began with a bit of political theater designed to separate his role as military leader from his role as civic leader and president.

When he rode into New York for that first inauguration, Washington, acting the part, wore the costume of a civilian, having packed his military uniform away. To underscore the point, he wore a suit of republican homespun on the day of his inauguration. Later in his presidency, during the so-called Whiskey Rebellion of 1794, Washington did don his uniform again, and in fact rode at the head of troops—but he conscientiously labeled them the "republican . . . Army of the Constitution." In his sixth annual message to Congress following the Whiskey Rebellion, Washington praised an army whose civilian character he emphasized: "It has been a spectacle, displaying to the highest advantage, the value of Republican Government, to behold the most and least wealthy of our citizens standing in the same ranks as private soldiers; pre-eminently distinguished by being the army of the constitution. . . . Nor ought I to omit to acknowledge the efficacious and patriotic co-operation, which I have experienced from the chief magistrates of the states, to which my requisitions have been addressed."[81] Washington was perhaps protesting too much; by late 1794 most of the serious fears that Washington was a would-be military dictator had melted away. Still, the opposition press continued to hammer away at what they considered Washington's imperial tendencies, portraying him as an "embryo-Caesar," a "Cromwell"—even a King George IV.[82]

But Washington had learned sobering lessons from Roman history, principally what mistakes to avoid as a republican leader. As a modern-day Roman, his political philosophy was more closely related to that of Cicero, whose *On Obligations* in English translation arrived in his library at Mount Vernon in 1759, and to a lesser extent of Cato the Younger, than it ever was to Julius Caesar's.[83] Washington did admire Caesar as a military leader and, as he himself put it, "a man of a highly cultivated understanding and taste."[84] According to William Fairfax, Washington had read Caesar's *Commentaries on the Gallic Wars* as a young man, and he even ordered a bust of the intrepid general in 1761.[85] But Washington drew the line at hero worship and empire building, and he never said, as John Adams and Hamilton (according to Jefferson) did, that Caesar was "the greatest man who ever lived."[86] Though he regularly used the word *empire* to describe the rising United States, Washington used it in the somewhat contradictory sense that Jefferson did, of an "Empire of liberty," rather than in a Caesarian sense.[87] He had no ambitions to be emperor or even king; he shared the republican Roman's abhorrence of monarchy, which the hapless Col. Nicola discovered too late during the Revolution.

Claiming to speak for a group in the officer corps, Nicola expostulated on the injustices done the Army by Congress and on "the weakness of republics" in a letter to General Washington in May 1782. What was needed was a monarch, in fact if not in name. "Some people," Nicola continued, "have so connected the ideas of tyranny and monarchy as to find it very difficult to seperate them . . . [but] I believe strong arguments might be produced for admitting the title of king, which I conceive would be attended with some material advantage."[88] Washington's immediate reply crackled with indignation. He was filled with "astonishment" at Nicola's suggestion, which he was compelled to "view with abhorrence, and reprehend with severety." It was in fact "big with the greatest mischiefs that can befall my Country. . . . Let me conjure you then . . . to banish these thoughts from your Mind, and never communicate, as from yourself, or any one else, a sentiment of the like Nature."[89] Like Caesar, Washington made a show of refusing the diadem—he secured a written statement that his letter of refusal had been sealed and sent—but in his case, the refusal was genuine. He no more wanted to be a king than he wanted to be an emperor.

An exchange with the slave poetess Phillis Wheatley also showed up Washington's chariness about monarchy. Wheatley had written a poem in honor of Washington that suggested a "crown, a mansion, and a throne that shine/With gold unfailing, Washington be thine!"[90] Washington initially wanted to see the poem published as an example of her "great poetical genius" but then decided against it.[91] At his army headquarters, Washington met with Wheatley, whom he treated with great courtesy, befitting a republican general but not a monarch. Washington may have taken his anti-imperial and anti-monarchical bearings off the failed political career of Caesar, but more than any other Roman figure, Washington resembled Cincinnatus, defender of the Roman republic.

WASHINGTON AND CINCINNATUS

When Lord Byron dubbed Washington "the Cincinnatus of the West," he was only acknowledging what Americans had long noticed, namely that Washington bore an uncanny likeness to the semi-mythical Roman general, dictator, and farmer.[92] Lucius Quinctius Cincinnatus had been called from his plow in 458 B.C., when he was picked by the Senate to save the Roman army from its barbarian enemies. Granted dictatorial powers for six months, Cincinnatus made quick work of the invading Aequi and then gave up those powers after a mere fifteen days. He promptly returned to his farm, hitched up his oxen, and plowed himself into legend.

Two thousand years later, Americans familiar with Roman history watched farmer Washington leave his own plow (a leaden one he had invented) to take command of the Continental Army in 1775. When it offered him the commission, the Continental Congress expressed its hope that Washington would "cheerfully . . . resume the character of our worthiest citizen" after hostilities with Britain were over. Washington replied with classical republican assurances: when he and his compatriots "assumed the soldier we did not lay down the citizen," and they longed for the time when "the establishment of American liberty upon the most firm and solid foundations shall enable us to return to our private stations."[93] Toward the end of his first season in command, Washington complained of the lack of public virtue: "such a dirty, mercenary spirit pervades the whole [war effort] that I should not be at all surprised at any disaster that may happen."[94] He also insisted to the president of Congress, in a message that wrapped the classical republican image of Cincinnatus in biblical prose, "I have no lust after power but wish with as much fervency as any Man upon this wide extended Continent, for an oppertunity of turning the Sword into a plow share."[95] After he proved himself trustworthy, Congress issued proclamations on December 12, 1776, and again on September 17, 1777, authorizing Washington to use whatever means he thought necessary to maintain the peace and supply his army, including martial law—in essence making him dictator. (Roman tradition had it that Cincinnatus himself had been made dictator a second time, in 439 B.C.) Though armed with unprecedented powers, Washington was for the most part restrained in exercising them. He did stir up some resentment when he ordered farmers within seventy miles of the army to sell their wheat to the army, even threatening to seize the grain of any who refused in return for rock-bottom prices.[96] But this was an exception to Washington's general policy of restraint. In fact, he was so lenient on New Jersey Tories that radicals there were frustrated he was not harsher. During the winter at Valley Forge, Congressman Charles Carroll wrote that "Washington is so humane and delicate that I fear the common cause will suffer."[97] But Washington was working for the common cause in his own way, by taking pains not to be seen as a man on horseback trampling down his country's liberties. He was convinced that in the long run, showing classical republican restraint would do more political good than simply taking what his army needed, even when he was authorized to do so. He exercised that restraint right up to his resignation from the army.

Washington's farewell address to the Continental Congress in December 1783 subtly reminded them that he had promised to resign when he accepted the command he thought was beyond his abilities in 1775. Indeed, he almost made it sound as though retirement had been his goal all along. "The great events on which my resignation depended having at length taken place," he said, "I resign with satisfaction the Appointment I accepted with diffidence. . . . I here offer my Commission, and take my leave of all the employments of public life."[98]

It was not a great speech, as resignation speeches go, but it got his points across. Washington had been called from his private domestic life into public service; he had taken command reluctantly, fought the good fight, and was fulfilling his promise to resign when the enemy was defeated. With the war won, it was time to beat his sword into a plowshare; now, as always, he was being duly submissive toward the civil authorities. To his brother John Augustine, Washington had written of his impatience to "put a period not only to my military Service, but also to my public life."[99] He later expressed this impatience in his discarded first inaugural address: "After I had rendered an account of my military trust to Congress and retired to my farm, I flattered myself that this unenviable lot was reserved for my latter years. I was delighted with agricultural affairs."[100]

Six years after war's end, Washington was again called out of private life, when he was elevated to the presidency by a unanimous vote of the electoral college. In 1792, at the end of his first term, he was ready to leave office. Washington had James Madison write a rough draft of a farewell address based on a detailed outline Washington gave him. Prevailed upon by his subordinates—including both the Federalist Hamilton and the Republican Jefferson—Washington allowed himself to be reelected unanimously once again. By the end of his second term he had made up his mind to leave for good, and leave he did. Washington was afraid that he might not live out a third term and that his death in office would set a bad precedent. (It turned out, of course, that his fears were justified: Washington only lived three years beyond his retirement, a year shy of a third presidential term.) As noted, Washington was exquisitely sensitive to the example his actions and words would set for future presidents. He reiterated the sentiments he had expressed to James Madison at the start of his presidency in a letter to the English historian Catharine Macaulay Graham: "In our progress toward political happiness my station is new; and, if I may use the expression, I walk on untrodden ground. There is scarcely any part of my conduct wch. may not hereafter be drawn into precedent."[101]

Washington was intent on establishing a precedent of presidential resignation, and he wanted to be a republican father to the American people, not simply their elected monarch. Jefferson had similar concerns: when he read the proposed constitution, he worried that a perpetually reelected president might turn out to be "a bad edition of a Polish king."[102] So by saying farewell in 1796, Washington ensured that the American president would never become a bad edition of any kind of king, even an elected one. (Franklin Roosevelt, the only president to break Washington's example of retiring after the second term, was portrayed in newspapers of the 1940s wearing a king's crown; in 1951, the Constitution was amended to insure that Washington's precedent would never be broken again.) It was because Washington willingly gave up his extraordinary civil and military powers that Byron called him the "Cincinnatus of the West." Even his old nemesis from the Revolution, George III, was moved by his resignations to call him the greatest character of the century.[103] At the end of the war, a group of Revolutionary officers was formed who called themselves the Society of the Cincinnati. They picked Washington for their first president, and their pidgin Latin motto was (and is) *omnia relinquit servare republicam*—"he gave up all to serve the republic."

Many of the Roman civic ideals that Washington embodied have been summed up tidily by Bruce Thornton and Victor Davis Hanson: "The citizen-soldier whose republican virtues were created by and nourished on the farm and were expressed actively in a just war, a war fought not for private glory or national aggrandizement, but for freedom and autonomy."[104] The Roman exemplars of these qualities who most influenced Washington, in their virtues and vices, were Julius Caesar, Marcus Tullius Cicero,

Marcus Porcius Cato, and of course Cincinnatus. In the realm of political thought, Washington's ideas closely mirrored classical republican concepts found in Joseph Addison's Anglo-Roman play *Cato,* in Cicero's *On Obligations,* and in a substantive outline of Seneca's *Morals,* all of which were on the bookshelves in his Mount Vernon study.

WASHINGTON AND CLASSICAL POLITICAL RHETORIC

American political rhetoric in the late eighteenth century was a riot of classical allusions. There were the shopworn pen names— "Publius," "Cato," "Brutus," "Fabius"—and others that were not so common, such as "Aristides" and "Epaminondas." Many a patriot was a "Cicero" or a "Cato," and a daring commander like Benedict Arnold was the "Hannibal of the North" (while he was still a hero, that is); even a losing general could at least be a "Fabius."[105] Every shady character was a "Catiline," the scheming demagogue whose plot to seize power was exposed by Cicero; President Jefferson once received an anonymous letter "to give you a warning about [Aaron] Burr's intrigues . . . be thoroughly persuaded B. is a new Catalina."[106] It is a measure of how classical, and indeed how Roman, the culture of the founding was that a paragraph in a 1786 letter from Washington to Jefferson concerning a statue depicting him "in the garb of antiquity" was followed immediately by a discussion of the classically named Society of the Cincinnati.[107]

George Washington's political rhetoric was indeed filled with classical elements, though he was, as John Adams acerbically pointed out, "not a scholar." But Washington picked up bits of classical learning through the course of his self-education, and more importantly, he absorbed classical teachings on political life through what appears to have been deeper study of Cicero and Seneca than historians have credited him with. He acquired classical tastes and mental habits partly by inspiration—that is, simply by breathing the common rarefied air of the eighteenth century— but also by reading and by active self-improvement.

Washington read history intentionally, including English-

language histories of Greece and particularly of Rome, his whole
adult life. He put considerable stock in what he called "classical
knowledge." By the time of the French and Indian War, he had
already read a translation of Caesar's *Commentaries on the Gallic Wars.* After his marriage Washington insisted on having his
stepson John Parke Custis educated in antiquities at Mount Vernon before sending him to boarding school, and he later demanded that any tutor of his step-grandson, George Washington
Parke Custis, "must be a classical scholar."[108] Washington acquired for himself five different multi-volume histories of Rome,
including Gibbon's *Decline and Fall,* which was published coin-
cident with the American Revolution between 1776 and 1783, as
well as Plutarch's ubiquitous *Lives of the Noble Grecians and Romans.* At the time of his marriage, he inherited from Martha's
first husband the *Lives of the Twelve Caesars,* probably an English
translation of Suetonius's famous study; Washington also inherited Cicero's *On Obligations,* and his later thinking and policy
prescriptions reflected Ciceronian ideals.[109]

Like many literate Americans, and nearly all the founders,
Washington's life and letters were laced with classical allusions.
Washington repeatedly used "Cicero" and "Fabius" as counter-
signs, paroles, and watchwords during the Revolution.[110] He
named his horses and slaves for famous Romans, like the plow-
horse he called Pompey, after Julius Caesar's rival in the last years
of the Republic.[111] Caesar himself lent his name to a strong-
willed slave of Washington's. "I see by the last weeks report that
Caesar has been absent six days," Washington wrote in 1796, toward the end of his presidency when he was re-charting his own
course on slavery. "Is he a runaway? If so, it is probable he will
escape altogether, as he can read, if not write."[112] For a time
Washington engaged in the distasteful habit of naming the most
impotent beings on his plantations after the most powerful ancient and mythical figures: other slaves on the Washington farms
were called Hercules and Paris, after Greek heroes.

Washington surrounded himself with other bits of Romanesque
paraphernalia. In 1760, on retiring from military service, he ordered a bust of Julius Caesar; the following year Washington sent
to England for busts of Sallust, Terence, and Horace, along with

a Latin grammar and two Latin-English dictionaries.[113] The same invoice to his British factor included an order for a "Groupe of Aeneas carrying his father out of Troy."[114] Washington's crest bore the inscription "*exitus acta probat*," a quotation from Ovid meaning "the outcome justifies the act"; that crest was reproduced on his bookplate and also on the personal seal he carried with him at all times for his correspondence.[115] He even presided over a children's performance of Shakespeare's *Julius Caesar* at Mount Vernon, with George Washington Parke Custis in the role of Cassius.[116]

Washington called up classical figures in literary and historical allusions in his personal correspondence. To the Marquis de Lafayette he wrote that

> Men of real talents in Arms have commonly approved themselves patrons of the liberal arts and friends to the poets of their own as well as former times. . . . Alexander the Great is said to have been enraptured with the Poems of Homer and to have lamented that he had not a rival muse to celebrate his actions. Julius Caesar is well known to have been a man of a highly cultivated understanding and taste. Augustus was the professed and magnificent rewarder of poetical merit, nor did he lose the return of having his atcheivments immortalized in song. The Augustan age is proverbial for intellectual refinement and elegance in composition; in it the harvest of laurels and bays was wonderfully mingled together.

Washington went on at considerable length recounting other patrons of learning from the ancient to the modern eras.[117] Washington had been making allusions of this kind since adolescence; while still in his teens, Washington returned a reference to Joseph Addison's play *Cato* in a letter from his coquettish neighbor Sally Fairfax by writing, "I should think my time more agreable spent believe me, in playing a part in Cato, with the Company you mention, and myself doubly happy in being the Juba to such a Marcia, as you must make."[118] (In *Cato* Juba and Marcia are star-crossed—and unconsummated—lovers.) But this was a lighthearted effort to ingratiate himself with an engaging correspondent. Washington also knew how to put classical republican rhetoric and thought to more serious political purpose, which he did repeatedly throughout his career, not only with

Addison's *Cato* but also with Cicero's *On Obligations* and Seneca's *Morals.*

WASHINGTON AND ADDISON'S *CATO*

Washington quoted and paraphrased Joseph Addison's *Cato* all his life; next to the Bible, it is the most-quoted literary production in Washington's writings. It influenced his mind and manners perhaps as much as any single work. Between *Cato* and his *Spectator* essays, which Washington also read conscientiously, Addison probably affected Washington more than any other individual thinker. Washington wrote the Comte de Grasse, who was at the time going through a court martial, that he was "under full persuasion that the enquiry will throw additional lustre on your character. 'It was not in your power to command success; but you did more, you deserved it.'"[119] In *Cato,* the hero says to the future traitor Sempronius, "'Tis not in mortals to command success,/But we'll do more, Sempronius; we'll deserve it" (Act I, Scene 2).[120]

Twice during the uncertainties of his early command in 1775, Washington fell back on this couplet from *Cato.* In October he wrote Rhode Island's governor that a naval captain's "Voyage has been unfortunate, but it is not in our Power to Command Success, tho' it is always our duty to deserve it."[121] In early December Washington used the lines again, this time with a kind of eerie prescience. Washington reminded Benedict Arnold, before that gifted commander turned his coat: "It is not in the Power of any Man to command Success; but you have done more—you have deserved it."[122] During the desperate winter of 1777, Washington even decided to have the play performed by his officers at Valley Forge. Like so many of his decisions, this one had a didactic intention behind it: Washington hoped his men would learn political-military lessons from the performance. In Addison's play, the hero Cato must deal with a rebellion in his ranks; as Fortune would have it, Washington had to do the same at Newburgh, New York, in 1783. Cato, like Washington, exposed the plot, but unlike his Roman counterpart, who put his mutinous soldiers to death, Washington managed to forestall an American mutiny. He did this by shaming his officers and reminding them of his own sacrifices; he also fumbled with a pair of reading glasses, a perfect bit of political theater that "brought forth Roman tears" from American eyes, to adapt a line from Pope's prologue to *Cato*.[123]

Two years earlier, when the British threatened to shell Mount Vernon during the war, Lund Washington bought them off and earned, instead of thanks, a stern rebuke from his cousin George. "It would have been a less painful circumstance to me," he wrote, "to have heard, that in consequence of your non-compliance with their request, they had burnt my House, and laid the Plantation in ruins."[124] The Master of Mount Vernon was possibly thinking of these lines, spoken by Cato: "I should have blush'd if Cato's House had stood/Secure, and flourish'd in a Civil-war" (Act IV, Scene 4).[125] Washington was also fond of this trio of lines spoken by Addison's Cato: "Thy steddy temper, Portius,/Can look on guilt, rebellion, fraud, and Caesar,/In the calm lights of mild Philosophy" (Act I, Scene 1).[126] After the Revolution, he wrote to Chastellux that "I am at length become a private citizen of America, on the banks of the Patowmac; where under my own Vine and my own Fig-tree, free from the bustle of a camp and the intrigues of a court, I shall view the busy world, 'in the calm light of mild philosophy', and with that serenity of mind, which the Soldier in his pursuit of glory, and the Statesman of fame, have not time to enjoy."[127] After leaving the presidency, he informed Charles Cotesworth Pinckney that "for myself I am now seated in the shade of my Vine and Fig tree, and altho' I look with regret on many transactions which do not comport with my ideas, I shall, notwithstanding 'view them in the calm lights of mild philosophy', persuaded, if any great crisis should occur, to require it, that the good sense and Spirit of the Major part of the people of this country, will direct them properly."[128] In a two-week period in 1797, Washington quoted the same line from *Cato* to Rufus King, David Humphreys, and the Earl of Buchan.[129] His most dramatic use came in that speech to his mutinous officers at Newburgh. "Let me entreat you, gentlemen, on your part not to take any measure which, viewed in the calm light of reason, will lessen the dignity and sully the glory you have hitherto maintained."[130]

The relation of public virtue and vice to private lives was a subject on which Washington frequently ruminated. He often quoted verbatim these lines spoken by Cato: "When Vice prevails, and impious men bear sway,/The Post of honour is a private station" (Act IV, Scene 4).[131] To his secretary of war, Washington complained that the "difficulty to one, who is of no party, and whose sole wish is to pursue, with undeviating steps a path which would lead this Country to respectability, wealth and happiness is exceedingly to be lamented." Yet such was "the turbulence of human passions in party disputes; when victory, more than truth, is the palm contended for, 'that the Post of honor is a private Station.'"[132] In circumstances of turbulent party passions—when local and personal interests were pursued at the expense of the public good, when passion dominated reason, in short when political vice prevailed—Washington, like Cato, hankered after a private life. That these were not merely platitudinous classical tags but had serious political import behind them, is reinforced in letters from June 1796, when Washington had the end of his presidency in plain view. Once again juxtaposing political vice (manifested in party strife) with private virtue, Washington quoted Addison's *Cato* to his aide and authorized biographer David Humphreys: "But these [newspaper] attacks, unjust and unpleasant as they are, will occasion no change in my conduct; nor will they work any other effect in my mind, than to increase the anxious desire which has long possessed my breast, to enjoy in the shades of retirement the consolation of having rendered my Country every service my abilities were competent to. . . . When you shall think with the poet [Addison] that 'the post of honor is a private station,' and may be inclined to enjoy yourself in my shades (I do not mean the shades below, where, if you put it off long, I may be) I can only tell you that you will meet with the same cordial reception at Mount Vernon that you have always experienced at that place."[133]

Washington reproduced the same line in a letter to Hamilton dealing with his Farewell Address. "Having from a variety of reasons (among which a disinclination to be longer buffited in the public prints by a set of infamous scribblers),'" he wrote, "taken my ultimate determination 'To seek the Post of honor in a private Station' I regret exceedingly that I did not publish my valedictory address the day after the Adjournment of Congress."[134] He used this quotable line from *Cato* to reflect the republican principle that when political vice predominates, retirement is honorable. He was also implying that his own retirement was in the best republican tradition because it came after a long career—more than four decades—of public service. Having done his own duty, Washington had earned the reward of retiring to private life at his own version of Tusculum, Mount Vernon. Addison has Cato speak these words over the body of his dead son who has fallen in battle: "Thanks to the Gods! my Boy has done his duty." That is the best a Roman can do: to sacrifice his life for his country fighting against tyranny and trusting in Fortune, or as Addison renders it, in "Providence." Lucius says: "To urge the Foe to battel,/(Prompted by blind rage and wild despair)/ Were to refuse th' awards of Providence,/And not to rest in Heav'ns determination" (Act II, Scene 1).[135]

The trouble with Providence for the Romans was that its determinations were often inscrutable. Portius, Cato's son, characterizes his father's teachings about Providence by observing that the "ways of Heav'n are dark and intricate;/Puzzled in mazes, and perplext with errors,/Our understanding traces 'em in vain."[136] Washington did his level best throughout his trying public career to cultivate a stoical reliance on the will of Providence. Occasionally he used the Anglicized Roman term "fortune" instead of the more Christian-sounding "Providence." We will deal with Washington's complex conception of Providence at greater length; for now we note only that Washington blended pagan and Christian notions of Providence. He adopted the Roman teaching on the inscrutability of Providence, to which he added an unwavering belief, more Christian than pagan, that Providence was benign rather than morally indifferent. In September 1758, during the Braddock campaign, when Washington was thinking of *Cato* and quoting it to Sally Fairfax, he wrote to a friend, "All is lost, if the ways of Men in power, like the ways of Providence are not Inscrutable; and, why [are] they not? for we who view the Action's of great Men at so vast a distance can only form conjectures agreable to the small extant of our knowl-edge and ignorant of the comprehensive Schemes intended; mis-take, plaugily, in judging by the Lump."[137]

The inscrutability of Providence became a recurrent theme in Washington's writings. Like Addison's Portius, he believed that "the ways of Providence are inscrutable, and Mortals must sub-mit."[138] He expressed this sentiment to secular and religious correspondents over four decades, from John Robinson during the French and Indian War (1758) to Rev. Bryan Fairfax, to whom he wrote "we know little of ourselves, and still less of the ways of Providence" in the last year of his life.[139]

Occasionally, however, Washington thought he could discern Purpose in events, particularly during the Revolution. In 1778 he wrote of the conspicuous direction of Providence but then made a little joke about his inability to comprehend the entire divine plan: "The hand of Providence has been so conspicuous in all this, that he must be worse than an infidel that lacks faith, and more wicked, that has not gratitude enough to acknowledge his obligations, but, it will be time enough for me to turn preacher, when my present appointment ceases; and therefore, I shall add no more on the Doctrine of Providence."[140] When he could not read the providential plan, Washington tried to bear up under his ignorance like Cato and other good Stoics: "I look upon every dispensation of Providence as designed to answer some valuable purpose, and I hope I shall always possess a suffi-cient degree of fortitude to bear without murmuring any stroke which may happen."[141] While Cato the Younger was, as Samuel Eliot Morison correctly pointed out, "Washington's favorite character in history," his political principles also reflected those articulated in Cicero's *On Obligations*, which made its way into his library in 1759.

WASHINGTON AND CICERO'S *ON OBLIGATIONS*

Recall that Thomas Jefferson singled out two ancient political thinkers, Aristotle and Cicero, as influences on what he called the "common sense" of the subject of American independence—and, one might add, of early American political thought generally. Washington owned a commentary on Aristotle and Cicero's *On Obligations* (*De Officiis*) which he catalogued as "Tullys Offices."[142] Much of his behavior and not a little of his political philosophy were Ciceronian. If he did not read his copy of *On Obligations,* Washington in some osmotic way internalized its teachings. Cicero's belief in the virtues of agrarian life, in natural law and justice; his emphasis on friendship as the political bond of states; on the civic value of education in both theory and practice; on nonpartisanship—all of these have their place in Washington's political philosophy.

In his *On Obligations,* Cicero sang the praises of the farming life, which he contrasted with the baser sorts of commerce and artisanship. Washington echoed these sentiments in his public addresses and correspondence. For Cicero, there was something vaguely sordid (the Latin word is *sordidi*) about non-agricultural vocations such as speculative finance and hired manual labor. No self-respecting citizen, he wrote, would engage in the manual arts, "for no workshop can have anything liberal about it."[143] A fragment from Washington's discarded first inaugural contains these lines: "We shall not soon become a manufacturing people. Because men are ever better pleased with labouring on their farms, than in their workshops. . . . Hence it will be found more beneficial, I believe, to continue to exchange our Staple commodities for the finer manufactures we may want, than to undertake to make them ourselves."[144] Only honest farmers merited Cicero's unqualified praise, and this sentence from the first book of *On Obligations* distills his thoughts on agriculture: "But of all the occupations by which gain is secured, none is better than agriculture, none more profitable, none more delightful, none more becoming to a freeman."[145]

Cicero had also emphasized the public responsibilities of a freeman in *On Obligations.* Though such a man might be inclined to stay put on his farm, Cicero stressed the claims that justice had on him, and what he owed to his country. Though men who refused to heed their country's call might seem to "steer clear of the one kind of injustice, they fall into the other: they are traitors to social life, for they contribute to it none of their effort, none of their means."[146] Private life has its attractions, according to Cicero, but "the fundamental principles of justice" demand that "the common interests be conserved."[147] "The life of retirement," he went on, "is easier and safer and at the same time less burdensome or troublesome to others, while the career of those who apply themselves to statecraft and to conducting great enterprises is more profitable to mankind."[148] Cicero echoed this theme when he praised Cato the Elder, who "might surely have remained at Tusculum in the enjoyment of the leisurely life of that healthful spot so near Rome. But he . . . preferred, though no necessity constrained him, to be tossed by the billows and storms of our public life even to an extreme old age, rather than to live a life of complete happiness in the calm and ease of such retirement."[149] Shortly after his election to the presidency, Washington wrote a revealing letter to Catherine Macaulay Graham, admitting that, like Cicero, he would rather have stayed at Mount Vernon, but justice, his country, and the general interests of mankind pulled him away. If "I had been permitted to indulge my first and fondest wish, I should have remained in a private Station," he wrote, but "our new Government seemed to be the last great experiment for promoting human happiness."[150]

Cicero, like Aristotle before him, posited affection as the bond of states. To Aristotle it had been "friendship"; to Cicero it was "fellowship." "For there is a bond of fellowship," he wrote in *On Obligations,* "uniting all men together and each to each. This bond of union is closer between those who belong to the same nation, and more intimate still between those who are citizens of the same city-state."[151] We have already seen how Washington relied on friendship to hold the young nation together. He also repeatedly stressed education as a means of breaking down sectional prejudices. This was especially true of his prescriptions for a national university, which had a peculiarly Ciceronian ring to them. In the first chapter of *On Obligations,* Cicero reminded his son Marcus that he had been studying a full year "in Athens, and you should be fully equipped with the practical precepts and the principles of philosophy; so much at least one might expect from the pre-eminence not only of your teacher but also of the city; the former is able to enrich you with learning, the latter to supply you with models."[152] Washington wanted a national university in the federal capital "where the Youth from *all parts* of the United States might receive the polish of Erudition in the Arts,

Sciences and Belle Letters; and where those who were disposed to run a political course, might not only be instructed in the theory and principles, but (this Seminary being at the Seat of the General Government) where the Legislature wd. be in Session half the year, and the Interests and politics of the Nation of course would be discussed, they would lay the surest foundation for the practical part also."[153] This combination of theoretical and practical education in the political capitol was also, as Richard Brookhiser points out, the kind of self-education Washington strove to give himself.[154] Washington was also keenly concerned that his step-grandson George Washington Parke Custis make the most of his higher educational opportunities and fulfill the obligations incumbent on one in his situation; the hortatory tone of the letters to his ne'er-do-well grandson is thoroughly Ciceronian as well, including warnings against "light reading" and to cultivate a due "sense of your duties to God and man."[155]

Cicero's greatest contribution to early American political thought, undoubtedly the reason Jefferson included him in his list of worthies who had influenced the political theory of the Declaration of Independence, was the doctrine of natural law. In his *Laws* (named after Plato's work but different in tone and orientation), Cicero wrote: "Law is the highest reason, implanted in Nature, which commands what ought to be done and forbids the opposite. This reason, when firmly fixed and fully developed in the human mind, is Law."[156] This natural law, or law of nature as the Declaration puts it, was for Cicero "of universal application . . . valid for all nations and all times" and could be known by all rational men; we "need not look outside ourselves for an expounder or interpreter of it."[157] Washington relied on his own apprehension of the natural law when wrestling with the question of British treatment of American rights prior to the Revolution. In a letter to his Tory friend Bryan Fairfax in 1774, Washington claimed reliance on his own native sense of natural law and justice more than any tutoring in constitutional law. An "innate spirit of freedom first told me," he insisted, "that the measures, which administration hath for some time been, and now are most violently pursuing, are repugnant to every principle of natural justice; whilst much abler heads than my own hath fully convinced me, that it is not only repugnant to natural right, but subversive of the laws and constitution of Great Britain itself." Washington, apparently feeling the prick of conscience, went on to compare the arbitrariness of Britain's treatment of the Americans to Southerners' treatment of their own African slaves. The "crisis is arrived when we must assert our rights, or submit to every imposition, that can be heaped upon us, till custom and use shall make us as tame and abject slaves, as the blacks we rule over with such arbitrary sway."[158] On another occasion Washington wrote to Fairfax that he was not simply asserting an individual opinion: he found "at the same time, that the voice of mankind is with me."[159] Following natural law thinkers from Cicero through Augustine to Thomas Aquinas, Washington mused, "Law can never make just [that] which in its nature is unjust."[160]

Cicero also exhibited the characteristically Roman traits of pragmatism and eclecticism. Regarding public service, he insisted that "it is not enough to possess virtue, as if it were an art of some sort, unless you make use of it . . . and its noblest use is the government of the State, and the realization in fact, not in words, of those very things that the philosophers, in their corners, are continually dinning in our ears. For there is no principle enunciated by the philosophers—at least none that is just and honourable—that has not been discovered and established by those who have drawn up codes of law for States."[161] And writing to his son Marcus, Cicero signaled his desire to "follow chiefly the Stoics, not as a translator, but, as is my custom, I shall at my own option and discretion draw from those sources in such measure and in such manner as shall suit my purpose."[162] Cicero was picking over Greek philosophy for useful principles rather than following any particular school slavishly. This eclectic turn of mind is quintessentially Roman—and very American, too.

Like Cicero, time and again Washington demonstrated a pragmatic and eclectic bent, an impatience with unnecessary abstraction, a high regard for the vocation of statecraft, and a knack for grasping the essential points in any argument. Discussing political economy with James Warren, Washington wrote in frustration that it "has long been a speculative question among Philosophers and wise men, whether foreign Commerce is of real advantage to any Country . . . but the decision of this question is of very little importance to us; we have abundant reason to be convinced, that the spirit for Trade which pervades these States is not to be restrained." It "behooves us then to establish just principles" and the necessity of "a controuling power is obvious; and why it should be withheld is beyond my comprehension."[163] Like Cicero, Washington commended his fellow countrymen for discovering the need for principles of "just" political economy "in fact, not in words." Many of Washington's attitudes and much of his political thinking concerning the American experiment in republicanism were Roman, indeed Ciceronian, in character. Yet even more of Washington's political thought and behavior reflected the *Morals* of Lucius Annaeus Seneca (ca. 3 BC–65 AD).

WASHINGTON AND SENECA'S *MORALS*

Around age seventeen Washington acquired a copy of Seneca's *Morals by Way of Abstract,* an English translation of several of Seneca's treatises, including "Of Benefits," "Of a Happy Life," "Of Anger," "Of Clemency," and the philosophical "Epistles."[164] It seems that Washington read this lengthy abridgment (over five hundred pages) with care and that he absorbed its principles and played them out in his career. The chapter titles alone taught Washington "There can be no Happiness without Virtue" (III); "Philosophy is the Guide of Life" (IV); "The Due Contemplation of Divine Providence is the Certain [Cure] of all Misfortunes" (VIII); "The Blessings of Temperance and Moderation" (XV); "The Blessings of Friendship" (XVIII); "The Contemplation of Death makes all the Miseries of Life easie to us" (XXI); and "Against immoderate Sorrow for the Death of Friends" (XXIII).[165] Richard Norton Smith notes that the "adolescent Washington examined Seneca's *Dialogues*" as well, driven by "an almost pathetic desire for social polish."[166] Descriptions of the virtuous man abound in Seneca's *Morals,* and the portrait they paint is one remarkably like the mature George Washington. Particularly striking is this line: "He that Judges aright, and perseveres in it, enjoys a perpetual Calm: he takes a true Prospect of things; he observes an Order, Measure, a *Decorum* in all his Actions: He has a benevolence in his Nature; he squares his Life according to Reason; and draws to himself Love and Admiration."[167]

Washington, though hotheaded by nature, always aimed at calm, particularly the philosophic calm that comes from giving reason preeminence over the passions. Toward the end of his presidency he lamented that the "restless mind of man can not be at peace; and when there is disorder within, it will appear without, and soon or late will shew itself in acts. So it is with Nations, whose mind is only the aggregate of those of the individuals, where the Government is Representative, and the voice of a Despot, where it is not."[168] During the French and Indian War, William Fairfax applauded the young Washington for "that philosophic mind you have already begun to practice."[169] Jefferson, despite his shortchanging of Washington's intellect, admired this trait in Washington. "His passions were naturally strong; but his reason, generally, stronger," he wrote years after Washington's death.[170] Washington himself indicated that he was passionate by nature: "The favourable sentiments which others, you say, have been pleased to express respecting me, cannot but be pleasing to a mind who always walked on a straight line, and endeavoured as far as human frailties, and perhaps strong passions, would enable him, to discharge the relative duties to his Maker and fellow-men, without seeking any indirect or left handed attempts to acquire popularity."[171]

But acquire popularity he did. Though during his second presidential term especially he had his share of journalistic detractors (Adams recounted Washington's "impatience under the lash of scribblers"), Washington also managed to draw to himself the admiration and even love of many of his countrymen.[172] In his quest for philosophic calm, Washington also took his cues from Seneca, who was convinced that the "true Felicity of Life, is to be free from Perturbations; to understand our Duties toward God, and Man."[173] Washington, by sublimating his "perhaps strong" passions to his reason, was trying to free himself of "perturbations" while not neglecting his duties "toward God, and Man." What might have been a personal liability Washington turned, by dint of self-discipline, into a political asset. Washington's ability to keep his passions in check was even more helpful in an age when Roman Stoicism was so admired. He also managed to make second nature the admonition of his youthful Rules of Civility: "In all Causes of Passion admit Reason to Govern," which might be considered the moral of his life.[174]

Washington had his own preference for a private life over the life of public service strengthened by reading Seneca. Vice President Adams was convinced that Washington was shamming, that he really yearned to be in the spotlight, and that he got his model of the "excellent hypocrite" of antiquity from the third chapter of Charles Rollin's popular *Ancient History* (which Washington did in fact own).[175] But this was just another example of how Adams's preoccupation with his own place in history could make impartial judgments impossible for him. (Adams even absurdly suggested that after leaving the presidency Washington "longed to return to public bustle again" because "my popularity was growing too splendid, and the millions of addresses to me from all quarters piqued his jealousy.")[176] Nor did Adams have the benefit, as we do, of access to Washington's voluminous private correspondence, which overwhelmingly demonstrates Washington's sincere desire to retire from public life.

Moreover, Washington had to be argued into standing for office a second time by his advisors, including the Federalist Hamilton *and* the Republican Jefferson. (Like their English counterparts, eighteenth-century American politicians "stood" for office; only later did the more vulgar but accurate locution of "running" come into use.) His shockingly brief second inaugural address—it was a testy two paragraphs long—talked only of duty and punishment for dereliction of duty. The brevity and tone of this address are a subtext that communicates Washington's indifference to power and his desire to be at Mount Vernon rather than in the president's house. After reading it, Washington swore the oath of office and trudged off for four more years of what he privately called "slavery."[177]

Personal virtue and rationality were one thing; but what of corporate virtue? Could a whole people be expected to "square their lives according to reason"? In "Of a Happy Life," Seneca wrote disparagingly of the common people's tendency to follow their feelings rather than their judgment or, as Jefferson put it in a famous letter, their "hearts" rather than their "heads."[178] Following Aristotle, who classed democracy among the deficient regimes, Seneca was skeptical of the people's judgment. Questions of political good and happiness were "not to be decided by *Vote*," according to Seneca. "Nay, so far from it, that Plurality of Voices is still an Argument of the Wrong; the Common People find it easier to Believe, than to Judge."[179] Washington had his own misgivings. "It is among the evils, and perhaps is not the smallest, of democratical governments, that the people must *feel*, before they will *see*," he wrote to Henry Knox on the eve of the Constitutional Convention. Too much passion and too little reason made for misguided government. Though he was perhaps more confident than Seneca about the people's political instincts, Washington shared the classical republican preference for reason over the passions. He also shared Madison's conviction in *Federalist* 55 that "had every Athenian citizen been a Socrates, every Athenian assembly would still have been a mob."[180] For Washington it was one of the shortcomings of democracy that its citizens' emotions had to become "roused" before they could think clearly.[181]

But Washington still believed that the people needed to be encouraged to link virtue with their happiness and to pursue that happiness as their inalienable right. Seneca, in his "Of a Happy Life," wrote of the pursuit of happiness some two millennia before Locke and Jefferson did.[182] In the first chapter of Seneca's abridged treatise, Washington read the following: "There is not anything in this World, perhaps, that is more Talk'd of, and less Understood, than the Business of a *Happy Life*. . . . We live . . . in a Blind and Eager Pursuit of it."[183] For Seneca and the Romans, the pursuit of happiness was inevitably linked with virtue—a possible reason that they thought it was easy to pursue but difficult to attain. Seneca claimed that "Human Happiness is founded upon *Wisdom*, and *Virtue*," and, more pointedly, "There can be no Happiness without Virtue."[184]

This belief became such a part of Washington's political creed that he quoted Seneca nearly word for word in his First Inaugural. "There is no truth more thoroughly established than that there exists in the economy and course of nature, an indissoluble union between virtue and happiness; between duty and advantage."[185] Toward the end of his second term, Washington was more convinced than ever of the link between virtue and happiness. "Republicanism is not the phantom of a deluded imagination," he wrote to Edmund Pendleton in 1795. "On the contrary, laws, under no form of government, are better supported, liberty and property better secured, or happiness more effectually dispensed to mankind."[186] As we shall see, Washington supplemented the classical republican axiom that individual virtue leads to corporate happiness with the modern belief, common to both British Enlightenment liberalism and Protestant Christian political theory, that religion could be used to moderate the democratic passions.

CONCLUSION

Rousseau reminds us that the ancient political philosophers "spoke incessantly about mores and virtue; ours speak only of commerce and money."[187] Rousseau might have had in mind the famous funeral oration of Pericles, in which he reminded the Athenians that "one's sense of honour is the only thing that does not grow old, and the last pleasure, when one is worn out with age, is not, as the poet said, making money, but having the respect of one's fellow men."[188] George Washington had plenty to say about commerce and money; in that respect he was a modern political thinker. But he was also classically republican in character, and he embraced many of the political postulates of antiquity as well, including honor (and its correlate, fame) and private and public virtue.

John Adams was onto something when he accused Washington of stealing his notions of selfless public virtue from the Romans. Washington did in fact trace his classical republican virtues off Roman patterns, although his sources were probably Cicero, Seneca, and Addison's *Cato* rather than Rollin's history, as Adams thought. Washington's limited exposure to ancient history might not have been a necessary condition for his classical republican political thought; perhaps Clinton Rossiter was correct when he claimed that "the Americans would have believed just as vigorously in public morality had Cato and the Gracchi never lived."[189] But Roman moralizing from Seneca reinforced Washington's private republican virtues, and his notions of public virtue were so Ciceronian that they might have been lifted verbatim from the copy of *On Obligations* in his study at Mount Vernon. Some of the classics of political philosophy were therefore sufficient, if not necessary, conditions for his republicanism. Washington quoted from Cicero's *On Old Age* and Addison's *Cato*, paraphrased Seneca, and emulated the best political morality of the noble Romans taught in his histories of Rome and in Cicero's *On Obligations*.[190] He exhibited a classicism that was both studied—as when he resigned his commission like Cincinnatus—and natural, or perhaps we might say, second nature. He overlaid his natural Stoicism and the civic-mindedness that was instilled in him growing up in colonial Virginia with a modest amount of Latinate learning, all of which combined to make him the foremost Roman in an age that worshiped antiquity.

Washington's classical republicanism showed itself in the following ways: in his predilection for agricultural life, both for himself and as a priority for the burgeoning nation; in his encouragement of friendship as the bond of American union; in his stoical personal ethical code; in his anxiety to give up power; in his admiration for a "balanced" regime not unlike the Roman republic's mixed constitution; in his belief in the inscrutability of fortune or "Providence"; in his martial orientation that yet subordinated the military to civil command; in his preference for private life over public service; and finally, in his willingness to sublimate his desire for retirement in favor of public service.

Yet Washington was hardly a cookie-cutter republican. If, as James Kloppenberg asserts, "classical republicans called for independent citizens to protect fragile civic virtue against the threat of corruption represented by the extension of executive power," then Washington was not a typical classical republican. He never embraced the strong states-rights position of other Virginia classical republicans like Thomas Jefferson. Nor was he overly concerned with perceived threats to individual rights from the new, stronger federal government. It is notable that neither his annual address to Congress in 1790 nor 1791 dwelt on the ratification of the Bill of Rights, perhaps the single most important change of the American constitutional landscape during his eight years as chief executive. Instead, Washington consistently backed a stronger union of states, voted during the Constitutional Convention for a more powerful executive than the nation eventually got, and, as president, set various precedents for an independent and vigorous chief executive—all manifestations of British liberal ideology, the subject of the next chapter.

CHAPTER 3

BRITISH LIBERALISM, REVOLUTION, UNION, AND FOREIGN AFFAIRS

An innate spirit of freedom first told me, that the measures, which administration hath for some time been, and now are most violently pursuing, are repugnant to every principle of natural justice; whilst much abler heads than my own hath fully convinced me, that it is not only repugnant to natural right, but subversive of the laws and constitution of Great Britain itself.

Washington to Bryan Fairfax, 1774

The young George Washington fancied himself an English gentleman in the making. He hankered after a career in the British navy, referred to England as "home" (though he had never been there), risked life and limb in the French and Indian War defending the interests of George II, whom he called "the best of kings." During that war he also befriended a young British officer named Thomas Gage. He read and absorbed Joseph Addison's Anglo-Roman play *Cato* and Addison's liberal essays "through no. 143" in *The Spectator.* Washington also spent many hours at Belvoir, home of his aristocratic neighbors the Fairfaxes; they became his foster family, his sponsors, and his models of British gentility and liberal sentiment. When he inherited Mount Vernon (named for British Admiral Lord Vernon), Washington enlarged the modest farmhouse into a "mansion house," replaced the rough Virginia rail fences with English hedgerows, planted English-style pleasure gardens, and added a deer park, that quintessential feature of a rural English estate.

But by the mid-1770s Washington had turned away from Britain, both literally and figuratively. He had become convinced that the ministry of George II's grandson George III, instead of representing the best of kings, was out to reduce the American colonies to "abject slavery." Deploying British liberal arguments against the policies of Crown and Parliament, Washington sent a letter to his old friend, now General Thomas Gage, military governor of Massachusetts. Echoing John Locke, Washington said he stood on the "honourable" principle of consent, the "original Fountain of all Power." And he warned his Tory benefactor George William Fairfax that "Americans will never be tax'd without their own consent." As the Revolution neared, the Fairfaxes sold Belvoir and moved back home, to England. When Washington remodeled Mount Vernon in the 1770s, he moved the mansion's entrance from the east to the west. No longer looking back to his roots in England, his home now faced the American frontier, and the future. Convinced that the time-honored principles of British liberalism actually favored the upstart colonies, George Washington had become that strange thing: a conservative revolutionary.[1]

BRITISH ENLIGHTENMENT LIBERALISM

David Humphreys, Washington's only authorized biographer, saw his subject standing intellectually in the line of British Enlightenment liberal thinkers, particularly John Locke.[2] In his outline for Washington's life during the 1760s, Humphreys wrote that Washington's "political creed" at the time of the Stamp Act (1766) amounted to a compendium of Lockean liberal political theory: "Locke &c—result of their theorems into short political Creed."[3] Humphreys's assessment was accurate on two counts. First, Washington's political theory was indeed heavily derived from British liberal arguments propounded by Locke and others— Addison, Algernon Sydney, the Scotsmen James Burgh, Adam

Smith, and David Hume—and second, it did amount to a short political creed. Washington himself said, "In politics, as in religion my tenets are few and simple."[4] What were the political tenets Washington drew from British liberal thinkers like John Locke and worked into his political creed along with the tenets of classical republicanism and Protestant Christianity?

Liberalism as propounded and lived by Britons during the early modern period stressed, as its name implies, *liberty* above all: particularly liberty of citizens from control by the state. Like so many labels, *liberalism* can obscure as much as it illuminates. Unfortunately, that is especially true of a term whose meaning has changed often, coming to mean something quite different in our own time than it meant during the founding. But speaking traditionally and simply, a liberal is one who believes in freedom of thought and action. Such a belief in liberty led to a belief in limited government among various British thinkers and writers of the seventeenth and early eighteenth centuries. Because of the priority they placed on liberty, some of these thinkers, including John Locke, one of the intellectual grandfathers of the American Revolution and "America's Philosopher," have also been described as "classical liberals."[5] (Here "classical" refers not to antiquity, as it does in "classical republicanism," but to a body of early modern libertarian thought articulated by the likes of Adam Smith, Immanuel Kant, Locke, and others; it should not be confused with contemporary European or American "liberalism.") According to James Kloppenberg, Locke's "sober Puritanism" informed one tradition of British liberalism, but one that produced a different branch of liberalism than that descended from the "stark individualism of Hobbes."[6]

British liberals in the seventeenth and eighteenth centuries thought the state should play a fairly minimal role in day-to-day life. Even Hobbes himself, though his *Leviathan* was hardly a prescription for minimalist government, said that the "greatest liberty of subjects, dependeth on the silence of the law."[7] And Locke had written in his *Second Treatise of Government* that people create the civil government "only with an intention in every one the better to preserve himself his Liberty and Property."[8] Hobbes, Locke, and others believed that government was necessary to secure domestic tranquility and rights—particularly property rights—and for foreign defense. These two concepts, of course, loom large in the Preamble of the federal Constitution; in this sense the written U.S. Constitution is the inheritor of British liberal political philosophy and the unwritten British constitution.

Another concept that marked British Enlightenment liberalism was "a democratic, individualistic, and contractual conception of the origins and limits of governmental power," according to the historian Lance Banning.[9] The political theorist Eldon Eisenach has explained that early modern liberal politics were characterized by the following familiar institutions: "revolution in defense of liberty, legislative protection of personal rights, and, most important, a political executive bounded by law, institutions, and morality."[10] Like the other ideologies present at the time of the American founding, British Enlightenment liberalism was not *sui generis*: it did not come from nowhere and was itself indebted to prior ideologies. For example, James Kloppenberg has noted that the fundamental tenets of Enlightenment liberalism "descend directly from the cardinal virtues of early Christianity: prudence, temperance, fortitude, and justice."[11] But in this chapter we will focus on Washington's liberal theory and practice of a revolution in defense of liberty and of natural rights, his conception of a strong American union with correspondingly strong executive powers to protect those rights, and his extension of that liberal theory into the realm of international relations or what at that time was called "foreign affairs."

"LIFE, LIBERTY, AND PROPERTY": LIBERALISM AND REVOLUTION

One can describe the American war for independence as Edmund Burke described the English conflict of the seventeenth century, as a revolution "prevented, not made." The Irish-born Burke, of course, sided with the colonies in the 1770s. He argued before Parliament that an "Englishman is the unfittest person on earth to argue another Englishman into slavery" and noted that Americans were "not only devoted to liberty, but to liberty according to English ideas, and on English principles."[12] George Washington took a Burkean tack with his neighbors the Tory Fairfaxes, in the years preceding the Revolution. He complained to Bryan Fairfax in 1774 of the "Invasion of our Rights and Priviledges by the Mother Country" and of "every imposition, that can be heaped upon us." Believing that British policy violated both "natural justice" and the "constitution of Great Britain itself," he concluded that the "crisis is arrived when we must assert our rights."[13] Washington was resting his conclusion, just as Burke had, on the two theoretical legs of natural law and British liberalism.

During the Revolutionary period, George Washington repeatedly invoked the stock concepts of British Enlightenment liberalism: a state of nature, happiness as an end of government (an idea as classical as it is modern), consent as the only legitimate source of government authority, and government's role in protecting natural rights. Though he did not invent the concept of a state of nature, among British liberals it was John Locke who was most responsible for giving that concept its currency with the American founders. Washington had the two volumes of Locke's *Essay concerning Human Understanding* (the best-known Lockean work in the eighteenth century) and *Some Thoughts concerning Education* at Mount Vernon and had access to Locke's *Two Treatises of Civil Government* in the library of his stepson John Parke Custis.

Yet even if he never read a page of Locke's *Two Treatises,* Washington had available to him other works that presumed liberal explanations of the origins, growth, and the proper constitution of political society. He had those *Spectator* essays by Addison, access to a number of works from the canon of Western political theory and from more ephemeral literature such as political pamphlets and newspapers. Perhaps just as important, simply by being an active public intellectual in eighteenth-century America, Washington was continually exposed to British liberal political concepts and absorbed their ideology in that way as well. For example, sitting in the president's chair during the Federal Convention, Washington heard James Madison, his young friend and political advisor, invoke the social contract, a useful liberal fiction well known to all the delegates. On June 19, 1787, Madison said, if "we consider the Federal Union as analogous to the fundamental compact by which individuals compose one society, and which must, in its theoretic origin at least, have been the unanimous act of the component members, it cannot be said that no dissolution of the compact can be effected without unanimous consent." Washington also listened to James Wilson of Pennsylvania refer to the state of nature and the social contract in a speech on June 8.[14] He reiterated that notion of a voluntary social contract in his discarded first inaugural address two years later. If officials of the new federal government should "overleap the known barriers of this Constitution and violate the unalienable rights of humanity," Washington predicted that "it will only serve to shew, that no compact among men (however provident in its construction and sacred in its ratification) can be pronounced everlasting and inviolable." He also echoed the language of *Federalist* 48, predicting that "no Wall of words, that no mound of parchm[en]t can be so formed as to stand against the sweeping torrent of boundless ambition on the one side, aided by the sapping current of corrupted morals on the other."[15]

Other elements of Lockean political theory recur in Washington's writings. Locke had stressed the value of improvements to land and grounded the legitimacy of private property ownership (contra Rousseau) on such improvement in his *Second Treatise*: "The Grass my Horse has bit; the Turfs my Servant has cut; and the Ore I have digg'd in any place where I have a right to them in common with others, become my *Property*, without assignation or consent of any body. The *labour* that was mine, removing them out of that common state they were in, hath *fixed* my *Property* in them."[16] For Locke, nature was superabundant but inefficient and wasteful. What was needed was the organizing and cultivating hand of man to harness that natural fecundity and to produce foodstuffs and other benefits for himself and his kind—Adam toiling by the sweat of his brow in the garden for his daily bread.

Washington was continually ringing the changes on the benefits and necessity of agricultural improvement and private property. To a group of Roman Catholics, Washington spoke of his hopes for the blessings of "a Divine Providence" on "agriculture, [and] improvements at home and respectability abroad."[17] He insisted to his stepson John Parke Custis that "land is the most permanent estate we can hold, and most likely to increase in its value."[18] And note the Lockean undercurrents in this hymn to agricultural improvement he sent to Jefferson: "If we wisely & properly improve the advantages which nature has given us, we may be benefitted by their [Europeans'] folly—provided we conduct ourselves with circumspection, & under proper restriction, for I perfectly agree with you, that an extensive speculation . . . or the introduction of any thing which will divert our attention from Agriculture, must be extremely prejudicial, if not ruinous to us." Washington then posited a stronger federal government as a guarantor of agricultural enrichment and even civic virtue. "I conceive under an energetic general Government," he predicted, "such regulations might be made, and such measures taken, as would render this Country the asylum of pacific and industrious characters from all parts of Europe—would encourage the cultivation of the Earth by the high price which its products would command—and would draw the wealth, and wealthy men of other Nations, into our own bosom, by giving security to property, and liberty to its holders."[19]

Such concern for American liberties in general, and property rights in particular, had been evident in Washington's thought since the mid-1760s. In 1765, only two years after the end of the French and Indian War and fully a decade before Lexington and Concord, Washington was beginning to express unease over the colonies' situation. In a letter to Martha's uncle, Washington wrote of the perception by colonists of the "direful attack" upon British-American liberties Parliament was then making, particularly through the Stamp Act. He explicitly referred to that act as "ill judgd" and implicitly endorsed the opinion of many that it was "unconstitutional."[20]

It was in this context that Washington's work with George Mason on Virginia's nonimportation association and Fairfax Resolves began. By the early spring of 1769, American merchants in Massachusetts, Pennsylvania, Maryland, and elsewhere were protesting the British duties on imports. Washington received a letter from a Maryland merchant enclosing a description of the Philadelphian's nonimportation association. In post haste he forwarded the information to Mason at Gunston Hall, suggesting such an association for Virginia. "At a time when our lordly Masters in Great Britain will be satisfied with nothing less than the deprication of American freedom, it seems highly necessary that some thing shou'd be done to avert the stroke and maintain the liberty which we have derived from our Ancestors; but the manner of doing it to answer the purpose effectually is the point in question," wrote Washington. A nonimportation association seemed to fit the bill. "This, if it did not effectually withdraw the Factors from their Importations, wou'd at least make them extremely cautious in doing it, as the prohibited Goods could be vended to none but the non-associator, or those who wou'd pay no regard to their association; both of whom ought to be stigmatized, and made the objects of publick reproach."[21] In this letter, called by Flexner "a major milestone of Washington's road to Revolution," he was already propounding the seemingly contradictory line of reasoning of America's leading conservative-liberals, that they were merely trying to protect ancient British liberties in the face of an innovative king and Parliament.[22]

Washington also hinted that he was ready to embrace force as a legitimate remedy to the economic and constitutional injustices. The use of arms was legitimate, he argued, especially since constitutional arguments had fallen on deaf English ears, though perhaps Americans should use economic sanctions before taking up arms. "Addresses to the Throne, and remonstrances to parliament, we have already, it is said, proved the inefficacy of," he wrote Mason. Yet "how far then their attention to our rights and priviledges is to be awakened or alarmed by starving their Trade and manufactures, remains to be tryed."[23] Of course economic sanctions turned out not to be effective enough for the most radical patriots, but that spring of 1769 Washington and Mason at least put the wheels in motion.

The two were serving together as Justices in the Fairfax County Court in mid-April, and on the evening of April 18 Mason accompanied Washington to Mount Vernon, where he remained for three days while the two worked out the blueprint for a nonimportation association.[24] From his home at Gunston Hall, Mason wrote Washington with further changes on April 23, which Washington made to their prior drafts and took with him on his way to the General Assembly in Williamsburg at month's end. By May 16 Washington and his fellow burgesses had endorsed resolutions reasserting the colonials' exclusive right to tax themselves and objecting to recent parliamentary policies toward the colonies. The following day, Lord Botetourt dissolved the House of Burgesses, whereupon Washington apparently led a group of the more radical burgesses to the Apollo Room of the Raleigh Tavern. Washington was appointed to a committee for preparing a resolution of nonimportation, which he had ready-made in the form of the articles he and Mason had drawn up the previous month at Mount Vernon. They were promptly adopted by the rump session of the Burgesses.[25] These resolutions included language stating that the "Merchants, Traders, Gentlemen, and other principal Inhabitants of the Colony of Virginia . . . deeply affected with the Grievances and Distresses with which his Majesty's American Subjects are oppressed, and dreading the evils which threaten the Ruin of themselves and their posterity, by reducing them from a free and happy people to a Wretched & miserable State of Slavery," were concerned over their mounting debts to "their Brethren the Merchants & Manufacturers of Great Britain" and would boycott various British goods "from motives of Interest justice, & Friendship . . . to obtain Redress of those Grievances under which the Trade & inhabitants of America at present Labour."[26]

The 1774 Fairfax Resolves, on which Washington and Mason again collaborated, gave a clear and succinct summary of what was, in effect, the unwritten British-American constitution. Article I of the Resolves stated that "our Ancestors, when they left their native Land, and setled in America, brought with them (even if the same had not been confirmed by Charters) the Civil-Constitution and Form of Government of the Country they came from; and were by the Laws of Nature and Nations, entitled to all it's Privileges, Immunities and Advantages; which have descended to us their Posterity, and ought of Right to be as fully enjoyed, as if we had still continued within the Realm of England." Here Mason and Washington were advancing an argument that New Englanders had made a decade earlier. James Otis, for example, in his "Rights of the British Colonies Asserted and Proved" (1764), asserted, "Every British Subject born on the continent of America, or in any other of the British dominions, is by the law of God and nature, by the common law, and by act of parliament, . . . entitled to all the . . . rights of our fellow subjects in Great-Britain."[27]

The twenty-four resolves went on to assert more fundamental civil rights for British-Americans, and to reproduce classic tenets of British liberal political philosophy, consent of the governed expressed through representation conducing to the people's pursuit of happiness: "Resolved that the most important and valuable Part of the British Constitution, upon which its very Existence depends, is the fundamental Principle of the People's being governed by no Laws, to which they have not given their Consent, by Representatives freely chosen by themselves; who are affected by the Laws they enact equally with their Constituents; to whom they are accountable, and whose Burthens they share; in which consists the Safety and Happiness of the Community." They also expressed, in the seventeenth resolve, a desire that "no Slaves ought to be imported into any of the British Colonies on this Continent; and we take this Opportunity of declaring our most earnest Wishes to see an entire Stop for ever put to such a wicked cruel and unnatural Trade."[28] The two principal authors of the Resolves apparently were convinced that the transatlantic slave trade had to stop because the very liberties they were contending for were being denied to Africans, though they stopped short of calling for manumission or abolition within the colonies. Mason would go on to argue against slavery on moral and religious grounds on the floor of the Constitutional Convention, while Washington, who presided over that meeting, would free his own slaves in the final revision of his will in 1799.

Two days after he and Mason wrapped up the Fairfax County Resolves, Washington sent this carefully phrased communication to his Tory neighbor Bryan Fairfax, a descendent of the county's namesake, showing he had mastered the logic and particulars of the Resolves. "I observe, or think I observe," Washington began, "that government is pursuing a regular plan at the expense of law and justice to overthrow our constitutional rights and liberties." As he went on at length, Washington marshalled his arguments to show Fairfax that in his mind it was constitutional principle that was at stake, not pennies.

> Sir, what is it we are contending against? Is it against paying the duty of three pence per pound on tea because burthensome? No, it is the right only, we have all along disputed, and to this end we

have already petitioned his Majesty in as humble and dutiful manner as subjects could do. Nay, more, we applied to the House of Lords and House of Commons in their different legislative capacities, setting forth, that, as Englishmen, we could not be deprived of this essential and valuable part of a constitution. If, then, as the fact really is, it is against the right of taxation that we now do, and, (as I before said,) all along have contended, why should they suppose an exertion of this power would be less obnoxious now than formerly? . . . If I was in any doubt, as to the right which the Parliament of Great Britain had to tax us without our consent, I should most heartily coincide with you in opinion, that to petition, and petition only, is the proper method to apply for relief; because we should then be asking a favor, and not claiming a right, which, by the law of nature and our constitution, we are, in my opinion, indubitably entitled to.

Washington then brought out his biggest rhetorical guns. "I think the Parliament of Great Britain hath no more right to put their hands into my pocket, without my consent, than I have to put my hands into yours for money," he argued, and concluded by saying that nonimportation was something the colonists "have a right to do, and no power upon earth can compel us to do otherwise, till they have first reduced us to the most abject state of slavery that ever was designed for mankind."[29]

This tightly reasoned letter shows the solid layman's grasp of British constitutionalism that Washington possessed by the mid-1770s. Indeed, it is perhaps his best statement of liberal political theory from the Revolutionary period, and moreover it is a composition entirely his own, though the underlying ideas show signs of indebtedness to the tutorial in British constitutionalism he received from Mason. (A month later Washington referred to "abler heads than my own," who had convinced him that British measures had become unconstitutional, and it now seems apparent that those heads belonged to George Mason and Patrick Henry.)[30] By claiming to perceive—or merely to think he perceived—"a regular plan at the expense of law and justice to overthrow our constitutional rights and liberties," Washington was anticipating the Lockean argument of the Declaration of Independence. Two years later Jefferson and his colleagues in Congress were to assert that they perceived a "long train of abuses" consciously designed to subvert British American liberties and "to reduce them under absolute Despotism." Washington claimed that Americans had gone through the proper channels with both Houses of Parliament, and argued, again in anticipation of the Declaration, that American grievances were not over "light and transient causes," as that document was to put it. These were serious and deliberate attempts to threaten American rights—rights they held under the law of nature (Jefferson's "Laws of Nature and of Nature's God") and under the British constitution. And since Americans had a right to be taxed only with their consent, petition was an inappropriate form of protest. Nonimportation was the appropriate and rightful response to violation of such a basic, natural right. Using similar British liberal arguments, the New York provincial congress informed Washington shortly after he took command of the Continental Army that "at a time when the most loyal of his Majesty's Subjects, from a regard to the Laws & the Constitution by which he sat on the throne, felt themselves reduced to the unhappy necessity of taking up arms to defend their dearest rights & privileges; and while they deplored the calamities of a divided empire, they rejoiced in the appointment of a gentleman [Washington], from whose abilities & virtues they were taught to expect both security & peace."[31]

As he internalized the rationale of these British liberal arguments and complained to Bryan Fairfax of the "abject slavery" being imposed on Americans, Washington began to feel the stirrings of conscience. For why, if white Americans were endowed with natural rights, were not their African slaves so endowed? A month later he again wrote to Fairfax, telling his friend that "an innate spirit of freedom first told me, that the measures, which administration hath for some time been, and now are most violently pursuing, are repugnant to every principle of natural justice . . . [and] repugnant to natural right." Disclaiming a solution of his own, Washington went on, "I shall not undertake to say where the line between Great Britain and the colonies should be drawn; but I am clearly of opinion, that one ought to be drawn, and our rights clearly ascertained. . . . [T]he crisis is arrived when we must assert our rights, or submit to every imposition, that can be heaped upon us, till custom and use shall make us as tame and abject slaves, as the blacks we rule over with such arbitrary sway."[32]

If their sway was purely arbitrary, there was nothing in nature that could justify whites enslaving blacks in violation of their natural rights. The same "innate spirit of freedom" surely spoke to Africans as clearly as it did to Europeans and their descendants. When, just a few years later, he was forced to acquiesce to armed black soldiers fighting alongside white troops in his patriot army—and to admit that they fought just as well—it constituted evidence that Washington had begun to unlearn some of the race prejudice that was so systemic in colonial Virginian culture. The evolution in his thinking regarding slavery and race relations was perhaps the sole instance of a marked change in Washington's political philosophy broadly considered. Meanwhile, Washington continued to complain about British usurpations. In the autumn of 1774 he wrote to Capt. Robert Mackenzie of the British danger posed to "those valuable rights and privileges, which are essential to the happiness of every free state, and without which, life, liberty, and property are rendered totally insecure."[33]

This formula of "life, liberty, and property" was, of course, vintage John Locke. In the second of his *Two Treatises of Government,* Locke penned what became the mantra of Washington and the American revolutionaries: "Man, being born, as has been proved, with a title to perfect freedom and uncontrolled enjoyment of all the rights and privileges of the law of nature equally with any other man or number of men in the world, hath by nature a power . . . to preserve his property—that is, his life, liberty and estate."[34] Thus to Washington the struggle for American liberty, though the ideology upon which it was based might be characteristically British, was universal in scope: "The Cause of Virtue and Liberty is Confined to no Continent or Climate, it comprehends within its capacious Limits, the Wise and good, however dispersed and seperated in Space or distance," he wrote at the Revolution's outset.[35]

Eight years later, at the war's end, Washington warned in his Circular to the States that the "Treaties of the European Powers with the United States of America, will have no validity on a dissolution of the Union. We shall be left nearly in a *state of Nature,* or we may find by our own unhappy experience, that there is a natural and necessary progression, from the extreme of anarchy to the extreme of Tyranny; and that arbitrary power is most easily established on the ruins of Liberty abused to licentiousness."[36] The security of liberty was the primary engine that had driven all of Washington's revolutionary efforts. As he put it to a group of German-Americans shortly before resigning his commission, the "establishment of Civil and Religious Liberty was the Motive which induced me to the Field."[37]

In the post-Revolutionary period, Washington became increasingly alarmed that the rights he had fought to secure were threatened by certain combinations of persons in the states. After learning of Shays's Rebellion in western Massachusetts, he complained to Madison that if "there exists not a power to check them [Shaysites] what security has a man for life, liberty, or property? . . . Thirteen Sovereignties pulling against each other, and all tugging at the foederal head will soon bring ruin on the whole; whereas a liberal, and energetic Constitution, well guarded and closely watched, to prevent incroachments, might restore us to that degree of respectability and consequence, to which we had a fair claim, and the brightest prospect of attaining."[38]

On December 26, 1786, Washington wrote a pair of letters to Henry Knox and David Humphreys further decrying the threats to the state constitutions. Mixing his metaphors, an agitated Washington wrote to Knox that there "are combustibles in every State, which a spark might set fire to. In this State, a perfect calm prevails at present, and a prompt disposition to support, and give energy to the foederal System is discovered, if the unlucky stirring of the dispute respecting the navigation of the Mississippi does not become a leaven that will ferment, and sour the mind of it."[39] In the years of his first retirement, Washington thus became increasingly pessimistic about the prospects of American liberties, ever more convinced that they could only be preserved under a stronger "foederal" union.

THE "FABRICK OF FREEDOM AND EMPIRE": LIBERALISM AND UNION

In 1862 the secessionist legislature at Richmond commissioned a Great Seal for their newly formed Confederate States of America featuring a portrait of George Washington at its center. It was a curious choice for a disunionist Congress to make, because the single greatest commitment in Washington's political life was to the American union he fathered, presided over, and, in his Farewell Address, prayed to God would be "perpetual."[40] Washington's appreciation for American union even predated his efforts during the "founding" period of the 1770s and 1780s and stretched back nearly as far as Benjamin Franklin's Albany Plan of Union in 1754. The Confederates would have done better to choose as their standard-bearer Washington's attorney general, Edmund Randolph, who said "I am not really an American. I am a Virginian."[41]

The received scholarly view is that until middle age, George Washington was a narrow-minded Virginia provincial whose eyes were forced open by command of the Continental Army beginning in 1775. One historian commends Washington and Benjamin Franklin for their "rapid" transition "from imperial and provincial loyalties to national consciousness" in the mid-1770s.[42] Yet we have noted that as early as 1756, when he was only a twenty-four-year-old militia major, Washington was writing to political figures of the need for an American "union" and for cooperation among the colonies. Recall that he wrote to Virginia's governor that spring, "Nothing I more sincerely wish than a union of the colonies in this time of eminent danger, and that you may find your assembly in a temper of mind to act consistently with their preservation."[43] Though he may have seen American "union" as an important feature of imperial federalism, or simply in military terms at that time, Washington was nevertheless thinking in terms of consolidating constituent powers. He had first been impressed as a teenaged Virginia surveyor and then militia officer by the largely untapped potential of the North American continent, provided a more centralized government and network of infrastructure could be built. Twenty years later, when friction between Great Britain and her colonies was heating up, Washington warned George William Fairfax not to underestimate the growing American commitment to colonial union: "The Ministry may rely on it that Americans will never be tax'd without their own consent, that the cause of Boston, the despotick Measures in respect to it I mean, now is and ever will be considered as *the cause of America* (not that we approve their conduct in destroyg. the Tea) and that we shall not suffer ourselves to be sacrificed *by piece meals* though god only knows what is to become of us."[44] Around the same time Washington wrote to another Fairfax, this time his friend Bryan, that "nothing but unanimity in the colonies (a stroke they did not expect) and firmness" could prevent taxation of the colonies by Parliament.[45]

After the Revolution, Washington more than ever envisioned an expanding and even imperial America, though he used the term *empire* in the counterintuitive way that Jefferson referred to an "empire of liberty."[46] Washington talked enthusiastically of a rising American "empire," referring to it some forty times after the Revolution. In the autumn of 1783 he wrote to Chastellux with the metaphors of a political surveyor: "I shall not rest contented 'till I have explored the Western Country, and traverse those lines (or great part of them) which have given bounds to a New Empire."[47] One of the longest letters in his private correspondence was written the following year to the Rev. John Witherspoon, president of the College of New Jersey at Princeton and a former colleague in the Continental Congress; the letter concerned Washington's western land holdings. Washington wrote glowingly of his thirty thousand acres of "rich bottom lands" in the west and of his desire to rent those lands and strike a "bargain" with immigrant religious communities who would help settle a new American "empire." Disavowing any desire to profit through means that were "speculative," Washington wrote, "I will only add, that it would give me pleasure to see these Lands seated by particular Societies, or religious Sectaries with their Pastors. It would be a means of connecting friends in a small circle, and making life, in a new and rising Empire."[48]

Washington, Jefferson, and the founders had two principal conceptions of empire available to them, the ancient Roman empire and the early modern British empire. Washington's "empire" was to be more liberal than the empire of either Rome or London: whereas Great Britain was using her empire to subjugate and control lands and peoples around the globe, America's "rising Empire" would expand westward and create a safe zone for dispossessed freedom-loving peoples everywhere. In his General Orders of April 18, 1783, announcing a cessation of hostilities, the general could

> not help wishing that all the brave men (of whatever condition they may be) who have shared in the toils and dangers of effecting this glorious revolution, of rescuing Millions from the hand of oppression, and of laying the foundation of a great Empire, might be impressed with a proper idea of the dignifyed part they have been called to act (under the Smiles of providence) on the stage of human affairs: for, happy, thrice happy shall they be pronounced hereafter, who have contributed any thing, who have performed the meanest office in erecting this steubendous *fabrick* of *Freedom* and *Empire* on the broad basis of Indipendency; who have assisted in protecting the rights of humane nature and establishing an Asylum for the poor and oppressed of all nations and religions.[49]

In December of that year he told a group of new Irish immigrants that the "bosom of America is open to the oppressed and persecuted of all Nations and Religions."[50] America was to be an empire of liberty, certainly; but it was also to be an asylum of liberty, a refuge where civil and religious liberties would be protected—again, the very motives that he said drove him "to the field" at the Revolution's outset. In his Circular to the States at the war's end, Washington noted that the newly independent American states were "not only surrounded with every thing which can contribute to the completion of private and domestic enjoyment, but Heaven has crowned all its other blessings, by giving a fairer oppertunity for political happiness, than any other Nation has ever been favored with."[51] Rather than taking other continents by force, as the British had done, the United States would carve out a vast territory on North America, improve unproductive lands, people those lands with freedom-loving and rights-bearing individuals, and benefit from the products of their labor.

But what to do about the Native American peoples already present on the continent? Though they might not have held and improved land like good Lockeans, Washington conceded that the Indians had natural rights but only gradually became willing to include them in the American political experiment.[52] The conduct of pro-British Indians during the Revolution (and years before, of Indian opponents in the French and Indian War) had left a bitter taste in Washington's mouth, and he was in no mood, at least in 1783, to consider them as potential American citizens. In September of that year he communicated his ideas "of the line of Conduct proper to be observed not only towards the Indians, but for the government of the Citizens of America, in their Settlement of the Western Country (which is intimately connected therewith)." "Indian Affairs," as he called them, were to be handled firmly, but not in such a way that would be "pregnant of disputes . . . with the Savages." Indians were to be considered a people "deluded" by the British, and Washington recommended a policy of containment, particularly as non-native Americans pushed westward. His military experience and appreciation of political "oeconomy," as much as just war theory, dictated this policy:

> At first view, it may seem a little extraneous, when I am called upon to give an opinion upon the terms of a Peace proper to be made with the Indians, that I should go into the formation of New States; but the Settlmt. of the Western Country and making a Peace with the Indians are so analogous that there can be no definition of the one without involving considerations of the other. [F]or I repeat it, again, and I am clear in my opinion, that policy and oeconomy point very strongly to the expediency of being upon good terms with the Indians, and the propriety of purchasing their Lands in preference to attempting to drive them by force of arms out of their Country; which as we have already experienced is like driving the Wild Beasts of the Forest which will return us soon as the pursuit is at an end and fall perhaps on those that are left there; when the gradual extension of our Settlements will as certainly cause the Savage as the Wolf to retire; both being beasts of prey tho' they differ in shape. In a word there is nothing to be obtained by an Indian War but the Soil they live on and this can be had by purchase at less expence, and without that bloodshed, and those distresses which helpless Women and Children are made partakers of in all kinds of disputes with them.

Americans were willing to let bygones be bygones, Washington said, and live under a kind of geographical apartheid for a time. "As we prefer Peace to a state of Warfare," he continued to Duane, "we will draw a veil over what is past and establish a boundary line between them and us beyond which we will endeavor to restrain our People from Hunting or Settling."[53]

During the period between the Revolution and his presidency, Washington considered the Native American tribes primarily in military and foreign relations terms, not in political terms. Washington's apartheid-like attitude might only have been reinforced when the first U.S. Congress placed Indian Affairs under the purview of the Secretary of War rather than the Secretary of State.

As president he began by insisting that then-current treaties with the Indians were to be honored and nullified a questionable land-grab in western Georgia between the Yazoo and Mississippi rivers in the summer of 1790. That August, Washington unilaterally negotiated the Treaty of New York with the Creek Nation, which returned to them most of the territory Georgia was claiming. It did not endear him to western Georgians, but it demonstrated that Washington considered existing treaties with the Indians as valid as those with other foreign nations and that, in terms of international relations, American interests would be served by mollifying the Creeks, who were threatening war if the Georgia scheme went through.

By the third year of his presidency, Washington appeared to recommend preparing the "undeluded" Indians to be de-tribalized and possibly become citizens. In his third annual address to Congress, Washington dropped his former recommendations and substituted language of incorporation.

> It is sincerely to be desired that all need of coercion, in future, may cease; and that an intimate intercourse may succeed; calculated to advance the happiness of the Indians, and to attach them firmly to the United States.
>
> In order to this it seems necessary: That they should experience the benefits of an impartial administration of justice. That the mode of alienating their lands[,] the main source of discontent and war, should be so defined and regulated, as to obviate imposition, and, as far as may be practicable, controversy concerning the reality, and extent of the alienations which are made. That commerce with them should be promoted under regulations tending to secure an equitable deportment towards them, and that such rational experiments should be made, for imparting to them the blessings of civilization, as may, from time to time suit their condition. That the Executive of the United States should be enabled to employ the means to which the Indians have been long accustomed for unit-

ing their immediate Interests with the preservation of Peace. And that efficatious provision should be made for inflicting adequate penalties upon all those who, by violating their rights, shall infringe the Treaties, and endanger the peace of the Union.

A System corrisponding with the mild principles of Religion and Philanthropy towards an unenlightened race of Men, whose happiness materially depends on the conduct of the United States, would be as honorable to the national character as conformable to the dictates of sound policy.[54]

The "rational experiments" Washington had in mind for the Indian tribes seem to have been based on the principles and technology of British political economy, including improvement of their rich but fallow lands with a vigorous commerce flowing out of the heartland to American and world markets. Thus modern farming techniques and "commerce" would convey the blessings of "civilization" to the Indians and "firmly attach" them to the United States as members of the westward-wending union.

Keen to learn the latest scientific methods of farming and animal husbandry, Washington corresponded with Arthur Young, the leading British agriculturalist of the post-Revolutionary and early industrial periods. Through his correspondence and reading, he kept abreast of British inventions and agricultural innovations by "'Turnip' Townsend, Jethro Tull, and Coke of Norfolk."[55] Washington yoked his admiration for British farming techniques to the Lockean understanding of ownership of land through the admixture of labor. That is one way he justified his own acquisition of the best interior lands following the French and Indian War: he argued that he had laid them off himself, in essence mixing his labor with the as-yet unproductive acres, and now held legitimate title to them. (Some of those lands, however, were in disputed Indian territories, a fact that Washington kept quiet.) Washington thus sought to harness his own—and America's—classical republican enthusiasm for farming and agriculture to modern British methods of production and ship the excess produce to the growing urban centers on the east coast and across the Atlantic. Washington himself had all the enthusiasm of a Cato or Cincinnatus for the farming life, and he played up this enthusiasm in his correspondence with Farmer Jefferson, for example, but he also realized that an energetic central government was needed to secure the right to that property and to liberty—both mainstays of a Lockean liberal political theory.

According to Garrett Sheldon's study of James Madison, the institutional expression of Lockean liberalism in early America was "centralized federalism."[56] Such centralization was thought necessary to secure the rights retained by the people after moving out of a state of nature into a state of society and creating a government. This was a theoretical grid that Washington laid over the American experience. He clearly accepted the liberal notions of Hobbes, Locke, and other social contractarians that pre-societal individuals, as well as individual nations at all times, were in a position of insecure equality in a "state of nature." After independence was declared, Washington consistently backed efforts at strengthening the federal arrangement haltingly begun with the Articles of Confederation to alleviate this insecurity. He saw the none-too-united states after the Revolution existing in a situation analogous to individuals in Locke's state of nature. "The Treaties of the European Powers with the United States of America," he wrote in the Circular to the States, "will have no validity on a dissolution of the Union. We shall be left nearly in a state of Nature." He feared that the newly won freedom might be squandered and the people's rights lost to an even worse tyranny that might be erected "on the ruins of Liberty abused to licentiousness."[57] It was this fear that drove Washington to accept, against his will, appointment to the Constitutional Convention in 1787. Justifying his actions to Lafayette, he wrote that the "pressure of the public voice was so loud, I could not resist the call to a convention of the States which is to determine whether we are to have a Government of respectability under which life, liberty, and property will be secured to us."[58] After the convention adjourned, Washington's signed letter accompanying the proposed constitution contained a quintessentially Lockean statement of the social contract and its application to the unique American circumstances of centralized federalism: "Individuals entering into society, must give up a share of liberty to preserve the rest. The magnitude of the sacrifice must depend as well on situation and circumstance, as on the object to be obtained. It is at all times difficult to draw with precision the line between those rights which must be surrendered, and those which may be reserved; and on the present occasion this difficulty was encreased by a difference among the several states as to their situation, extent, habits, and particular interests."[59]

During the ratification debates six months later, Washington wrote another constitutional lecture to Lafayette that reads like a primer of social contractarian thought. "Now, although it is not to be expected that every individual, in Society, will or can ever be brought to agree upon what is, exactly, the best form of government," he wrote,

> yet, there are many things in the Constitution which only need to be explained, in order to prove equally satisfactory to all parties. For example: there was not a member of the convention, I believe, who had the least objection to what is contended for by the Advocates for a *Bill of Rights* and *Tryal by Jury*. The first, where the people evidently retained every thing which they did not in express terms give up, was considered nugatory as you will find to have been more fully explained by Mr. Wilson and others: And as to the second, it was only the difficulty of establishing a mode which should not interfere with the fixed modes of any of the States, that induced the Convention to leave it, as a matter of future adjustment.[60]

This position comported well with Hamilton's argument in *Federalist* 84, that the constitution—that is, the form of the government—"is itself, in every rational sense, and to every useful purpose, A BILL OF RIGHTS."[61] To Washington it was not the writing down of constitutional prohibitions (the "parchment barriers" so disparaged in *The Federalist Papers*) that secured rights, it was an energetic government, and ultimately, a virtuous people.

By the time of his presidential inauguration, Washington had reluctantly come around to the position that a bill of rights should be allowed if it would calm the popular mind, so long as the amendments were consistent with both freedom and government efficiency. In the discarded draft of his inaugural address, Washington wrote, "Certain propositions for taking measures to obtain explanations and amendments on some articles of the Constitution, with the obvious intention of quieting the minds of the good people of these United States, will come before you [Congress] and claim a dispassionate consideration. Whatever may not be deemed incompatible with the fundamental principles of a free and efficient government ought to be done for the accomplishment of so desirable an object."[62] In that inaugural draft, Washington also invoked a venerable British liberal phrase used by James Harrington in his *Commonwealth of Oceana* (1656) regarding the superiority of "a government of laws" and not of men. (John Adams had invoked Harrington in his *Novanglus* essays in 1775, as would John Marshall in his 1803 opinion in *Marbury v. Madison*.) Washington wrote that his own careful study of all the written arguments pro and con concerning the new constitution had "resulted in a fixed belief that this Constitution, is really in its formation a government of the people; that is to say, a government in which all power is derived from, and at stated periods reverts to them, and that, in its operation, it is purely, a government of Laws made and executed by the fair substitutes of the people alone."[63]

In a 1790 missive to the British historian Catherine Macaulay Graham, Washington expressed a British liberal view of the origin and purposes of the American government, complete with a Lockean social contract designed to secure the right to pursue happiness, another invocation of Harrington, and a measure of Burkean prudence:

> The establishment of our new Government seemed to be the last great experiment for *promoting human happiness by reasonable compact in civil Society*. It was to be, in the first instance, in a considerable degree a government of accommodation as well as a government of Laws. Much was to be done by *prudence*, much by *conciliation*, much by *firmness*. Few who are not philosophical spectators can realize the difficult and delicate part which a man in my situation had to act. All see, and most admire, the glare which hovers round the external trappings of elevated office. To me there is nothing in it, beyond the lustre which may be reflected from its connection with a power of promoting human felicity.[64]

Washington occasionally partook, as he did here, in the optimism about human improvement so prevalent in Enlightenment liberalism. In August of 1786, he confessed to Lafayette, "I indulge a fond, perhaps an enthusiastic idea, that as the world is evidently much less barbarous than it has been, its melioration must still be progressive; that nations are becoming more humanized in their policy, that the subjects of ambition and causes for hostility are daily diminishing, and, in fine, that the period is not very remote, when the benefits of a liberal and free commerce will, pretty generally, succeed to the devastations and horrors of war."[65] Yet that optimism, as we have seen, was soon tempered with a heavy dose of realism following Shays's Rebellion; by year's end, Washington was complaining of the "inconsistency and perfidiousness" of human nature.[66]

Washington was by no means indifferent to the protection of liberties, civil and religious, later in his presidency. During the crisis over the Neutrality Proclamation in his second term, Washington took care not to infringe the people's right to free speech. Unlike his presidential successor John Adams, who was to sign the infamous Alien and Sedition Acts into law following the "XYZ Affair" with France, Washington took no action on a draft proclamation by John Jay urging him to "recommend" that citizens cease speaking publicly in any way that would offend the warring governments of England and France.[67] Still, to Washington's mind there was a difference between an unrepresentative, tyrannical government suspending its subjects' rights and a duly elected legislature or executive in a representative republic curtailing certain rights. During the Adams administration, Washington stopped short of denouncing the Alien and Sedition laws as unconstitutional and even suggested there was a conspiracy by disloyal persons "endeavoring to dissolve the union" that might justify them, though he was very circumspect about his opinions, even in private.[68]

As president, Washington labored to maintain American neutrality in all spheres, domestic and foreign. Although he had spent eight agonizing years and half his net worth from 1775 to 1783 expelling the British from North America, some of Washington's critics considered him unduly pro-British during his presidency. The Francophile Jefferson became convinced that President Washington was too influenced by Alexander Hamilton, Robert Morris, and other factors of the "British interest," or at least that is the impression he gave to the French envoy "Citizen" Genet.[69] But the reality was that in cabinet meetings Washington deferred as much or more to Jefferson than to Hamilton, and he resisted impulses to align the United States too closely to either the British or the French. To Washington's mind, the American ship of state had to be kept out of the turbulent waters of European politics altogether.

"A SENSE OF OUR OWN INTEREST": FOREIGN AFFAIRS

In 1805, with the Indispensable Washington safely dead and buried, John Adams gloated to Benjamin Rush,

> My maxim, which you know I have preached and inculcated for thirty years and which Jefferson has been mean enough to steal from me and display as his own, [is] "friendship and commerce with all nations, alliances with none." Washington learned it from me, too, as you very well know, and practiced upon it, as far as he could, to my certain knowledge and by my constant advice at a time when he consulted me in everything, to the infinite jealousy of Hamilton. . . . I am always mortified when I see my administration supported by the name, opinion, or authority of that man [Washington], great and good as he certainly was.[70]

Like so much of Adams's posturing, this claim was absurd. After a few early consultations with the first vice president, Washington essentially proceeded to ignore him on all matters foreign and domestic for the remainder of his two terms. However, Adams's description of Washington's policy of neutrality was closer to the mark. At the outset of his presidency in August 1790, Washington was writing to Lafayette, "It seems to be our policy to keep in the situation in which nature has placed us, to observe a strict neutrality, and to furnish others with those good things of subsistence, which they may want, and which our fertile land abundantly produc[es], if circumstances and events will permit us so to do."[71] At the end of his trying second term, after the uproar caused by the supposedly pro-British Jay Treaty, Washington wrote to Jay himself, "We are an Independent Nation, and act for ourselves. Having fulfilled, and being willing to fulfil, (as far as we are able) our engagements with other Nations, and having decided on, and strictly observed a Neutral conduct towards the Belligerent Powers, from an unwillingness to involve ourselves in War. We will not be dictated to by the Politics of any Nation under Heaven, farther than Treaties require of us."[72]

Washington's ideas regarding American neutrality and his sense of the place of the United States in the wider world were extensions of his liberal political theory, mixed with a faith in American exceptionalism that recalled the original Puritans themselves. As we have noted, Washington saw America as a haven for the world's heavy-laden, a place where they could come and exercise their civil and religious rights and have them protected. "Rather than quarrel abt territory," Washington wrote to David Humphreys, "let the poor, the needy, & oppressed of the Earth; and those who want Land, resort to the fertile plains of our Western Country, to the Second Land of Promise, & there dwell in peace, fulfilling the first & great Commandment [to 'increase and multiply']."[73] The pristine quality of the American west, which in his day began on the far side of the Alleghenies, evidently caused Washington to think of the place of America in the community of nations in almost millennial terms. Americans were enacting a new providentially scripted drama that would usher in a new age. The frontier was, as he described it to the Marquis de Lafayette, flowing "with milk and honey," a new Promised Land for a new political Israel. Settlers would have to cross their own version of the Jordan River, the "Potomac and James river," but they would come out on the other side.

Washington was as dazzled by the vision of America as "a city on a hill" as that old New England Puritan John Winthrop had been, and he wrote to Humphreys, Lafayette, and others with the combined enthusiasm of a booster and a Protestant revivalist preacher. His sense of the exceptional situation of the United States, both in political and geographical terms, led to his policy of neutrality in international affairs. In order to function as an "asylum of pacific and industrious characters from all parts of Europe," America would have to hold herself apart from European affairs. While Washington wished to see and encourage European immigration, he was also concerned that American political and moral principles might be infected with European principles "unfriendly to republican Governmnt."[74] That is why he continually lobbied (vainly, as it turned out) for a national university in the capitol, to counteract any anti-republican strains that might be carried by European immigrants and to inoculate America's political leaders against them by education.

Washington also transferred the Lockean notion of a state of nature to the international scene and accepted the prevailing liberal theory that individual nations are always in a state of natural equality, and therefore potential hostility, with one another. In an international state of nature, force was the only lingua franca understood by all. And in an insecure world, the fledgling United States needed time to mature and strengthen her internal union before she would be able to resist the aggression of other states. Those nations—perhaps including recent allies like France—would be governed by naked self-interest, so the United States would have to engage in clear-eyed realism and consult her own self-interest in foreign affairs. This meant, in the early stages of her national existence, avoiding entanglement in European power-politics. "Interest," as Washington repeatedly said, was the polestar by which he intended to navigate the American vessel. Interest, that is, coupled with a uniquely American sense of justice and mission. "Our detached and distant situation invites and enables us to pursue a different course," Washington wrote. "If we remain one People, under an efficient government, the period is not far off, when we may defy material injury from external annoyance; when we may take such an attitude as will cause the neutrality we may at any time resolve upon to be scrupulously respected; when belligerent nations, under the impossibility of making acquisitions upon us, will not lightly hazard the giving us provocation; when we may choose peace or war, as our interest guided by our justice shall Counsel."[75]

Throughout his presidency, Washington became increasingly convinced of the importance of "interest" in foreign affairs. In the same way he had thought it naive to rely on soldiers' mere patriotism disconnected from their financial interest during the Revolution, so he thought nations could not be trusted to act out of simple benevolence. They would always act in their own self-interest, just as the French had acted in aiding the American colonies during their war for independence from England. It was not magnanimity so much as genetic animosity towards the British that caused the French to throw in with the Americans on that earlier occasion. That is why, after the alliance with France during the Revolution Washington resisted pressure from Lafayette and the Congress for a joint Franco-American venture to conquer Canada. France, however, had her own set of interests and would be in a state of nature toward the United States after independence was won, and Washington effectively squelched the hoped-for invasion.

CONCLUSION

From the Revolution forward, Washington continually beat the drum for American neutrality in international relations and for an exceptional United States uniquely situated to protect civil and religious liberties. One of his strongest statements of American neutrality came in the Farewell Address, in which he famously insisted not that we should avoid "entangling alliances" (that phrase was Jefferson's) but that it was, and should be, "our true policy to steer clear of permanent Alliances."[76] (It is striking that for a century and a half American foreign policy followed this advice, until the United States joined the NATO alliance in 1949.) His thinking about the union and what was necessary to sustain and expand it contained recognizable elements of British liberal political thought and economy of the Enlightenment era. Barry Schwartz has pointed out that Washington embodied the Whig "public virtues," including love of liberty, along with the institutional expressions of those virtues, including supremely the balance of power.[77] Having fought a revolution against imperial Britain in the name of traditional British liberties, Washington reluctantly assumed "the chair of government" twice, at a constitutional convention that produced a stronger central government empowered to secure rights and then as a powerful executive protector of the people's rights, rather along the lines of the British theorist Bolingbroke's Patriot King. Americans paid an awkward compliment to Washington's liberal office when they kept the tune to the traditional anthem "God Save the King," but changed the lyrics to "God Save Great Washington."

CHAPTER 4

PROTESTANT CHRISTIANITY, PROVIDENCE, AND THE REPUBLIC

The establishment of Civil and Religious Liberty was the Motive which induced me to the Field [of battle].

Washington to the Reformed German
Congregation of New York, 1783

And to the care of that Providence, whose interposition and protection we have so often experienced, do I chearfully commit you and your nation, trusting that he will bring order out of confusion.

Washington to the Marquis de Lafayette, 1792

From the time he took command of the Continental Army, George Washington was ringed with a religious halo in many minds, and his sainted image has been conscripted to serve an American civil religion ever since. A Revolutionary woodcut produced in 1778 at Lancaster, Pennsylvania, featured an angel carrying a picture of Washington and trumpeting the German words *Das Landes Vater*—"Father of the Country," the first time that title was applied to him. Throughout the remainder of the eighteenth century, Washington was compared to Moses—liberator, lawgiver, and leader of the ancient Hebrews—more often than he was compared to the Roman Cincinnatus. John Marshall even hinted in his eulogy that Washington's passion from a Friday to a Sunday was reminiscent of the death of Jesus Christ. Beyond the religious images that were thrust upon him, Washington deliberately leveraged his character, offices, and moral authority to help create the ritual and liturgy of what Benjamin Franklin called an American "publick religion."

Washington was a lifelong Anglican, both by profession and by temperament, though the evidence for his orthodoxy is ambiguous. He preferred to stand rather than kneel in prayer, attended church but seems seldom to have taken communion, never referred to Christ in his correspondence, and died without requesting a clergyman, a Bible, or prayer. Yet he was a thoroughly religious man who quoted the Bible more than any other source, borrowed liberally from the Anglican *Book of Common Prayer,* and was firmly convinced a benign Providence ruled the affairs of nations and had presided over the birth of the United States. He complained that "Religious controversies are always productive of more acrimony and irreconcilable hatreds than those which spring from any other cause" but insisted that religion in general, and Christianity in particular, were essential props of the young republic.

Throughout his public career, Washington did his best to encourage them both while holding the reins of power tightly against sectarian squabbling. As soon as he took command of the Continental Army in the Puritan stronghold of Boston, Washington outlawed the anti-Catholic Guy Fawkes Day celebrations and ordered attendance at divine service. At war's end, he wanted to see each departing soldier presented with a congressionally approved Aitken Bible, the first Bible published in North America. He incorporated Christian symbolism in his first inauguration but while president, reassured New England Jews that the new constitutional government was religion-blind. Through such actions and by filling his public papers and speeches with references to the guiding hand of Providence and other reverential but nonsectarian phrases, Washington balanced public piety with religious liberty in uniquely American ways.[1]

AN ANGLICAN TEMPERAMENT

George Washington was an Anglican from cradle to grave. Though he has been claimed as one of their own by Roman Catholics, Baptists, modern Evangelicals, and even Swedenborgians, Washington was a member of the Church of England, which after the Revolution became the Protestant Episcopal Church, his entire life.[2] On April 5, 1732 (Old Style), the infant George Washington, aged two months, was baptized into the Anglican church.[3] Sixty-eight years later, on December 14, 1799, Washington died suddenly after a brief illness; no Anglican clergyman was present at his death, but the funeral performed for him four days later was a mixture of Anglican and Masonic rituals.

During the course of his life, Washington maintained active membership in the Anglican communion and, as his biographer Fitzpatrick put it, was "a consistent, if not always regular churchgoer." Moreover, he signed the oath of conformity to the established church in 1756 and was a parish vestryman and warden of Pohick Church and Christ Church in Alexandria, within Truro Parish. In the eighteenth century, the vestry was as much a civil office as a religious one, responsible for taxation, poor relief, upkeep of church buildings, parish land boundaries, and the like; even Jefferson—no orthodox Christian he—was a vestryman for a period of time.[4] In these connections Washington "witnessed the practical working of the Episcopal system and its value to the social well-being of both the individual and society."[5] During his years as U.S. president, Washington went to church more religiously, although it is difficult to say whether from a desire to set an example, greater accessibility of churches in New York and Philadelphia, or genuine piety. When he lived at Mount Vernon, where the nearest church was nine miles distant, Washington attended service less frequently, visiting, transacting business, and even fox-hunting instead of going to church many Sundays.[6] On average he seems to have attended church roughly once per month during his adult life.[7] His habit of abstaining during communion earned Washington a rebuke from the pulpit of Dr. James Abercrombie, assistant rector of Christ Church in Philadelphia, for not setting a better example. Washington "afterwards never came on the morning of Sacrament Sunday, tho' at other times, a constant attendant in the morning," according to Abercrombie himself.[8] Privately, Washington admitted the justice of Abercrombie's criticism. Yet he was "always serious and attentive" during divine service, in the words of Rev. William White, also of Christ Church.[9] And his belief in the efficacy of prayer was demonstrated repeatedly; according to Paul Boller, Washington "seems, in fact, to have been perpetually at prayer."[10] The Anglican *Prayer Book* made perpetual prayer easier, containing forms of prayers for almost every occasion in life.

In addition to the habit of prayer, his Anglican upbringing imparted a moderating spirit to the young Washington that stayed with him as he matured. As the 1769 *Book of Common Prayer* expressed the posture of the Anglican Church, "It hath ever been the wisdom of the Church of England, ever since the first compiling of her Publick Liturgy, to keep the mean between the two extremes, of too much stiffness in refusing, and of too much easiness in admitting any variation from it."[11] Washington's moderation and even gentlemanliness were largely the result of his immersion in the balanced ethos of the Anglican liturgy and religious culture; he seems to have agreed with Charles II, for whom Anglicanism was "the only religion for gentlemen."[12] While he was in some ways a model Anglican gentleman himself, Washington did not force his beliefs on others or demand that those around him emulate his actions. Washington demonstrated religious tolerance toward hired laborers at Mount Vernon, for example, writing to his farm manager that if they were good workmen they "may be Mahometans, Jews or Christian of an[y] Sect, or they may be Athiests [*sic*]."[13] In political terms this moderation expressed itself in his employment of nonsectarian religious language while commander in chief of the Continental Army and later president, his consistent nonpartisanship in the midst of increasing bipolarity in the early republic, and his severe warnings against the baneful spirit of party in the Farewell Address.

Washington's indifference to the personal religion of his workers did not signal an indifference to the importance of religion on a large scale in society, however. Washington consistently preached the virtues of religion as a conservative social force at the state and national levels, and he continued to do so even after Virginia began its constitutional modifications leading toward disestablishment of the Anglican Church in 1776 and after the United States institutionalized non-establishment in the First Amendment to the Constitution in 1791. In 1776, the Virginia convention approved George Mason's state Bill of Rights with its Article XVI assertion that "all men are equally entitled to the free exercise of religion, according to the dictates of conscience."[14] In 1784 Patrick Henry led efforts to introduce in the Virginia legislature a general assessment bill for supporting teachers of the Christian religion. This resulted in a public relations campaign to reject the bill orchestrated by Mason and James Madison, who wrote his famous "Memorial and Remonstrance against Religious Assessments" in 1785 to defeat it. Washington, declining to endorse the Memorial, explained to Mason, "Altho, no man's sentiments are more opposed to *any kind* of restraint upon religious principles than mine are; yet I must confess, that I am not amongst the number of those who are so much alarmed at the thoughts of making people pay towards the support of that which they profess, if of the denomination of Christians; or declare themselves Jews, Mahometans or otherwise, and thereby obtain proper relief." That was his position regarding the principle of the matter: state financial support for the Christian religion, yes; intolerance toward dissenters, no. But in practice, he said that "as the matter now stands, I wish an assessment had never been agitated, and as it has gone so far, that the Bill could die an easy death; because I think it will be productive of more quiet to the State, than by enacting it into a Law; which, in my opinion, would be impolitic, admitting there is a decided majority for it, to the disquiet of a respectable minority. In the first case the matter will soon subside; in the latter, it will rankle and perhaps convulse, the State."[15]

Though he was just as liberal as Mason, Madison, Jefferson and other anti-assessment Virginians regarding the free exercise of religion, Washington was more conservative regarding public support for religion, financial or otherwise. To Washington, Christianity was a crucial support of republican government in Virginia, and it was to be supported monetarily. He did not view such support as "restraint" upon religious belief or practice and even exempted non-Christian conscientious objectors. Yet to Washington the stability of a republican state was paramount, and since the matter had begun to "convulse" Virginia, he preferred to see Henry's bill quietly expire. His position during the assessment controversy in Virginia demonstrated Washington's Anglican sensibilities: the Christian church was a conservative force and contributed to the general public good; therefore professing Christians, who were in the majority in society, should be willing to pay to support it, while dissenters of the minority non-Christian religions could be exempted. If after 1785 it had become "impolitic" to tax Virginians to support Christian ministers, Washington continued to believe in the social utility of Christianity. He also believed that signs of public gratitude were owed to God for his providence in conducting the United States safely through the Revolution. He therefore continued to invoke the deity in language that was harmonious with that of the biblical religions Judaism and Christianity, and particularly his own Protestant tradition.

"PROVIDENCE" AND PROTESTANT POLITICAL RHETORIC

In his many communications dealing with God and public affairs, Washington employed a wide gamut of religious language, from mildly theistic terminology to the phraseology of ultra-orthodox Protestant believers. Washington's favorite word for describing both God and God's relation to the world was "Providence." (Douglas Southall Freeman dryly noted that over the course of his life, Washington referred to Providence alternately as "he, she, and it,"—he being God, she being lady Fortune, and it some mysterious force that science might someday explain.)[16] Though not a biblical term per se, "Providence" had by the eighteenth century become a commonplace among lay Protestants and was studied as a distinct branch of doctrinal theology by American divinity students and clergy.[17] It was used in at least two senses by American Protestants, as a name for God but more frequently as a description of his benevolent action in the world, usually rendered in that context as "divine Providence." This was the sense in which the Continental Congress used "the Protection of divine Providence" in the Declaration of Independence; it was one of their significant additions to Jefferson's original draft. The Anglican *Prayer Book* used it to describe God's care for his creatures through Christ: "We offer unto thy divine Majesty the sacrifice of praise and thanksgiving, lauding and magnifying thy glorious Name for such thy preservation and providence over us, through Jesus Christ our Lord. *Amen.*"[18]

Washington used a variety of names for Providence, but his favorite locution was "divine Providence," which he used nearly two dozen times. Echoing the Declaration, Washington answered a congressional address in 1782 by saying, "I feel very sensibly, this fresh assurance of the esteem and confidence of Congress; and thank them most cordially for their good wishes and recommendation of me to the protection of divine Providence."[19] At the Revolution's end the following year, the general wrote to Rev. John Rodgers: "Glorious indeed has been our Contest . . . but in the midst of our Joys, I hope we shall not forget that, to divine Providence is to be ascribed the Glory and the Praise."[20] Divine Providence was God's action in the world, his intervention in human affairs on behalf of Washington and his country. In addition to God's action, "Providence" was also God himself, and Washington even occasionally referred to Providence with the pronoun "he." During the upheavals of the French Revolution, he wrote to Lafayette, "to the care of that Providence, whose interposition and protection we have so often experienced, do I chearfully commit you and your nation, trusting that he will bring order out of confusion, and finally place things upon the ground on which they ought to stand."[21] Washington here slipped into the mode of the Judeo-Christian scriptures, which referred to God with the masculine pronoun. Such references were unusual, though not unheard of, among the founders; even the deist Jefferson occasionally personalized Providence, speaking of "the ways of Providence, whose precept is to do always what is right, and leave the issue to *him.*"[22] In his fourth annual message to Congress, Washington predicted that their work "will tend to strengthen and confirm their [constituents'] attachment to that constitution of Government, upon which, under Divine Providence, materially depend their Union, their safety and their happiness."[23] Washington's "Providence" was a far cry from the Roman *fortuna* or a weak deistic or Unitarian non-interventionist god; it (sometimes "he") was closer to the personal god of the Hebrew and Christian scriptures, sounding a familiar note with Protestants in the Reformed (Calvinistic) and Anglican traditions.

Besides "Providence," Washington employed other locutions from the Anglican *Book of Common Prayer* in political contexts. Nine times, for example, he referred to "Almighty God," a favorite name for the deity among the compilers of the *Book of Common Prayer*, who used it in prayers of thanksgiving and, after 1789, in prayers for Congress in their American edition.[24] In his General Orders for April 15, 1783, Washington instructed the chaplains and brigades to "render thanks to almighty God for all his mercies, particularly for his over ruling the wrath of man to his own glory, and causing the rage of war to cease among the nations," thereby combining language from the *Prayer Book* and the seventy-sixth Psalm.[25] In a letter on religious liberty from his first presidential term, Washington prayed, "May the father of all mercies scatter light, and not darkness, upon our paths, and make us all in our several vocations useful here, and in His own due time and way everlastingly happy."[26] This was precisely the name for God from a prayer of general thanksgiving in the 1769 and 1789 editions of the *Book of Common Prayer*: "Almighty God, Father of all mercies, we, thine unworthy servants, do give thee most humble and hearty thanks."[27]

Even phrases that sound Masonic on first hearing were near-copies of *Prayer Book* names for the Judeo-Christian God. Washington's "great Governor of the Universe" was scarcely distinguishable from "the supreme Governor of all things," used in a prayer for a "time of War and Tumults" in the 1789 *Book of Common Prayer*. During the final stage of the struggle over ratification of the Constitution, Washington wrote to Benjamin Lincoln that the "great Governor of the Universe has led us too long and too far on the road to happiness and glory, to forsake us in the midst of it."[28] Washington used grandiloquent titles for God such as this in his general orders to his Revolutionary troops and in his annual messages to Congress. Six times he used variants of "ruler of the universe" to refer to the deity, including references to the "Almighty ruler of the universe" in his General Orders of May 1778; the "Supreme Ruler of the Universe" in a letter to Reformed Germans in New York in 1783; and the "great ruler of the Universe" in a presidential address in 1793.[29] Washington described a personal, intervening and political God when he addressed Congress the following year and urged them to "unite, therefore, in imploring the Supreme Ruler of nations to spread his holy protection over these United States, to turn the machinations of the wicked to the confirming of our constitution; to enable us, at all times, to root out internal sedition, and put invasion to flight; to perpetuate to our country that prosperity, which his goodness has already conferred; and to verify the anticipations of this government being a safeguard to human rights."[30] Twice he mentioned "the ruler of the universe" in his final annual address to Congress in 1796, which began: "Fellow Citizens of the Senate and House of Representatives: In recurring to the internal situation of our Country, since I had last the pleasure to Address you, I find ample reason for a renewed expression of that gratitude to the ruler of the Universe, which a continued series of prosperity has so often and so justly called forth."[31] But none of these usages by Washington was more grandiloquent than the 1789 *Prayer Book*'s formulation "O Lord, our heavenly Father, the high and mighty Ruler of the universe," in "A Prayer for the President of the United States, and all in civil Authority."[32]

Finally, only three months before his death, Washington wrote an eerily prescient letter to his kinsman Burges Ball that was expressed in Anglican prose. "I was the *first,* and am now the *last,* of my fathers Children by the second marriage who remain," he wrote. "When I shall be called upon to follow them, is known only to the giver of life."[33] A prayer "For a Recovery from Sickness" in the 1769 *Prayer Book* began, "O God, who art the giver of life. . . ."[34]

In addition to his use of recognizably Anglican formulae from the *Prayer Book*, Washington often phrased his public addresses in ways that were reminiscent of Protestant language more generally and Reformed Protestant language specifically. For example, in a letter to the attorney general in which he was deliberating whether to stand for a second term as president, Washington wrote, "As the allwise disposer of events has hitherto watched over my steps, I trust that in the important one I may soon be called upon to take, he will mark the course so plainly, as that I cannot mistake the way."[35] This sort of language, easily and frequently mistaken by modern readers for "deistic" god-talk, was in fact precisely how Reformed believers spoke of their Calvinist God in the eighteenth century. Compare Washington's "allwise disposer of events" with the language of his Revolutionary colleague the Rev. John Witherspoon, author of several religious proclamations on behalf of the Continental Congress. Writing about an official day of fasting and prayer, Witherspoon, who was a staunch evangelical Presbyterian and Madison's Hebrew tutor at Princeton, noted, "Setting apart this day, and applying ourselves to the duty of fasting and prayer, implies a confession of the power and providence of God. It implies that we believe in him as the almighty Creator and righteous Governor of the world; the supreme Disposer of every event, and sovereign Arbiter of the fate of nations."[36] Such Protestant diction came easily, one might even say naturally, to Washington, given his upbringing in a commonwealth with an established Protestant religion which he publicly professed.

THE BIBLE AND POLITICAL RHETORIC

Examination of the thirty-seven typeset volumes of Washington's writings reveals that the literary source he quoted and paraphrased most frequently—more even than his favorite play, Addison's *Cato*—was the Bible. Washington was especially fond of agrarian biblical metaphors such as "wheat and tares," turning "swords into ploughshares," and sitting in peace under a "vine and fig tree." The latter phrase, which he directly quoted thirty-seven times, was his favorite literary image—an interesting choice for a man who spent so many years of his life making war, not peace.[37] Washington selected Micah 4:4, a visionary description by an Old Testament prophet of the "last days." In the passage immediately preceding that verse, Micah speaks of a time when God "shall judge among many people, and rebuke strong nations afar off; and they shall beat their swords into plowshares, and their spears into pruninghooks: nation shall not lift up a sword against nation, neither shall they learn war any more."[38]

Washington adapted those prophetic lines on several occasions as president. In a 1791 letter to Catherine Macaulay Graham, he combined the allusion from Micah with the New Testament verses Matthew 24:6 and Mark 13:7, predicting "wars and rumors of wars": "The United States enjoy a scene of prosperity and tranquillity under the new government," he wrote her, "that could hardly have been hoped for under the old . . . while you, in Europe, are troubled with war and rumors of war, every one here may sit under his own vine and none to molest or make him afraid."[39] Around that time Washington also wrote to la Luzerne in France that the United States, "at this great distance from the Northern parts of Europe, hear of Wars and rumors of Wars, as if they were the events or reports of another Planet."[40] (Washington's complacency was soon shattered, however; in just a few years' time, the war between France and England would threaten to overleap the moat of the Atlantic and draw the United States into the conflict.) Even after he was out of office, Washington continued to be concerned about undue French influence on America and expressed his worry in biblical cadences. If the French were to possess Louisiana and the Floridas, Washington predicted "that there will be 'no peace in Israel'" to Governor Jonathan Trumbull in the summer of 1799.[41]

Peace was a continuing biblical refrain in Washington's political correspondence. On accepting his commission as commander of the Continental Army, Washington combined classical and biblical elements in his speech to Congress. Although it "may be said that this is an application for powers that are too dangerous to be Intrusted," Washington could only reply "that desperate diseases require desperate Remedies; and with truth declare, that I have no lust after power but wish with as much fervency as any Man upon this wide extended Continent, for an oppertunity of turning the Sword into a plow share."[42] In his general orders to the troops of April 1783, Washington borrowed from Psalm 76:10 ("Surely the wrath of man shall praise thee; the remainder of wrath shalt thou restrain"): "The several Brigades will render thanks to almighty God for all his mercies, particularly for his over ruling the wrath of man to his own glory, and causing the rage of war to cease among the nations."[43] In 1795, when his presidential administration was winding down, Washington expressed a tentative hope that "wars would cease, and our swords would soon be converted into reap-hooks, and our harvests be more abundant, peaceful, and happy." But he went on to strike a note not unlike those sounded in gloomy American jeremiad sermons: "Alas! the millenium will not I fear appear in our days." Human nature itself seemed to mitigate against blithe optimism, on both individual and national scales. Washington continued, the "restless mind of man can not be at peace; and when there is disorder within, it will appear without, and soon or late will shew itself in acts. So it is with Nations, whose mind is only the aggregate of those of the individuals, where the Government is Representative, and the voice of a Despot, where it is not."[44] In 1786 he counseled John Jay: "We must take human nature as we find it, perfection falls not to the share of mortals. . . . We have probably had too good an opinion of human nature in forming our confederation. Experience has taught us, that men will not adopt & carry into execution, measures the best calculated for their own good without the intervention of a coercive power."[45] Washington was no religious enthusiast; his hopeful visions were always tempered by a vague Protestant sense of original sin, or at least of human frailty and contingency. Washington was ever, to use Peter Henriques's term, a realistic visionary, and his realism owed not a little to Protestant and ultimately Augustinian notions of intrinsic human sinfulness.[46]

The topic of constitution-making also elicited biblical language and themes from Washington. He compared separating good elements from bad in the Virginia and Confederation governments with the separation of the wheat from the tares in the last days prophesied by Christ in Matthew 13:25. Writing from Philadelphia at the end of May 1776, he noted, "We have, no doubt, some good parts in our present constitution; many bad ones we know we have, wherefore no time can be misspent that is imployed in seperating the Wheat from the Tares."[47] During the ratification debates on the federal Constitution, Washington confessed his worries that "there are persons, who, upon finding they could not carry their point by an open attack against the Constitution, have some sinister designs to be silently effected" but also offered that "I trust in that Providence, which has saved us in six troubles yea in seven, to rescue us again from any imminent, though unseen, dangers."[48] This "Providence" whom Washington trusted to protect the Constitution was none other than the biblical god of Abraham, Isaac, and Jacob—and Job. That suffering servant had been told, in Job 5:19: "He [God] shall deliver thee in six troubles: yea, in seven there shall no evil touch thee."

Washington also combined the language of the Gospels from Luke 1:28 and the *Book of Common Prayer* to describe his sense of awe at the revolutionary century in which he lived. "We of the present age are very highly favored," he wrote in language reminiscent of Mary's Magnificat in the Gospels (Luke 1:28). "The rapidity of national revolutions appear no less astonishing, than their magnitude. In what they will terminate, is known only to the great ruler of events; and confiding in his wisdom and goodness, we may safely trust the issue to him," he concluded.[49]

Over the course of his long public career, and especially during the Revolutionary War years, Washington's public and private correspondence were filled with biblical prose. Especially in communications about serious and even grave political matters, Washington frequently expressed himself in biblical idioms and rhythms. But it was in a letter to Lafayette on the settlement of the American west, a topic of the greatest importance to Washington, that he struck the mother lode of biblical allusions. In one sentence alone he quoted Genesis 1:28, Exodus 3:8, Isaiah 40:3–4, and Matthew 11:28: "I wish to see the sons and daughters of the world in Peace and busily employed in the more agreeable amusement of fulfilling the first and great commandment, *Increase and Multiply*: as an encouragement to which we have opened the fertile plains of the Ohio to the poor, the needy and the oppressed of the Earth; any one therefore who is heavy laden, or who wants land to cultivate, may repair thither and abound, as in the Land of promise, with milk and honey: the ways are preparing, and the roads will be made easy, thro' the channels of Potomac and James river."[50] All of which makes Samuel Eliot Morison's claim that he had "found no trace of Biblical phraseology" in Washington's letters more than a little puzzling.[51]

Washington's biblical quotations were weighted in favor of

the Old Testament, the larger of the two testaments and the one dealing most explicitly with national and political matters. On not a few occasions, however, Washington quoted from the New Testament and from the words of Jesus recorded in the Gospels. In what he intended as his final legacy to his country, the Circular Letter to the States at the end of the Revolution, Washington gave Christ himself a prominent and unusual place in American public religion.

"WASHINGTON'S LEGACY": THE CIRCULAR LETTER TO THE STATES, JUNE 1783

Although the Address of September 1796 is rightly thought of as *the* Farewell Address, Washington's Circular Letter to the States of June 1783 deserves to be read alongside it. These two documents together provide a fuller statement of Washington's core politico-religious beliefs about the new nation than either piece does individually. Washington himself paired the two documents when he hoped that the Farewell Address might provoke the same "endulgent reception of my sentiments" that had been given "on a former and not dissimilar occasion."[52] William B. Allen, editor of a judicious volume of Washington's writings, has noted the importance of the Circular in "carrying directly to his countrymen a coherent vision of the unfinished work which lay before them in the aftermath of peace."[53] Washington mistakenly expected this to be his final political statement, and as such the Circular reveals much of his mind regarding what was needed for Americans of 1783 "to establish or ruin their national Character forever" and the role of religion in establishing that character.[54]

Washington presumed that when he resigned his commission as commander in chief of the Continental Army, his circular letter would be his "last official communication" before leaving the public stage for a much-longed-for "domestic retirement"; thus it became known as his "Legacy" until supplanted by the Farewell Address thirteen years later.[55] The Circular was directed to the governors of the thirteen newly independent states and was delivered to them six months before Washington returned his commission as commander of the Army. In it Washington wished to express his sentiments respecting some important subjects connected with the "tranquility" (the word foreshadows the "domestic tranquility" in the Constitution's Preamble) and "mutual felicitation" of the United States.[56]

The Circular was typically Washingtonian in that it was seasoned with various expressions of thankfulness to an active deity: three to "Heaven," and two each to "Providence" and "God."[57] But it contained two anomalous religious references to "the pure and benign light of Revelation" and "the Divine Author of our blessed Religion."[58] The latter reference was especially unusual, because it was one of only two public utterances in which Washington referred specifically to Jesus Christ. The other was a speech to the Delaware Chiefs from 1779, in which he said that they did "well to wish to learn our arts and ways of life, and above all, the religion of Jesus Christ. These will make you a greater and happier people than you are."[59] (Washington, however, made no references to Christ in his private correspondence.)[60]

In the Circular to the States, Washington elaborated on this "Divine Author": he was one who demeaned himself with "Charity, humility and [a] pacific temper of mind," characteristics that Washington hoped Americans would humbly imitate.[61] These characteristics point to a person of history who left behind a record of his conduct that is capable of imitation.[62] Henry Cabot Lodge, along with many zealous believers before and since, thought this was an undeniable reference to Jesus Christ and therefore proof of Washington's personal orthodoxy.[63] More germane to Washington's political philosophy is how he put this reference to Christ to political use in the Circular. A fuller quotation reads: "I now make it my earnest prayer, that God would have you, and the State over which you preside, in his holy protection, . . . and finally, that he would most graciously be pleased to dispose us all, to do Justice, to love mercy, and to demean ourselves with that Charity, humility and pacific temper of mind, which were the Characteristicks of the Divine Author of our blessed Religion, and without an humble imitation of whose example in these things, we can never hope to be a happy Nation."[64]

Here Washington took a text from the Hebrew scriptures, Micah 6:8, and updated it for a political purpose. He borrowed language from the Old Testament that was rendered in the Authorized or "King James" Version of the Bible he used, "what doth the Lord require of thee, but to do justly, and to love mercy, and to walk humbly with thy God?" Washington proceeded to inform the Hebraic verse with Christian content, thus turning it into a prayer expressing his hope that God would help Americans in all the states to imitate Christ and therefore become a "happy Nation." Coming as it did in the final sentence of what he believed would be his final public utterance, this prayer is a significant indicator of the importance Washington placed on religion as an aid to civic virtue. It is a significant movement as well from Old Testament to New Testament religion, replacing Jehovah with an incarnate Christian god. During the 1770s and 1780s—the decades of constitution writing during the founding—American political writers cited the Bible more than any other source, overwhelmingly the Old Testament.[65] This is in keeping with the national blessings and curses God visits on the children of Israel in that testament, depending on their obedience or disobedience. In contrast, the New Testament's teachings are apolitical or transpolitical; indeed, the founder of Christianity himself insisted that his kingdom was "not of this world" (John 18:36).

So the gist of Washington's civil theology in the Circular was that beyond the progressive benefits of the Enlightenment, the imitation of Christ was necessary for political happiness in America. To be sure, Washington did not say that *belief* in Christ was a necessary condition for national happiness, only *imitation* of his moral virtues. Perhaps Christian practice, more than Christian faith, was required for that happiness. Moreover, Washington was speaking of corporate political happiness, not the salvation of individual souls. That task, as we shall see, Washington believed properly belonged to the clergy and private religious groups and individuals. But the import of what he wanted to be his last public statement is no less interesting for its political utility.

Equally intriguing is Washington's reference to the "benign light of Revelation." It appears at the end of a list of impressive advancements in human knowledge that have "increased the blessings of Society":

> The foundation of our Empire was not laid in the gloomy age of Ignorance and Superstition, but at an Epocha when the rights of

mankind were better understood and more clearly defined, than at any former period, the researches of the human mind, after social happiness, have been carried to a great extent, the Treasures of knowledge, acquired by the labours of Philosophers, Sages and Legislatures, through a long succession of years, are laid open for our use, and their collected wisdom may be happily applied in the Establishment of our forms of Government; the free cultivation of Letters, the unbounded extension of Commerce, the progressive refinement of Manners, the growing liberality of sentiment, *and above all, the pure and benign light of Revelation,* have had a meliorating influence on mankind and increased the blessings of Society. At this auspicious period, the United States came into existence as a Nation, and if their Citizens should not be completely free and happy, the fault will be intirely their own.[66]

For Washington, the foundation of the American empire was laid at a near-perfect moment in history, not in the kind of "gloomy age of Ignorance and Superstition" in which the Roman Empire, say, came into being. Eighteenth-century Americans were enlightened; they were not groping about in the gloom, as their predecessors had. At this point in the Circular, one might expect Washington to proceed on a skeptical, instead of a religious, trajectory, and in fact various commentators have read Washington in that way. In his seminal *Enlightenment in America,* Henry F. May even saw this section of the Circular (though he did not reproduce the phrase concerning "Revelation") as expressing an "essence of Enlightenment." May wrote that in "religion as in style of life he [Washington] was a man of the Moderate Enlightenment," an assessment that is accurate so far as it goes. But for Washington, the most important component of the foundation of the American Empire was revelation, and here he was expressing not the essence of the Enlightenment but the essence of Protestant Christianity, with its doctrine of *sola scriptura.* Readers of the late eighteenth century, who like Washington had grown up during the first Great Awakening, would have understood "Revelation" to mean the Bible, including the Old and New Testaments, and Washington singled out that scriptural revelation as "above all" the most important sustainer of American society. (In his discarded first inaugural address, Washington would refer to the "blessed Religion revealed in the word of

God.")[67] More than the ancient wisdom of classical republicanism, more than Enlightenment liberalism's commerce and the
rights of man, Protestant Christianity's revelation had done the
most to improve civil society.

Here Washington was expressing a more straightforward view
of religion's importance to the American founding than some of
its other architects. His vice president, John Adams, was at pains
to emphasize that one of the marks of the American government's enlightened modernity was its basis in nature, not the
supernatural. "The United States of America have exhibited,"
he wrote, "perhaps, the first example of governments erected
on the simple principles of nature; and if men are now suffi-
ciently enlightened to disabuse themselves of artifice, imposture,
hypocrisy, and superstition, they will consider this event as an era
in their history. . . . It will never be pretended that any persons
employed in that service [i.e., framing the American govern-
ments] had interviews with the gods or were in any degree under
the inspiration of Heaven, more than those at work upon ships
or houses, or laboring in merchandise and agriculture; it will forever be acknowledged that these governments were contrived
merely by the use of reason and the senses." Americans, Adams
said, were "too enlightened to be imposed on by artifice" and
preferred their government "without a pretense of miracle or
mystery."[68]

Washington was no fan of "superstition" either, and he too
saw it as a mark of progress that the American republic had come
of age in enlightened times. But Washington acknowledged the
hand of Providence in both the Revolution and the Federal Convention in ways that perhaps Adams did not. "The singular interpositions of Providence" during the Revolution and the successful perseverance of the continental army were "little short of
a standing miracle," he wrote at the war's conclusion.[69] Five
years later, after the Federal Convention had produced its work,
Washington wrote to Lafayette that it "appears to me, then, little
short of a miracle, that the Delegates from so many different
States (which States you know are also different from each other
in their manners, circumstances and prejudices) should unite in
forming a system of national Government, so little liable to well
founded objections."[70]

After the section in the Circular dealing with revelation, Washington sketched out, as he was to do in the Farewell Address, a sort of architect's rendering of the political edifice of the United States "as an Independent Power." Washington enumerated four "Pillars on which the glorious Fabrick of our Independency and National Character must be supported"—union, public justice, proper establishment of peace (the Revolutionary War had just ended), and a disposition toward national community—with "Liberty" as the "Basis" of the structure.[71] Religion was there as a sort of mortar, holding the entire structure together. In specific terms, the imitation of the moral virtues of Christ by American citizens was a necessary precondition for a stable polity and national political happiness. The theme of religion as a buttress to civil government was one Washington would sound again six years later, when he became first president of the more perfectly united states.

"INDISPENSABLE SUPPORTS": PROTESTANT CHRISTIANITY AND PRESIDENTIAL PRECEDENTS

Despite condescending attitudes from his presidential successors—recall that John Adams said he was too "illiterate" to run the country, Thomas Jefferson that his slow mind lacked "imagination"—Washington's political sagacity was especially evident in the public treatment of religion throughout his two groundbreaking terms as chief executive.[72] Washington had what was called "presence" in the eighteenth century, and he used it to inspire confidence and unity in the young nation. He had a special knack for using religion to accomplish those political ends, succeeding in this regard where his immediate presidential successors failed.

President Adams, by contrast, appeared to be a heavy-handed executive whose actions during his single term in office came off as self-righteous, puritanical, even establishmentarian. His signature on the Alien and Sedition Acts raised the specter of an established religion in shrewd constitutional thinkers like James Madison, who feared that threats to civil liberties would bleed over into threats to religious liberties as well.[73] President Jefferson had the opposite problem with religion. During the bitter

1796 and 1800 presidential contests against Adams, Jefferson's Federalist opponents called him an "atheist," and the label stuck. When he broke ranks with the precedent set by Washington and refused to issue religious proclamations, Jefferson added fuel to the fire. Despite the conciliatory rhetoric of his First Inaugural ("We are all republicans, we are all federalists"), Jefferson never managed to shed his image as an irreligious Jacobin. When news of his election reached New England, farm wives there buried family Bibles in their gardens to protect them from Jefferson's minions, who, they were told, would confiscate them after he took office, and his apparent lack of conventional religion put him out of step with Americans everywhere.[74]

In contrast to Adams and Jefferson, President Washington deftly used religion to foster unity in the infant United States. And although Jefferson and Madison, the third and fourth presidents, are invariably celebrated for their words outlining a new approach to church-state relations, it was George Washington who set the first precedents of a national public religion through finely staged ritual. It was he, and not they, who was considered the very embodiment of American civil-religious ideals. He gave religion a public face in government ceremonies, particularly in his first inauguration. Moreover, Washington contributed his own share of words to the uniquely American experiment in religious liberty in his proclamations and correspondence with religious constituents. He brought religious minorities—including Jews, Quakers, Catholics, and Baptists, and even majority Christian groups like Presbyterians who were upset with the godless Constitution—into the national fold with reassuring rhetoric in his letters to them. At the self-imposed end of his presidency, Washington's Farewell Address characterized religion and morality as "indispensable supports" of the young American republic.[75]

PROTESTANT RITUAL AND THE FIRST INAUGURATION

Washington was of course the first man inaugurated president of the United States, under the Constitution of 1787, over whose writing he had presided. He was responsible for much of the inaugural ceremony and ritual adopted in 1789 and perpetuated by succeeding presidents; he had to be, because the Constitution gave little guidance when it came time to invest the chief executive.[76] Drawing on British coronation traditions and republican colonial customs, the president-elect as always was conscious that his actions would set precedents, and he took care not to appear either too kingly or too common.[77]

The first inauguration ceremony fashioned by Washington, Madison, and his other counselors was rich with religious ritual and symbolism, consistent with both his appreciation for religion in public life and his eye for political staging. The basic elements of the inauguration ceremony have become ritualized expressions of American political culture and values. Washington's conduct at the outset of his administration showed his willingness to use religion to make the inauguration solemn, authentic, and legitimate and to strengthen the political order with Protestant rituals, including attendance at the Anglican church following his inauguration, and the use of Judeo-Christian language throughout his presidency.

In early 1789 Washington began confidential consultations with James Madison and others about the form of his inauguration and a suitable address to the Congress. By the end of April, Congress began its own arrangements and suggested an oath of office based on the constitutional language to be "administered by Robert R. Livingston, chancellor of the state of New York." They also recommended that "after the oath shall have been administered to the President, he, attended by the Vice President and the members of the Senate and House of Representatives, proceed to St. Paul's Chapel, to hear Divine Service, to be performed by the Chaplain of Congress already appointed."[78]

According to contemporary accounts, shortly after noon on April 30, 1789, churches throughout New York City were "opened, and prayers offered up to the Great Ruler of the universe for the preservation of the President," and church bells rang for half an hour, heralding the new president and the new nation.[79] An announcement in the *New York Daily Advertiser* of inauguration-day prayer meetings stated that the observance of such "religious solemnities" ensured that "the inauguration of our President and the commencement of our national charter will be introduced with the auspices of religion."[80] Shortly after midday, a procession of troops and political dignitaries escorted the president-elect to Federal Hall, where he was ushered to the balcony for the administration of the oath of office. Accounts of what happened next vary slightly, but according to one, Washington stepped toward the rail and the secretary of the Senate, Samuel Otis, raised up a crimson cushion supporting a Bible. Washington put his right hand on the Bible (it had been supplied by the Masons), which was opened to the Psalms. Chancellor Livingston proceeded with the oath: "Do you solemnly swear that you will faithfully execute the office of President of the United States and will to the best of your ability preserve, protect and defend the Constitution of the United States?" The President responded, "I solemnly swear," and repeated the oath, adding, "So help me God." He then bent forward and kissed the Bible before him.[81]

The company on the balcony retired to the Senate chamber, where the new president delivered his inaugural message. A third of the address, as Richard Brookhiser has observed, was devoted to a "discussion of the 'providential agency' at work in the founding."[82] It "would be peculiarly improper to omit in this first official Act," Washington began, "my fervent supplications to that Almighty Being who rules over the Universe, who presides in the Councils of Nations . . . that his benediction may consecrate to the liberties and happiness of the People of the United States, a Government instituted by themselves." He continued: "In tendering this homage to the Great Author of every public and private good, I assure myself that it expresses your sentiments not less than my own; nor those of my fellow-citizens at large, less than either: No People can be bound to acknowledge and adore the invisible hand, which conducts the Affairs of men more than the People of the United States. Every step, by which they have advanced to the character of an independent nation, seems to have been distinguished by some token of providential agency."[83]

Following the address, the president, members of Congress, and guests walked through the cheering crowd to St. Paul's Chapel for divine services conducted by the Rev. Dr. Samuel Provoost, the Protestant Episcopal Bishop of New York and congressional chaplain. "Prayers were offered and a *Te Deum* sung, and after the services [Washington] retired to the presidential mansion."[84] The public was then treated to a display of fireworks, a harbinger of America's love affair with incendiary patriotic displays.[85]

In the ensuing months, the First Congress grappled with proposals eventually shaped into the First Amendment non-establishment and free exercise of religion clauses. The day after it approved the final language of this amendment, the House adopted a resolution requesting the president to "recommend to the people of the United States a day of public thanksgiving and prayer, to be observed by acknowledging, with grateful hearts, the many signal favors of Almighty God."[86] Washington complied on October 3 with a proclamation designating November 26 as a day for public thanksgiving. He urged all Americans to "unite in most humbly offering our prayers and supplications to the great Lord and Ruler of Nations and beseech him to pardon our national and other transgressions."[87] Nearly every president thereafter, with only a few exceptions such as Thomas Jefferson and Andrew Jackson, followed this precedent of issuing religious day proclamations.

The tradition of presidential inaugurations begun in 1789 links oath-taking and religious ritual. In the manner adopted by Washington, which he borrowed from the common law, virtually every president has recited the constitutionally prescribed oath of office with his hand on the Bible. Washington apparently initiated another custom when he concluded the oath with the words "so help me God," though his alleged addition is currently under scholarly scrutiny.[88] These extra-constitutional words, found in many Anglo-American oaths, have subsequently been added by federal statute to the oaths for Supreme Court justices, federal employees, petitioners for naturalization, and others.[89] Those additional words have become so engrafted on presidential tradition that one commentator has even suggested that in "a real sense, then, we have a religious oath of office as a result of a constitutional amendment adopted through the precedent-setting action of the nation's first chief executive."[90] Though the framers omitted familiar religious rhetoric from the constitutional text, by his precedent-setting action, Washington reinserted it. In this particular respect, he was the architect of a visible and durable public role for religion in American political culture.

CORRESPONDENCE WITH RELIGIOUS CONSTITUENTS

In the days following his inauguration, Washington received a flood of congratulatory addresses from diverse sources, including state and local representative bodies, civic and fraternal organizations, educational institutions, and religious societies. In that era before press conferences, presidential responses to constituent letters and petitions were a favored and effective vehicle used by the early presidents to communicate their political principles and policies and to shape public opinion. President Washington made frequent use of this medium for articulating and disseminating his views. Among these exchanges were some two dozen with religious societies and congregations. Virginia Baptists, for example, wrote the president that there were "shouts of congratulation" and praise for Washington's services in war and peace and for his elevation to the chief magistracy.[91] Washington's replies here and elsewhere often contained quotations and paraphrases of what had been conveyed to him, with modest additions of constitutional interpretation.[92] These amicable exchanges show Washington trying to inspire life and meaning into the constitutional text, addressing vexing church-state disputes, commentating on American constitutional traditions pertaining to religion, and affirming liberty of conscience.

The plight of Quakers, Jews, Baptists, and other religious minorities excited Washington's sympathy for the bigotry and persecution they had endured, and he used his missives to these religious minorities to calm deep-rooted fears of discrimination that threatened to exclude them from the project of nation-building. His letter to the Protestant Episcopal Church celebrated flourishing religious pluralism: "It affords edifying prospects indeed to see Christians of different denominations dwell together in more charity, and conduct themselves in respect to each other with a more christian-like spirit than ever they have done in any former age, or in any other nation."[93] He reassured Methodist bishops that "it shall still be my endeavor . . . to contribute whatever may be in my power towards the preservation of the civil and religious liberties of the American People."[94] To Presbyterians he offered this homily on the duties of the pious citizen: "While all men within our territories are protected in worshipping the Deity according to the dictates of their consciences; it is rationally to be expected from them in return, that they will be emulous of evincing the sincerity of their profession by the innocence of their lives, and the beneficence of their actions: For no man, who is profligate in his morals, or a bad member of the civil community, can possibly be a true Christian, or a credit to his own religious society."[95]

Washington praised the Virginia Baptists for being "uniformly, and almost unanimously, the firm friends to civil liberty, and the persevering Promoters of our glorious revolution." He reaffirmed their sentiment that "every man, conducting himself as a good citizen, . . . ought to be protected in worshipping the Deity according to the dictates of his own conscience."[96] He favored the Quakers with the endorsement that "there is no Denomination among us who are more exemplary and useful Citizens." Although he candidly took exception to Quaker pacifism, he emphasized that the "liberty enjoyed by the People of these States, of worshipping Almighty God agreable to their Consciences, is not only among the choicest of their *Blessings,* but also of their *Rights.*"[97] Catholics, who had long borne the brunt of bitter discrimination in the New World, had reason to hope for a promising future; Washington assured them that all citizens are "equally entitled to the protection of civil Government" and honored the "patriotic part" they played in the War of Independence.[98]

Demonstrating an ability to speak the religious vernacular of his audience, Washington wrote to the Hebrew Congregation in Savannah, Georgia: "May the same wonder-working Deity, who long since delivering the Hebrews from their Egyptian Oppressors planted them in the promised land—whose providential agency has lately been conspicuous in establishing these United States as an independent nation—still continue to water them with the dews of Heaven and to make the inhabitants of every denomination participate in the temporal and spiritual blessings of that people whose God is Jehovah."[99] All American citizens,

Washington wrote to the Jews in Rhode Island, "possess alike liberty of conscience and immunities of citizenship."[100] There were many such messages sent out by Washington during his eight years in office, but three presidential messages stand out for their eloquent, robust statements of religious liberty.

In a May 1789 letter to the United Baptist Churches in Virginia, written only months before Congress drafted the First Amendment, President Washington wrote that if the Constitution "might possibly endanger the religious rights of any ecclesiastical Society" or if the national "Government might ever be so administered as to render the liberty of conscience insecure," then he would labor zealously "to establish effectual barriers against the horrors of spiritual tyranny, and every species of religious persecution."[101] Commentators have observed that this graphic imagery prefigured Jefferson's First Amendment "wall of separation between church and state," erected in an 1802 letter to the Baptist Association of Danbury, Connecticut. But although Washington's imagery superficially resembles Jefferson's better-known metaphor, his conceit differs from Jefferson's in one vital respect. Washington did not suggest that "effectual barriers" are normally desirable, nor did he argue that a barrier between religion and the civil state is a necessary precondition for religious liberty. Instead, he used the subjunctive mood to express a condition that he did not believe existed. If he had had the slightest concern that summer of 1787 that the Constitution would threaten religious rights, then "certainly I would never have placed my signature to it," he wrote, reminding the Baptists that "you, doubtless, remember that I have often expressed my sentiment, that every man, conducting himself as a good citizen, and being accountable to God alone for his religious opinions, ought to be protected in worshipping the Deity according to the dictates of his own conscience."[102] Rather than lobbying for a wall of separation between church and state, Washington expressed a willingness to "establish effectual barriers" to protect people of faith from "spiritual tyranny" and "religious persecution" if warranted by circumstances.[103]

In a November 1789 address to a New England Presbytery, Washington defused a criticism that had earlier threatened to blow up ratification of the Constitution. The Presbyterians lamented the absence of "some Explicit acknowledgement of the *only true God and Jesus Christ, whom he hath sent* inserted some where in the *Magna Charta* of our country."[104] Washington's reply provided insight on the subtle interplay between religion and the American constitutional order. The "path of true piety," he insisted, "is so plain as to require but little political direction. To this consideration we ought to ascribe the absence of any regulation, respecting religion, from the Magna-Charta of our country." Moreover, it was not the federal government's job to save sinners. "To the guidance of the ministers of the gospel this important object is, perhaps, more properly committed," he told them. "It will be your care to instruct the ignorant, and to reclaim the devious—and, in the progress of morality and science, to which our government will give every furtherance, we may confidently expect the advancement of true religion, and the completion of our happiness."[105]

The president dispelled the notion that the Constitution's lack of reference to a deity indicated hostility or indifference toward religion. True piety was a matter best left between an individual and his god; religious instruction was the responsibility of religious societies, not the civil state. The best and purest religion, in short, was most likely to flourish if left to the voluntary support of believers without the regulation or compulsion of the civil state. Religion and the state shared many concerns and objectives, but Washington assigned distinct and separate tasks to these two institutions. His lecture to the Presbyterian ministers on the compatibility of morality and science with "true religion" is also striking.

In perhaps his most eloquent, and certainly his most famous, pronouncement on religion, Washington celebrated the American spirit of religious freedom that allows every citizen, in the words of an ancient Hebrew blessing, to "sit in safety under his own vine and figtree, and there shall be none to make him afraid." This 1790 address to a Hebrew Congregation in Newport, Rhode Island, which Washington may have delivered in person, substantively described the distinctively American view of religious liberty.[106] "All possess alike liberty of conscience and immunities of citizenship," he said. "It is now no more that toleration is spoken of, as if it was by the indulgence of one class of people, that another enjoyed the exercise of their inherent natural rights. For happily the Government of the United States, which gives to bigotry no sanction, to persecution no assistance requires only that they who live under its protection should demean themselves as good citizens, in giving it on all occasions their effectual support."[107] Despite Washington's insistence that Christianity was a necessary support of republican government, the United States was to be no Christian Nation. All that was required of "good citizens" was that they demean themselves well, not profess any particular religion—or any religion at all. Washington here underscored the uniquely American contribution to religious freedom by jettisoning a regime of toleration in favor of one of liberty.

This notion is arguably the most profound innovation of the American experiment in religious liberty. The principle was first expressed in Article XVI of the Virginia Declaration of Rights of 1776. George Mason, Washington's coadjutor on the Virginia nonimportation association and the Fairfax Resolves, was the architect and chief draftsman of the Virginia Declaration. He had initially framed Article XVI in the language of religious toleration, but a young James Madison, recently seated in the Virginian legislature, successfully moved to replace "toleration" with the concept of absolute equality in religious belief and exercise.[108] Madison understood, as Washington did, that religious toleration is not synonymous with religious liberty. Toleration often assumes an established church and is always a revocable grant of the state rather than a natural, inalienable right.[109] In Madison's mind, the right of religious exercise was too important to be cast in the form of a mere privilege allowed by the state and enjoyed as a grant of governmental benevolence. Instead, he viewed religious liberty as a natural and inalienable right, possessed equally by all citizens—a right that must be beyond the reach of civil magistrates and subject only to the dictates of individual conscience.[110]

Washington unequivocally aligned himself with Madison and other advocates of religious liberty and opponents of the Old World regime of toleration. Writing to the followers of Emmanuel Swedenborg in January 1793, Washington reiterated the American insistence on "equal liberty" rather than mere toleration.

"In this enlightened Age and in this Land of equal liberty," he wrote, "every person may here worship God according to the dictates of his own heart," and "a man's religious tenets will not forfeit the protection of the Laws, nor deprive him of the right of attaining and holding the highest Offices that are known in the United States."[111]

In these letters, among the most eloquent he wrote, Washington articulated fundamental and enduring principles of religious liberty and church-state relations. They encapsulated his views on the prudential relationships between religious communities and the state, the role of religious citizens in civil society, and the contribution of religion to the social and political order. Washington was unquestionably supportive of organized religion in its diverse denominational forms. Though they were often couched in terms recognizable to Protestant Christians, his communications with diverse religious communities suggested Washington's acceptance of religious pluralism, and the substance of the letters advanced the concepts of religious liberty rather than toleration, voluntary religious exercise and belief, equality of sects, federal non-establishment, and a distinction between the tasks of the church and the state. Washington also used these addresses to reaffirm a national commitment to religious liberty and to quiet the fears of religious minorities that they would be excluded from the American project. These were messages of reconciliation and inclusion.

PRESIDENTIAL PROCLAMATIONS

As president, Washington also set a precedent of issuing religious proclamations, which was continued by President Adams before being abandoned by President Jefferson. In response to a House resolution citing precedents from the Bible and the Continental Congress, on October 3, 1789, Washington did "recommend and assign Thursday the 26th day of November next to be devoted by the People of these States to the service of that great and glorious Being, who is the beneficent Author of all the good that was, that is, or that will be."[112] The president recommended a "day of thanksgiving and prayer" and stated that it was "the duty of all Nations to acknowledge the providence of Almighty God, to obey his will, to be grateful for his benefits, and humbly to implore his protection and favor." These were stock concepts and phrases from the Anglican *Book of Common Prayer*, which frequently spoke of God's providence in its formulaic prayers, and almost invariably referred to "Almighty God."[113]

In 1791 the United States ratified the first amendment to the Constitution, guaranteeing non-establishment of religion at the federal level and the free exercise of religion. To Washington, then in the midst of his first term, the First Amendment did not preclude him as president from a variety of religious expressions, including issuing a number of religious proclamations. For example, on February 17, 1795, Washington issued a thanksgiving day proclamation recommending "to all religious societies and denominations, and to all persons whomsoever within the United States to set apart and observe Thursday, the 19th day of February next, as a day of public thanksgiving and prayer, and on that day to meet together and render their sincere and hearty thanks to the Great Ruler of Nations for the manifold and signal mercies which distinguish our lot as a nation, particularly for the possession of constitutions of government which unite and by their union establish liberty with order."[114] In addition to returning thanks to God for constitutions of ordered liberty, domestic tranquility, and prosperity, Washington's proclamation alluded to suppression of the Whiskey Rebellion and freedom from foreign entanglements, two subjects of special interest to him. President Adams would follow Washington's precedent and issue religious proclamations of his own, but that precedent was broken by President Jefferson, who thought that the First Amendment forbade the chief executive from such religio-political prescriptions. Washington, who on other occasions was not shy about exercising his executive privilege of constitutional interpretation, obviously did not think himself so prohibited by the Bill of Rights. Indeed, in his mind none of these state or national constitutional texts precluded verbal or financial support of religion, an important buttress of civil government. Nowhere in Washington's papers was this assertion made with more force or clarity than in his Farewell Address of 1796.

In that most influential of all his public proclamations, Washington voiced the prevailing sentiment of his day regarding the role of religion in public life: "Of all the dispositions and habits which lead to political prosperity, Religion and morality are indispensable supports." This line, perhaps more than any other in American public letters, has been used to justify an expansive role for religion in public life. It has become the *locus classicus* of the notion that religion is indispensable to social order and stability.

Contrary to popular belief, Washington's Address was never delivered orally. Instead, it appeared in Claypoole's *American Daily Advertiser* over his signature on September 19, 1796, some three years before his death in 1799.[115] Four key early American statesmen—Alexander Hamilton, James Madison, and John Jay (authors of *The Federalist Papers*), in addition to Washington himself—all had a hand in its creation, making it perhaps the single most representative document of the political philosophy of the elite American founders. Madison had drafted a brief address to be used at Washington's anticipated retirement from the presidency in 1792. Using Madison's old draft as a point of departure, Washington sent notes and instructions to Alexander Hamilton on May 15, 1796. With Washington's rough draft in hand Hamilton composed a draft which he went over with Jay; correspondence and revisions back and forth between Washington and Hamilton ensued, finally resulting in the printed version of the Address.[116] Pedantic debates have been held over the authorship of the Farewell Address, but we can say with confidence that while Hamilton did most of the drafting, Washington was the superintending intelligence behind all of its political philosophy and language. He reviewed drafts from Madison and Hamilton with great care, made substantial changes of his own, and published the Address over his signature as his final public statement.[117]

The language of the Farewell Address, and especially language from two paragraphs explicitly about religion, quickly entered the American political vernacular. They are worth quoting in full:

> Of all the dispositions and habits which lead to political prosperity, Religion and morality are indispensable supports. In vain would that man claim the tribute of Patriotism, who should labour to

subvert these great Pillars of human happiness, these firmest props of the duties of Men and citizens. The mere Politician, equally with the pious man ought to respect and to cherish them. A volume could not trace all their connections with private and public felicity. Let it simply be asked where is the security for property, for reputation, for life, if the sense of religious obligation *desert* the oaths, which are the instruments of investigation in Courts of Justice? And let us with caution indulge the supposition, that morality can be maintained without religion. Whatever may be conceded to the influence of refined education on minds of peculiar structure, reason and experience both forbid us to expect that National morality can prevail in exclusion of religious principle.

'Tis substantially true, that virtue or morality is a necessary spring of popular government. The rule indeed extends with more or less force to every species of free Government. Who that is a sincere friend to it, can look with indifference upon attempts to shake the foundation of the fabric[?][118]

These phrases on religion and government were immediately singled out by Americans for special recognition. In October 1796, just days after Washington published the Address, its religious language was quoted approvingly by William Loughton Smith in an anonymous pamphlet with the lengthy title *The Pretensions of Thomas Jefferson to the Presidency Examined; and the Charges against John Adams Refuted*. Smith, a staunch defender of Adams (and soon to be President Adams's ambassador to Lisbon), used lines from the Address to amplify his case against Jefferson in the upcoming presidential election. Smith compared the "virtuous Washington" with the allegedly impious Jefferson. Smith pointed to Jefferson's infamous claim in Query XVII of his *Notes on the State of Virginia* that it did him no injury for his neighbor to say "there are twenty gods, or no God."[119] Smith retorted: "What? do I receive no injury, as a member of society, if I am surrounded with atheists . . . ? Good God! is this the man the *patriots* have cast their eyes on as successor to the *virtuous Washington*, who, in his farewell address, so warmly and affectionately recommends to his fellow-citizens, the *cultivation of religion*?" With righteous indignation Smith invited readers to contrast Jefferson's "frivolous and impious passage" with "the following dignified advice from that true patriot [Washington];

'of all the dispositions and habits which lead to political prosperity, *religion* and *morality* are indispensable supports. In vain
would *that man* (he seems to point at Jefferson!) claim the tribute of patriotism, who should labor to subvert these great pillars
of human happiness.'"[120] Smith's pamphlet is a clear example
of the immediate resonance in American political culture of
Washington's religious language from the Farewell Address and
of the injection of that language into national politics mere
weeks after its publication.

Some five months later, Ashbel Green, a prominent Presbyterian clergyman and later president of the College of New Jersey at Princeton, delivered an address to Washington on behalf
of an ecumenical group of Philadelphia-area clergy on March 3,
1797. Green congratulated Washington on his career-long acknowledgment of the aiding hand of divine providence, and especially the first paragraph on religion, from "your affectionate
parting address," which he copied out at length. In his reply to
Green and the other clergymen, Washington reiterated his belief
that "*Religion* and *Morality* are the essential pillars of Civil society," deviating only slightly from his formulation in the Farewell
Address.[121] The wording in his letter to Green was, if anything,
stronger than that of the Farewell Address. In the Address, "religion and morality"—in the eighteenth century they invariably
went together—were "indispensable supports" of "dispositions
and habits," which in turn hold up "political prosperity." In the
reply to the clergy, Washington eliminated the intermediary dispositions and habits and described religion and morality themselves as essential pillars of civil society.

Immediately following Washington's death, in early January
1800 *The United States Oracle* newspaper in Portsmouth, New
Hampshire, began running already familiar language from the
Farewell Address in its masthead: "Of all the dispositions and
habits which lead to political prosperity, religion and morality
are indispensable supports." The influence of the Address and
particularly that section of it grew steadily throughout the nineteenth century. For instance, in 1862 President Lincoln, comply-
ing with concurrent resolutions from both houses of the Congress, issued General Orders No. 16, in which he commanded
extracts that included the paragraphs on religion to "be read to

the troops at every military post and at the head of the several regiments and corps of the Army."[122] The nineteenth century was rife with such examples, in which the religious language from the Address was singled out as especially noteworthy.

Nearly all of that religious language was suggested by Hamilton. Madison's original draft of a farewell address from June 1792 contained, by comparison, not one word on religion; Washington's first 1796 draft had one reference each to "Heaven" and to "Providence," along with the distinctly biblical phrasing in which he hoped "there will be none who can make us afraid."[123] There is much about religion in Hamilton's "Major Draft" of the Address, and Washington chose Hamilton's religious draft over Madison's secular one, allowing most of Hamilton's additions to stand in the final version. Washington did, however, remove this over-bold line of Hamilton's, which perhaps sounded establishmentarian: "Does it [national morality] not require the aid of a generally received and divinely authoritative religion?"[124] That question came at the end of the first paragraph on religion in Hamilton's Major Draft, a paragraph that questioned how national morality could exist in the absence of religion and asserted that religion is an "indispensable support" of political prosperity. Moreover, Washington insisted that any person who tries to subvert religion, one of the two "great Pillars," cannot "claim the tribute of Patriotism"—a startling claim itself.

The entire paragraph is insistent that national morality requires religion, and concludes by saying that "reason and experience both forbid us to expect that National morality can prevail in exclusion of religious principle." Here, unlike in his Circular to the States, Washington consciously placed religion as one of the supports of political prosperity. Thus in the Farewell Address he was even more explicit that religion has a vital structural position in holding up the republican edifice than he had been on that earlier occasion. Moreover, Washington observed that with "slight shades of difference, you have the same Religeon, Manners, Habits and political Principles," suggesting that Americans did have a de facto "generally received" religion which most of them thought "divinely authoritative," as Hamilton had written in less muted tones.[125]

Washington made another omission from Hamilton's Major Draft that concerned religion and civil society. Hamilton had asked, "Who that is a prudent & sincere friend to them [virtue and morality] can look with indifference on the ravages which are making in the foundation of the Fabric—Religion? The uncommon means which of late have been directed to this fatal end seem to make it in a particular of manner the duty of the Retiring Chief of a Nation to warn his country against tasting of the poisonous draught."[126] Washington shortened Hamilton's paragraph, removed the word "religion" from the final version, and then inserted a new short paragraph of his own:

> 'Tis substantially true, that virtue or morality is a necessary spring of popular government. The rule indeed extends with more or less force to every species of free Government. Who that is a sincere friend to it, can look with indifference upon attempts to shake the foundation of the fabric[.]
>
> Promote then as an object of primary importance, Institutions for the general diffusion of knowledge. In proportion as the structure of a government gives force to public opinion, it is essential that public opinion should be enlightened[.][127]

Hamilton had identified religion with the "foundation of the fabric" of the republic; Washington also considered religion to be that fabric. In fact, there is no other possibility, given the context of the preceding paragraph. As to the "ravages" being made in religion, the "uncommon means which of late have been directed to this fatal end" and the "tasting of this poisonous draught," suggested by Hamilton, Washington chose quietly to ignore them. Hamilton was probably referring to the recent French Revolution and its violent anticlerical and de-Christianizing effects; Washington passed over that reference in silence, perhaps for reasons of diplomacy or residual gratitude for French aid during America's own Revolution. And while his paragraph did not speak explicitly of "religion," as Hamilton's did, Washington clearly was warning against undermining religion and against "shaking the foundation of the fabric" of free government.

Furthermore, Washington inserted a paragraph where Hamilton had none, and that paragraph also implicitly deals with religion. "Promote then as an object of primary importance," Washington began, "Institutions for the general diffusion of knowledge." The question immediately arises: Why should such institutions be promoted? Or, in Washington's language, Why promote "*then* . . . Institutions for the general diffusion of knowledge"? The Northwest Ordinance suggests an answer. Washington's sentence contains an unmistakable echo of the Ordinance, which was passed in 1787 by the Confederation Congress and reaffirmed by the First Congress of the United States in 1789. Article Three of the Ordinance begins: "Religion, morality, and knowledge, being necessary to good government and the happiness of mankind, schools and the means of education shall forever be encouraged."[128] Washington was saying precisely what the Northwest Ordinance had said, and the logic of his three consecutive paragraphs is: (1) religion is an indispensable support of political prosperity; (2) the friends of free government should be concerned about attempts to weaken that support; and (3) religious education should therefore be promoted. This line of reasoning, and the conclusion that education involved the spread of religion, were axiomatic to most of the founders and Americans of Washington's time.[129] Washington so understood it, and he suggested that because religion was the foundation of the fabric of free government, it should be promoted through education.

As president, Washington realized that in the complex task of nation-building, simply getting the structure or institutions of government properly balanced was not enough. The "people" of the Constitution's Preamble had to be encouraged to think and, perhaps of greater importance in a democratic republic, to *feel* nationally. (Recall Washington's remark that it was "one of the evils, perhaps not the smallest, of democratical governments that the People must feel before they will see or act.")[130] Americans also had to feel something akin to religious reverence for the new constitutional order. Washington thus understood the difference between a constitution and constitutionalism, between the mere form of the government and the many sub-constitutional conditions, mores, and dispositions—Tocqueville's "habits of the heart"—that make up what might be called a people's constitutional morality. So Washington gave religion a public face in government ceremonies to help call up precisely those feelings of veneration for the new, more perfect constitutional union. In part he was trying to solve the problem addressed in *Federalist* 49 of how to encourage people to venerate a government that was a new thing under the constitutional sun.[131] It was, after all, a *novus ordo seclorum,* a new order for the ages.

From his first presidential acts—taking the prescribed oath of office with his hand on the Bible and adding the extra-constitutional "so help me God" to the end of that oath—to his Farewell Address, George Washington lauded the public benefits of religion and crafted a ritual of public religion for subsequent presidents and public officials to follow. He gave religion in general the same informal but essential role in sustaining the American republic in his Farewell Address that he had given Christianity in his Circular Letter to the States in 1783. In the Circular he had claimed that the revelation of the Bible was the most important boon to society in history and that the imitation of Jesus of Nazareth by Americans was necessary for their political happiness. In his Farewell Address of 1796, Washington crafted three successive paragraphs in which he insisted that religion and morality are essential supports of civil society, suggested that lovers of free government should take care that those supports not be undermined, and implied that promoting religion through education was a wise means of strengthening those supports. Irrespective of his personal orthodoxy or heterodoxy, Washington gave biblical religion an "indispensable" supporting role in his prescriptions for a healthy public order in the document containing his parting words to the American people. In that final address, Washington demonstrated the same painstaking care with which he had staged his first inaugural and the same regard for religious expression that he had shown in his correspondence with religious constituents from 1789 to 1796.

Indeed, throughout his two administrations Washington consciously fashioned a liturgy and ritual of American public religion. Always insistent that religion had a fundamental and "indispensable" part to play in the republic, at the same time Washington managed to promote toleration and religious liberty—no easy task. In his public actions, statements, and correspondence, President Washington struck an original balance and set precedents that future American presidents and politicians for the most part tried to maintain.

CONCLUSION

Michael and Jana Novak have observed that Washington's "vision of God was in good measure that of the Hebrew prophets and the psalmist. . . . His was a richly informed biblical mind—informed, perhaps, by the Anglican Book of Common Prayer (which is itself saturated with biblical references), which he knew from childhood on."[132] Little wonder, then, that Washington's political conduct and language were so often redolent of the Protestant Christian tradition. Indeed, his mind had absorbed the language and logic of Judeo-Christian thought his whole life, and these flowed out naturally in his political prose. Before the Revolution, he had bought himself "a beautifully printed thin Book of Psalms to carry in his coat pocket, and many of its descriptions of the Creator and Divine Architect" found their way into Washington's political lexicon.[133] His deployment of a multitude of religious phrases in public settings can also be seen as a conscious effort on his part to give an aura of sanctity to the union through Judeo-Christian incantations. Indeed, to Washington biblical religion was an essential ingredient in the American experiment, just as Protestant Christianity was an essential influence in early American political thought.

EPILOGUE

FAREWELLS

"FRIENDS AND FELLOW-CITIZENS": THE FAREWELL ADDRESS

George Washington made a career of saying farewell; he was, as Garry Wills put it, a "virtuoso of resignations."[1] Paradoxically, Washington gained power by pushing it away. But by 1796 he had had his fill of political power and was eager to replace the reins of civil government with those of his horses at Mount Vernon. On September 17, 1796, nine years to the day after the Constitutional Convention adjourned, Washington finished his farewell address and sent it off to the *American Daily Advertiser*, where it appeared two days later.

That document, as we noted at the book's outset, was a statement of Washington's political principles, and was in effect a transcript of his political philosophy. Jefferson ranked it with the Declaration of Independence and *The Federalist Papers* as the best guides to the distinctive Whig political philosophy of the United States. He thought it conveyed "political lessons of peculiar value," and he sought to follow its lessons of neutrality during his own two-term presidency.[2] Over the next century and a half, the Farewell Address would serve as a compendium of early American political thought, and it would be recited and studied by children and adults alike before falling out of vogue in the mid-twentieth century, around the time the United States joined the North Atlantic Treaty Organization, thus disregarding for the first time Washington's advice of no "permanent Alliances, with any portion of the foreign world."[3]

Its longevity would have pleased Washington, who wanted the Address to be a legacy of principle and policy for the toddling nation he had fathered. No less than today's politicians, Washington was also concerned about his own political legacy, and he used the Address as an *apologia* for his administration as well. First came the general themes vital to the country's well-being—union, independence, fidelity to the Constitution.[4] Moving to specific elements of American political culture, Washington argued for strict civilian control of a modest military, domestic nonpartisanship, the separation of powers, and the necessity of mediating institutions. Finally, he urged economic and foreign policies, including calls for balanced budgets, steady tax revenues, and neutrality (to which he devoted twelve paragraphs), ending with his belief that he had "been guided by the principles which have been delineated."[5] With dogged insistence he reminded his readers of the foreign policy outlined in his 1793 Neutrality Proclamation. These were the political principles Washington claimed to have navigated by during "forty five years of my life dedicated to" the service of "my Country." They were also the broad themes we noted in the introduction—union, liberty, and self-government under the Constitution, administered with virtue as an example to the world, all under the superintendence of a benevolent Providence. We have since seen how these principles and policies of Washington's reflected the political ideologies of classical republicanism, British Enlightenment liberalism, and Protestant Christianity.

Washington's overall political strategy had been to provide the time and conditions for the young nation "to settle and mature its yet recent institutions, and to progress without interruption, to that degree of strength and consistency, which is necessary to give it, humanly speaking, the command of its own fortunes," just as one might expect a father—political or otherwise—to do.[6] Indeed, the primary function of the Address was to give fatherly advice, and above all Washington encouraged what can be called the constitutional morality—that is, the political thinking, habits, and virtues—of his "Friends, and Fellow-Citizens." That accomplished, at the end of the Address Washington looked forward "with pleasing expectation" to retirement, but also with a kind of grim fatalism to being "consigned to oblivion" in "the Mansions of rest."[7]

"I George Washington": Last Will and Testament

According to Washington family lore, one night in July of 1799 the general dreamt of his own death; the next morning he sat down to amend his will to dispose of his property, and to dispose of himself.[8] He had already bequeathed a political legacy to the American people three years earlier. But Washington still had unfinished business with his countrymen, and even his last will and testament blurred the lines between private and public, containing posthumous lessons in republicanism for those with eyes to see between the lines. His will was to constitute a postscript to the Farewell Address on the themes of union, race, and citizenship. In his clear hand, Washington began, "In the name of God amen[.] I George Washington of Mt. Vernon, a citizen of the United States, and lately President of the same...."

Unlike his fellow Virginian and presidential successor Thomas Jefferson (who allegedly shelved the United States Code under "foreign laws" in his library), Washington emphasized his U.S. citizenship and presidency. He also began his will with an ancient Christian invocation of the deity, the same invocation the Pilgrims had used to begin their Mayflower Compact in 1620. Believing it would "not be displeasing to the justice of the Creator," in the will's second item Washington freed his slaves.[9] Jefferson, by contrast, began his will, "I, Thomas Jefferson, of Monticello, in Albemarle, being of sound mind...."[10] Though he, like Washington, had been an Anglican vestryman, in his final testament Jefferson made no mention of the Creator he had invoked in 1776 as the one who endowed all men with the right to liberty. Nor did he mention his own two-term presidency of those united states he had declared free and independent; indeed, he did not even think his national offices worth mentioning among the most important achievements inscribed on his tombstone. In his will Jefferson freed only five of his slaves, all males from the Hemings family.

Washington, however, left no doubt where he stood on the preeminence of the union, on the nullification controversy then threatening it, or on the institution of chattel slavery. He had supposedly once told Edmund Randolph that if slavery ever divided the country, "he had made up his mind to move and be of the northern."[11] As a young man, Washington unreflectively accepted the race distinctions endemic in colonial Virginia. He bought and sold slaves and offered rewards for runaways. After time spent in the north during the Revolution and as president, he changed his thinking. In 1786 he wrote that he never meant "to possess another slave by purchase" and wanted to see laws that would eradicate slavery by "slow, sure, & imperceptable degrees."[12] By 1799, when he revised his will, Washington's thoughts on slavery were closer to those of British abolitionists such as William Wilberforce and his Clapham Sect than they were to most of his Fairfax County neighbors. A dozen years earlier, Washington had been the largest slaveholder at the Constitutional Convention; now he became the only former delegate to free his slaves—even posthumously.[13]

Shortly after his death, his executors (and executrix, for he had included Martha) began to carry out the provisions of Washington's will. They saw to the simple funeral arrangements he had requested. They noted that he had set up a trust fund to provide financially for his freed slaves and their descendants, who were to "be taught to read and write, and brought up to some useful occupation," and perhaps to citizenship.[14] In these provisions, Washington implicitly rejected the repatriation schemes favored by other southern founders like Jefferson and Monroe, schemes that continued to be embraced as late as the Civil War. The executors noted, too, Washington's imperious tone in the will's slavery clause: "And I do moreover most pointedly, and most solemnly enjoin it upon my Executors hereafter named, or the Survivors of them, to see that *this* [cl]ause respecting Slaves, and every part thereof be religiously fulfilled . . . without evasion, neglect or delay."

His will also left Washington's library, correspondence, and Revolutionary papers to his favorite nephew, Bushrod Washington. The master of Mount Vernon wanted them in the hands of a blood relation who would put "my library of Books, and Pamphlets of every kind" to good use, as he himself had, up to the night before his death. Bushrod, who later sat on the Supreme Court, was a good choice; he inherited the library and papers along with the Washington legacy of acquiring "useful knowledge," as his uncle liked to put it, for public service.[15] Bushrod made the papers available to John Marshall, who used them in writing his biography of his old benefactor and commander-in-chief. Washington also left his stock in the Potomac Company to the "general government" of the United States to fund his treasured project of a national university in the District of Columbia. There he hoped American youth might learn political theories "friendly to Republican Governmt" and gain "knowledge in the principles of Politics."

Having begun his will with an invocation of the deity, Washington ended it with a benediction on his country. "In witness of all . . . of the things herein contained, I have set my hand and Seal, this ninth day of July, in the year One thousand seven hundred and ninety [nine] and of the Independence of the United States the twenty fourth." He had also given one last twist to the British lion's tail. English monarchs customarily dated their documents from the birth of Christ and also the year of their own accession to the throne. Washington republicanized the custom by emphasizing the independence of the United States.[16] His will was no testament of an elected monarch, done "in the reign of our Sovereign Lord King George, the sixteenth year, Anno Domini 1799," as it might have been written had Colonel Nicola gotten his wish at the end of the Revolution. Instead, it was simply the will of Citizen Washington, "lately President" of the United States. It was a fitting epitaph for the founder who, more than any other, had incarnated the political philosophy of the nation he had helped conceive.

Selections From the Last Will and Testament

[Original page numbers in brackets.]

"In the name of God amen[.] I George Washington of Mt. Vernon, a citizen of the United States, and lately President of the same, do make, orda[in] and declare this Instrument; w[hic]h is written with my own hand [an]d every page thereof subscribed [wit]h my name, to be my last Will and [Tes]tament, revoking all others. . . .

"Item Upon the decease [of] my wife, it is my Will and desire th[at] all the Slaves which I hold in [*my*] *own right*, shall receive their free[dom.] To emancipate them during [her] life, would, tho' earnestly wish[ed by] me, be attended with such insu[perab]le difficulties on account of thei[r interm]ixture by Marriages with the [Dow]er Negroes, as to excite the most pa[i]nful sensations, if not disagreeabl[e c]onsequences from the latter, while [both] descriptions are in the occupancy [of] the same Proprietor; it not being [in] my power, under the tenure by whic[h t]he Dower Negros are held, to man[umi]t them. And whereas among [thos]e who will receive freedom ac[cor]ding to this devise, there may b[e so]me, who from old age or bodily infi[rm]ities, and others who on account of [thei]r infancy, that will be unable to [su]pport themselves; it is [my] Will a[nd de]sire that all who [come under the first] and second description shall be comfor]tably cloathed and [fed by my heirs while] they live; and [3] that such of the latter description as have no parents living, or if living are unable, or unwilling to provide for them, shall be bound by the Court until they shall arrive at the age of twenty five years; and in cases where no record can be produced, whereby their ages can be ascertained, the judgment of the Court upon its own view of the subject, shall be adequate and final. The Negros thus bound, are (by their Masters or Mistresses) to be taught to read and write; and to be brought up to some useful occupation, agreeably to the Laws of the Commonwealth of Virginia, providing for the support of Orphan and other poor Children. And I do hereby expressly forbid the Sale, or transportation out of the said Commonwealth, of any Slave I may die possessed of, under any pretence whatsoever. And I do moreover most pointedly, and most solemnly enjoin it upon my Executors hereafter named, or the Survivors of them, to see that *this* [cl]ause respecting Slaves, and every part thereof be religiously fulfilled at the Epoch at which it is directed to take place; without evasion, neglect or delay, after the Crops which may then be on the ground are harvested, particularly as it respects [4] the aged and infirm; Seeing that a regular and permanent fund be established for their Support so long as there are sub-jects requiring it; not trusting to the uncertain provision to be made by individuals. And to my Mulatto man William (calling himself William Lee) I give immediate freedom; or if he should prefer it (on account of the accidents which have befallen him, and which have rendered him incapable of walking or of any ac-tive employment) to remain in the situation he now is, it shall be optional in him to do so: In either case however, I allow him an annuity of thirty dollars during his natural life, which shall be in-dependent of the victuals and cloaths he has been accustomed to receive, if he chuses the last alternative; but in full, with his free-dom, if he prefers the first; and this I give him as a testimony of my sense of his attachment to me, and for his faithful services during the Revolutionary War. . . .

"That as it has always been a source of serious regret with me, to see the youth of these United States sent to foreign Countries for the purpose of Education, often before their minds were formed, or they had imbibed any adequate ideas of the happiness of their own; contracting, too frequently, not only habits of dis-sipation and extravagence, but principles unfriendly to Republi-can Governmt. and to the true and genuine liberties [8] of man-kind; which, thereafter are rarely overcome. For these reasons, it has been my ardent wish to see a plan devised on a liberal scale which would have a tendency to sprd. systematic ideas through all parts of this rising Empire, thereby to do away local attach-ments and State prejudices, as far as the nature of things would, or indeed ought to admit, from our National Councils. Looking anxiously forward to the accomplishment of so desirable an ob-ject as this is (in my estimation) my mind has not been able to contemplate any plan more likely to effect the measure than the establishment of a UNIVERSITY in a central part of the United States, to which the youth of fortune and talents from all parts thereof might be sent for the completion of their Education in all the branches of polite literature; in arts and Sciences, in ac-quiring knowledge in the principles of Politics and good Gov-ernment; and (as a matter of infinite Importance in my judg-ment) by associating with each other, and forming friendships in Juvenile years, be enabled to free themselves in a proper degree from those local prejudices and habi[9]tual jealousies which have just been mentioned; and which, when carried to excess, are never failing sources of disquietude to the Public mind, and pregnant of mischievous consequences to this Country: Under these impressions, so fully dilated,

"Item I give and bequeath in perpetuity the fifty shares which I hold in the Potomac Company (under the aforesaid Acts of the Legislature of Virginia) towards the endowment of a UNIVERSITY to be established within the limits of the District of Columbia, under the auspices of the General Government. . . .

"To my Nephew Bushrod Washington, I give and bequeath all the Papers in my possession, which relate to my Civel and Military Administration of the affairs of t[his] Country; I leave to him also, such of my private Papers as are worth preserving; and at the decease of [my] wife, and before, if she is not inclined to retain them, I give and bequeath my library of Books, and Pamphlets of every kind. . . .

"The family Vault at Mount Vernon requiring repairs, and being improperly situated besides, I desire that a new one of Brick, and upon a larger Scale, may be built at the foot of what is commonly called the Vineyard Inclosure, on the ground which is marked out. In which my remains, with those of my deceased relatives (now in the old Vault) and such others of my family as may chuse to be entombed there, may be deposited. And it is my express desire that my Corpse may be Interred in a private manner, without parade, or funeral Oration. . . .

In witness of all, and of each of the things herein contained, I have set my hand and Seal, this ninth day of July, in the year One thousand seven hundred and ninety [nine] and of the Independence of the United States the twenty fourth."[17]

APPENDIX

A SELECTED INVENTORY OF WASHINGTON'S LIBRARY

Note: Book titles are italicized, pamphlet titles are in quotation marks. Titles have been selected from the various published inventories of GW's library, including those made by GW himself (ca. 1759, 1764), Lund Washington (1783), and the executors of GW's estate after his death (1799); as well as from "A Checklist of the Pamphlets in Bound Volumes in George Washington's Library," unpublished manuscript, comp. Ellen McAllister Clark, Library of the Society of the Cincinnati, Washington, D.C. For inventories and commentaries on GW's reading habits, see Benson J. Lossing, *Home of Washington,* 376 ff.; J. M. Toner, "Washington's Library and Manuscript Records," 71–111; Appleton P. C. Griffin, ed., *Washington Collection in the Boston Athenaeum*; Worthington Chauncey Ford, comp., *Inventory of the Contents of Mount Vernon*; Frances Laverne Carroll and Mary Meacham, *The Library at Mount Vernon*; Paul K. Longmore, "Appendix," *The Invention of George Washington,* 213–26; "List of Books at Mount Vernon, [Mount Vernon, c. 1764]," in Abbot et al., eds., *The Papers of George Washington,* Col. Ser., 7:343–50; and Stanley Ellis Cushing, *Washington Library Collection.* When the place and date of publication of a book that does not bear GW's authentic signature is listed, the suggestions of the editors of the Boston Athenaeum collection or those of the PGW have been followed and placed in brackets.

John Adams. *A Defence of the Constitutions of Government of the United States* (Philadelphia, 1787).
Joseph Addison and Sir Richard Steele. *The Spectator* (London, 1744).
Joseph Addison and Sir Richard Steele. *The Guardian* (Dublin, 1744).

[Francis] Bacon. *Essays.*

Isaac Backus. *A Church History of New England* (Providence, 1784).

William Bartram. *Travels Through North & South Carolina, Georgia, etc.* (Philadelphia, 1791).

Jeremy Belknap. *American Biography,* 2 vols. (Boston, 1794).

Jeremy Bentham. *Panopticon* (London, 1791).

George Berkeley. *Chain of Philosophical Reflections and Enquiries* (London, 1744).

The Bible (Oxford, 1783).

Offspring Blackhall. *The Sufficiency of a Standing Revelation in General, and of the Scripture Revelation in Particular* (London, 1717).

The Book of Common Prayer.

Hugh Henry Brackenridge. "An Eulogium of the Brave Men who have Fallen in the Contest with Great-Britain." Philadelphia, [1779].

George Buchanan. "An Oration upon the Moral and Political Evil of Slavery" (Baltimore, 1793).

Georges Buffon. *Natural History,* 2 vols. (London, 1792).

Miguel Cervantes. *The History and Adventures of the Renowned Don Quixote,* trans. Tobias Smollett, 4 vols. (London, 1786).

Marquis de Chastellux. *Travels in North America in the Years 1780, 1781, and 1782,* 2 vols. (London, 1787).

Marcus Tullius Cicero ("Tully"). *On Duties.*

William Cobbett. "A Little Plain English, Addressed to the People of the United States, on the Treaty, Negotiated with his Britannic Majesty" (Philadelphia, 1795).

Thomas Comber. *Short Discourses upon the Whole Common-prayer* (London, 1712).

Daniel Defoe. *A Tour Thro' the Whole Island of Great Britain* (London, 1748).

John Dryden. *Juvenal.*

John Dryden. *Miscellaneous Poems.*

Jonathan Edwards. "Observations on the Language of the Muhhekaneew Indians" (New Haven, 1788).

Adam Ferguson. *The History of the Progress and Termination of the Roman Republic,* 3 vols. (London, 1783).

Henry Fielding. *The History of Tom Jones,* 4 vols. (London, 1750).

Charles James Fox. "Substance of the Speech of the Right Honourable Charles James Fox, on Monday, December 1, 1783" (Dublin, 1784).

Edward Gibbon. *History of the Decline and Fall of the Roman Empire,* 6 vols. (London, 1783).

[Thomas Gordon and John Trenchard]. *Cato's Letters,* 4 vols.

Hugo Grotius. *The Rights of War and Peace* (London, 1738).

Alexander Hamilton, James Madison, and John Jay. *The Federalist,* 2 vols. (New York, 1788).

Henry Home [Lord Kames]. *The Gentleman Farmer* (Dublin, 1779).

Homer. *The Iliad,* trans. Alexander Pope (London, 1756).

Homer. *The Odyssey,* trans. Alexander Pope (London, 1758).

Horace. *The Lyric Works of Horace* (Philadelphia, 1795).

John Jay. "An Address to the People of the State of New-York, on the Subject of the Constitution" (New York, [1788]).

Thomas Jefferson. *Notes on the State of Virginia* (Philadelphia, 1794).

Samuel Johnson. *Dictionary of the English Language* ([London], 1786).

Juvenal. [*Satires*]. Trans. John Dryden et al.

John Locke. *An Essay concerning Human Understanding,* 2 vols. (London, 1775).

John Locke. *Some Thoughts concerning Education.*

James McHenry. "Brief Exposition of the Leading Principles of a Bank" (Baltimore, 1795).

John Milton. *Paradise Lost.*

John Milton. *Poems,* 2 vols.

Comte de Mirabeau. *Considerations on the Order of Cincinnatus* (London, 1785).

Jedediah Morse. "The Present Situation of other Nations of the World, Contrasted with our Own" (Boston, 1795).

Novum Testamentum (*New Testament*) (London, 1746).

Ossian. *The Poems of Ossian* (Philadelphia, 1790).

Ovid. *Epistles.*

Ovid. *Travels.*

Thomas Paine. *Common Sense* (Philadelphia, 1776).

Thomas Paine. *Rights of Man* (London, 1791).

Plato. *Works,* Vol. I.

Pliny [the Younger]. *Panegyric.*

Plutarch. *The Lives of the Noble Grecians and Romans,* 5 vols.

Plutarch. *Morals.*

Alexander Pope. *The Works of Alexander Pope,* 6 vols. (London, 1736).

Richard Price. "Observations on the Nature of Civil Liberty, the Principles of Government, and the Justice and Policy of the War with America" (Philadelphia, 1776).

Joseph Priestley. *Discourses Relating to the Evidences of Revealed Religion* (Philadelphia, 1796).

Alain René le Sage. *The Adventures of Gil Blas of Santillane,* 4 vols. (London, 1785).

Seneca. *Seneca's Morals by Way of Abstract,* ed. Sir Roger L'Estrange (London, 1746).

William Shakespeare. *Works.*

Granville Sharp. *The Just Limitation of Slavery in the Laws of God* (London, 1776).

Adam Smith. *An Inquiry into the Nature and Causes of the Wealth of Nations,* 3 vols. (Philadelphia, 1789).

Tobias Smollett. *A Complete History of England to 1748,* 11 vols. (London, 17[58–]60).

Temple Stanyan. *Grecian History,* 2 vols. (London, 1774).

Laurence Sterne. *The Beauties of Sterne.*

Ezra Stiles. "The United States Elevated to Glory and Honor" (New Haven, 1783).

[Suetonius?]. *Lives of the Twelve Caesars.*

Jonathan Swift. *Travels into Several Remote Nations of the World by Captain Lemuel Gulliver,* 2 vols. (London, 1727 [?]).

Jonathan Swift. *The Beauties of Swift* (London, 1782).

James Thomson. *The Seasons.*

St. George Tucker. "Reflections on the Policy and Necessity of Encouraging the Commerce of the Citizens of the United States of America" (Richmond, [1785]).

François Marie Arouet de Voltaire. *Voltaire's Letters* (Dublin, 1770).

Isaac Watts. *The Beauties of the Late Revd. Dr. Isaac Watts,* 2d ed. (London, 1782).

Noah Webster. *Sketches on American Policy* (Hartford, 1785).

John Wesley. "A Sermon on Original Sin" (Bath, 1783).

James Wilson. *An Introductory Lecture to a Course of Law Lectures* (Philadelphia, 1791).

Arthur Young. *Annals of Agriculture and Other Useful Arts,* 26 vols. (London, 1786–96).

NOTES

Preface

1. See Lombardi, "Measure of Washington," 72–78.

2. I use *ideologies* throughout not in the older, pejorative sense but simply to mean systems of thought.

3. Boorstin, "Washington and American Character," ix.

4. Fitzpatrick, ed., *Washington Himself*, 44.

5. Dalzell and Dalzell, *Washington's Mount Vernon*, 18.

6. See Knott, *Secret and Sanctioned*, 13–26.

7. John Adams to Benjamin Rush, January 25, 1806, in Schutz and Adair, eds., *Spur of Fame*, 47.

8. "British liberalism" will be used broadly, to encompass movements that professional historians have tended to separate, including social contractarians such as Thomas Hobbes and John Locke, Common Law thinkers, the libertarian Commonwealthmen or radical Whigs of the English Civil War period, and Scottish Enlightenment thinkers who were British though not English.

9. The "American founding" is often referred to as the period from roughly 1760 to 1805. See, for example, Lutz and Heinemann, eds., *American Political Writing*, 1:xi–xvi.

10. Smith, *Patriarch*, 365.

11. Flexner, *Washington: The Indispensable Man*, 3.

12. Johnson, *George Washington*, 4.

Introduction

1. Benjamin Franklin, *Autobiography*, in Lemay, ed., *Writings*, 1388. Franklin quotes from Cicero's *Tusculan Disputations* and Joseph Addison's *Cato*, James Thomson's poem "Winter" (1726) from *The Seasons*, and Proverbs 3:16–17. For GW's ownership of Thomson's *The Seasons*, see Griffin, *Catalogue*, 491.

2. Alexander Pope, "Prologue" to Addison, *Cato* (1730), 14.

3. Rev. Jonathan Mayhew, "The Snare Broken" (1766), quoted in Gummere, *American Colonial Mind*, 5.

4. Thomas Jefferson to Henry Lee, May 8, 1825, in Koch and Peden, eds., *Life and Writings*, 656–57.

5. Benjamin Rush quoted in Wood, *American Revolution*, 122.

6. On St. Paul's quotation of the Stoics Cleanthes and Aratus, see "Introduction" to Marcus Aurelius, *Meditations*, 29; and "Aratus," in Thomas, comp., *Dictionary of Biography*, 160.

7. See "Glorious things are spoken of thee, O city of God," Psalms 87:3 (KJV); and Marcus Aurelius, *Meditations*, 23, 68n.

8. Petrarch quoted in "Introduction" to Miller, trans., *De Officiis*, xiv.

9. See Hudson, "John Locke," in Hunt and McNeill, eds., *Calvinism and the Political Order*, 108–29. For Locke's quotation of Cicero, see Locke, *Two Treatises*, 1. Locke also paraphrased Cicero when he wrote, "Trade is wholly inconsistent with a gentleman's calling"; see Johnson, *History of the American People*, 177.

10. Compare GW's Circular to the States (1783), in Fitzpatrick, ed., *Writings of Washington* (hereafter WGW), 26:489 ("We may find by our own unhappy experience, that there is a natural and necessary progression, from the extreme of anarchy to the extreme of Tyranny; and that arbitrary power is most easily established on the ruins of Liberty abused to licentiousness") with Plato, *Republic*, 564a ("Tyranny is probably established out of no other regime than democracy, I suppose—the greatest and most savage slavery out of the extreme of freedom") and 562b ("'And does the greediness for what democracy defines as good also dissolve it?' 'What do you say it defines that good to be?' 'Freedom,' I said.").

11. Johnson, *History of the American People*, 146.

12. Hartz, *Liberal Tradition*, 42.

13. Fischer, *Paul Revere's Ride*, xvii.

14. Lutz, "Relative Influence," 190.

15. Kloppenberg, "Virtues of Liberalism," 9–10. However, at 10 Kloppenberg does assert that after the Constitution was made "the three streams almost immediately diverged."

16. Witte, *Religion and the American Constitutional Experiment*, 33.

17. GW, Circular to the States, June 1783, in WGW, 26:485.

18. In Humphreys, *Life of Washington*, 52; and Henriques, *Realistic Visionary*, xi.

19. GW to the Grand Lodge of Ancient, Free, and Accepted Masons of the Commonwealth of Massachusetts, April 24, 1797, in WGW, 35:439–40.

20. See GW to David Humphreys, July 25, 1785, in Rhodehamel, ed., *Washington: Writings*, (hereafter GWW), 580, where GW attributes his

refusal to write his autobiography to "a consciousness of a defective education."

21. Adams quoted in Boorstin, "Washington and American Character," xi; see also Johnson, *History of the American People,* 211.

22. See Benjamin Rush to John Adams, October 31, 1807, and Adams to Rush, November 11, 1807, in Schutz and Adair, eds., *Spur of Fame,* 96, 98.

23. GW quoted in Humphreys, *Life of Washington,* 48.

24. Thomas Jefferson to Dr. Walter Jones, January 2, 1814, in Peterson, ed., *Jefferson: Writings,* (hereafter TJW), 1318; see also Smith, *Patriarch,* 360.

25. See GW to the American Philosophical Society, December 13, 1783, in WGW, 27:269–70; see also editor's note, WGW, 18:11n.

26. GW to Samuel Griffin, April 30, 1788, in WGW, 29:481–82.

27. GW to George Chapman, December 15, 1784, in WGW, 28:13.

28. Garry Wills is virtually alone among modern scholars in seeing beyond the myths of Weems to the deeper truths he intended to teach about Washington; see Wills, *Cincinnatus.*

29. Morison, *Young Man Washington,* 12, 22.

30. Abigail Adams quoted in Brookhiser, *Founding Father,* 109.

31. See Beard, *Economic Interpretation;* Beard quoted in Stevens, *Provenance,* 99.

32. Bradley, "Political Thinking of Washington," 470.

33. See Longmore, *Invention of Washington.*

34. Thomas Jefferson, Resolution to the Board of Visitors, University of Virginia, March 4, 1825, in TJW, 479.

35. See Spalding and Garrity, *Sacred Union of Citizens;* see also Lucas, review of same, 1492–93.

36. See Wiencek, *Imperfect God.*

37. Higginbotham, ed., *Washington Reconsidered,* 3.

38. White, *Philosophy of the American Revolution,* 3.

39. Madison quoted in Johnson, *George Washington,* 82.

40. GW to Francis Fauquier, December 2, 1758, in WGW, 2:313–14; see also Fitzpatrick, *Washington Himself,* 116.

41. See GW to Richard Henry Lee, [1741?], in Allen, ed., *Washington: A Collection* (hereafter GWC), 5; GW to unnamed correspondent, [1749–50], in WGW, 1:19.

42. GW to Rev. Jonathan Boucher, July 9, 1771, in GWW, 141; see also Abbot et al., eds., *Papers of Washington* (hereafter PGW), Col. Ser., 3: 50–51.

43. Humphreys, *Life of Washington,* 35; see also Wiencek, *Imperfect God,* 4; *Mount Vernon Handbook,* 81.

44. GW to Annis Boudinot Stockton, August 31, 1788, in WGW, 30: 75, 76. GW's allusion is to this line spoken by Cato the Elder in Cicero's *On Old Age*: "Should this my firm persuasion of the soul's immortality prove to be a mere delusion, it is at least a pleasing delusion, and I will cherish it to my latest breath."

45. Crèvecoeur, "To the Abbé Raynal," *Letters from an American Farmer*, 30.

46. GW to Lafayette, August 15, 1786, in WGW, 28:520.

47. GW to Bryan Fairfax, August 24, 1774, in GWC, 38; GW to the Acting Secretary of War [Henry Knox], April 1, 1789, in WGW, 30:269.

48. Gregg and Spalding, eds., *Patriot Sage*, 17.

49. Kammen, "Introduction," in Freeman, *Washington: An Abridgement*, ed. Harwell, xx; see also Wills, *Cincinnatus*, xxi: GW "was the embodiment of stability within a revolution, speaking for fixed things in a period of flux."

50. Stevens, *Provenance*, 98.

51. Wilson quoted in Allen, "Standing Oak," 105.

52. Ellis, *Founding Brothers*, 120.

53. GW ["Proposed Address to Congress," 1789], in WGW, 30:297.

54. Longmore, *Invention of Washington*, ix.

55. Jefferson quoted in *Maxims of Washington*, 16.

56. Flexner, *George Washington*, 4:415.

57. Flexner, *George Washington*, 3:193.

58. GW to the Secretary of War, July 27, 1795, in WGW, 34:251.

59. John Adams to Benjamin Rush, June 21, 1811, in Schutz and Adair, eds., *Spur of Fame*, 181.

60. John Adams quoted in Vidal, *Inventing a Nation*, 169.

61. Thomas Jefferson, "Anas" (1818), in TJW, 673.

62. Johnson, *George Washington*, 4.

63. See Fahim, "Washington Letter," *New York Times*, April 26, 2007.

64. Chernow, *Hamilton*, 90.

65. See Phelps, *Washington and Constitutionalism*; and Higginbotham, *Uniting a Nation*, 84.

66. Morgan quoted in Wills, *Cincinnatus*, 93.

67. Longmore, *Invention of Washington*, 214.

68. GW, Farewell Address, September 19, 1796, in GWW, 963–64.

69. John Marshall, "Eulogy on Washington," 292–93.

70. GW to the Roman Catholics in the United States of America, [March 15], 1790, in GWC, 547.

71. GW to James Madison, May 5, 1789, in GWC, 531.

72. GW, Farewell Address, September 19, 1796, in GWW, 976.

1. A Political Life of Washington

Epigraph: GW to [Connecticut] Governor Jonathan Trumbull, August 30, 1799, in WGW, 37:349–50.

1. Sources for the prologue: Humphreys, *Life of Washington*, 44; GW, diary entry of December 13, 1799, in Flexner, *George Washington*, 4:456; Flexner, *Washington: The Indispensable Man*, 397; Custis, *Recollections of Washington*, 527; Ferling, *Setting the World Ablaze*, 43; GW quoted in Flexner, *George Washington*, 1:23; Fitzpatrick, *Washington Himself*, 28; and GW to Elizabeth Powell, quoted in Henriques, *Realistic Visionary*, 190.

2. GW to the Acting Secretary of War [Henry Knox], April 1, 1789, in WGW, 30:269.

3. Thomas Jefferson to Henry Lee, May 8, 1825, in Koch and Peden, eds., *Life and Selected Writings*, 657.

4. Johnson, *George Washington*, 10.

5. GW to Bushrod Washington, July 27, 1789, in WGW, 30:366. For GW's reference to "The Argus" newspaper, see GW to Alexander Hamilton, July 29, 1795, in WGW, 34:263n79.

6. Jefferson quoted in Achenbach, *Grand Idea*, 190–91; see also Smith, *Patriarch*, 174. The cartoon was titled "The Funeral of George Washington and James Wilson, King and Judge."

7. GW to Gov. Jonathan Trumbull, August 30, 1799, in WGW, 37: 349–50.

8. In Higginbotham, *Washington Reconsidered*, 1.

9. Humphreys, *Life of Washington*, 5.

10. GW was baptized April 5, 1732 (Old Style). Fitzpatrick, *Washington Himself*, 19.

11. Flexner, *Washington: The Indispensable Man*, 4; see also GWW, 1055.

12. Flexner, *George Washington*, 1:234.

13. Now some five hundred years old, Sulgrave Manor is owned by a joint British-American trust, which has restored and opened it to visitors.

14. Randall, *Washington: A Life*, 8–9.

15. Herndon and Weik, *Life of Lincoln*, 45.

16. Flexner, *Washington: The Indispensable Man*, 3.

17. GW to David Humphreys, July 25, 1785, in GWW, 580.

18. Baker, *Wilson: Life and Letters*, 1:49–50.

19. George and George, *Wilson and Colonel House*.

20. Humphreys, *Life of Washington*, 6.

21. Flexner, *George Washington*, 1:6.

22. Humphreys, *Life of Washington*, 7.

23. See GW to Rev. G. W. Snyder, October 24, 1797, in WGW, 36:519.

24. Thomas, Lord Fairfax, to Mary Ball Washington, 1748, quoted in Smith, *Patriarch*, 4.

25. Humphreys, *Life of Washington*, 6.

26. Humphreys, *Life of Washington*, 7.

27. GW, "Journey Over the Mountains," diary entries, March 11–31, 1748, in WGW, 1:5–7.

28. See Johnson, *George Washington*, 20–21.

29. GW, "Journey Over the Mountains," diary entries, March 11–31, 1748, in WGW, 1:8–9.

30. See GW to Lawrence Washington, May 5, 1749, in WGW, 1:13.

31. GW to unknown correspondent, [1749–50], in WGW, 1:17.

32. GW to [Virginia] Governor Robert Hunter Morris, April 9, 1756, in GWC, 21.

33. See Phelps, *Washington and Constitutionalism*, 23–61.

34. GW to Alexander Hamilton, September 1, 1796, in WGW, 35: 199–200.

35. Flexner, *George Washington*, 1:85.

36. GW to John Augustine Washington, July 18, 1755, in WGW, 1:152.

37. GW to Mrs. George William Fairfax, April 30, 1755, in WGW, 1:117.

38. Crèvecoeur, *Letters*, 340–41.

39. GW to [Virginia] Governor Robert Hunter Morris, April 9, 1756, in GWC, 21.

40. GW to George Mason, April 5, 1769, in WGW, 2:501.

41. "I think the more conspicuous the point of view a man is to appear in, the more pains should be taken to enlarge his mind and qualify him for a useful Member of Society." GW to Rev. Jonathan Boucher, June 5, 1771, in WGW, 3:43.

42. Fitzpatrick, *Washington Himself*, 125.

43. George III quoted in Novak and Novak, *Washington's God*, 6; see also Henriques, *Realistic Visionary*, 46.

44. See GW, Address to Congress on Resigning his Commission, December 23, 1783, in WGW, 27:284.

45. Chernow, *Alexander Hamilton*, 86.

46. John Marshall quoted in Chernow, *Alexander Hamilton*, 157.

47. GW to George Mason, March 27, 1779, in WGW, 14:301.

48. GW to Lund Washington, August 20, 1775, in WGW, 3:433.

49. GW to Joseph Reed, December 15, 1775, in WGW, 4:165.

50. GW to Lafayette, June 19, 1788, in WGW, 29:525.

51. GW to John Banister, April 21, 1778, in GWC, 99.

52. Smith quoted in Heilbroner, *Worldly Philosophers*, 53.

53. Heilbroner, *Worldly Philosophers*, 66.

54. GW to Joseph Reed, January 23, 1776, in WGW, 4:269.

55. Rush quoted in Chernow, *Alexander Hamilton,* 100.

56. See Col. Lewis Nicola to GW [May? 1782], in WGW, 24:273n81; GW to Col. Lewis Nicola, May 22, 1782, in WGW, 24:272–73.

57. GW, Circular to the States, June 1783, in WGW, 26:492.

58. In WGW, 26:222n38.

59. GW to Thomas Nelson, August 20, 1778, in GWW, 320.

60. GW, Circular to the States, June 1783, in WGW, 26:485.

61. Humphreys, *Life of Washington,* 35.

62. Flexner, *George Washington,* 1:234.

63. Humphreys, *Life of Washington,* 35.

64. GW to Lafayette, June 19, 1788, in WGW, 29:524.

65. See GW to Lt. Col. Tench Tilghman, April 24, 1783, in WGW, 26:358.

66. GWW, 1069.

67. GW to Henry Lee, October 31, 1786, in GWW, 608.

68. GW to James Madison, November 5, 1786, in GWW, 621–22.

69. Benjamin Franklin, Speech of June 30, 1787, in Madison, *Notes of Debates,* 227.

70. Van Buren quoted in Bowen, *Miracle,* 62.

71. Proceedings of the Confederation Congress, February 21, 1787, in Solberg, *Constitutional Convention,* 63–64.

72. James Monroe to Thomas Jefferson, quoted in Freeman, 6:140.

73. See Phelps, *Washington and American Constitutionalism,* 99–112.

74. Abigail Adams quoted in Flexner, *George Washington,* 3:200.

75. See Farrand, ed., *Records,* 3:271–72.

76. GW, Speech of September 17, 1787, in Madison, *Notes of Debates,* 655.

77. Rossiter, *Presidency,* 80.

78. Pierce Butler quoted in Rossiter, *Presidency,* 81.

79. Edmund Randolph, Speech of June 1, 1787, in Madison, *Notes of Debates,* 46.

80. Benjamin Franklin, Speech of June 4, 1787, in Madison, *Notes of Debates,* 65.

81. See also GW to Samuel Vaughan, March 21, 1789, in WGW, 30:237, where he calls his inauguration the "event which I have long dreaded."

82. Accounts of the Bible verses vary; this one is adapted from Riccards, *Republic,* 73–74. According to other accounts, the Bible, borrowed from St. John's Masonic Lodge, was opened to Genesis 49; see Bowen, "Inauguration of Washington," 828–30.

83. GW anecdote quoted in Flexner, *George Washington,* 3:212.

84. Henry Lee, 1789, quoted in Kinnaird, *Pictorial Biography,* 214.
85. GW to Catherine Macaulay Graham, January 9, 1790, in WGW, 30:495–96.
86. See White, *Federalists,* 486.
87. Kinnaird, *Pictorial Biography,* 229.
88. GW, Circular to the Supreme Executives of the Several States, June 8, 1789, in WGW, 30:344–45.
89. John Adams to Benjamin Rush, September 1807, in Schutz and Adair, eds., *Spur of Fame,* 95.
90. See Ellis, *Founding Brothers,* 48–80.
91. GW, Discarded First Inaugural Address, 1789, in GWC, 451–52.
92. For a discussion of the "Whiskey Insurrection," see PGW, Diaries, 1:170–98.
93. GW, Sixth Annual Message to Congress, November 19, 1794, in WGW, 34:34.
94. GW, Sixth Annual Message to Congress, November 19, 1794, in WGW, 34:29.
95. See generally, Greenstein, *Hidden-Hand Presidency.*
96. Jefferson quoted in Achenbach, *Grand Idea,* 190–91; see also Smith, *Patriarch,* 174.
97. See GW's diary entry of December 12, 1799: "At about ten o'clock [a.m.] it began to snow, soon after to hail, and then to a settled cold rain. Mercury 28 at night." Quoted in Flexner, *Washington: The Indispensable Man,* 396.
98. Adams quoted in Vidal, *Inventing a Nation,* 151.
99. GW to Sarah Cary Fairfax, May 16, 1798, in GWW, 1003.
100. GW, Last Will and Testament, [July 9, 1799], in WGW, 37:293.

2. Classical Republican Political Culture and Philosophy

Epigraphs: Seneca, *Epistles,* III, in L'Estrange, ed., *Seneca's Morals,* 385; and GW to James Anderson, December 21, 1797, in WGW, 36:113.

1. John Marshall, "Eulogy on Washington," [December 26, 1799], 296. (Most commentators wrongly attribute this eulogy to Richard Henry Lee, who delivered it on Marshall's behalf.)
2. See generally, Reinhold, *Classica Americana.*
3. Forbes, *Paul Revere,* 378; see also Johnson, *History of the American People,* 146.
4. See Johnson, *History of the American People,* 163.
5. See Dalzell and Dalzell, *Washington's Mount Vernon,* 78.
6. See Sheldon, *Political Philosophy of Madison,* xi, 78–97.
7. Thomas Jefferson to John Norvell, June 14, 1807, in TJW, 1176.

8. *Federalist* 9, 71.

9. Tocqueville, *Democracy in America,* 12.

10. John Adams to Arthur Lee, July 18, 1788, quoted in McCullough, *John Adams,* 397.

11. GW, Circular to the States, June 8, 1783, in WGW, 26:489.

12. Plato, *Republic,* 564a, in *Collected Dialogues,* 792.

13. GW to David Humphreys, March 8, 1787, in WGW, 29:173.

14. See generally, Aristotle, *Nicomachean Ethics* and *Politics,* in *Basic Works,* 935–1324.

15. Aristotle, *Politics,* 1279a-b, in *Basic Works,* 1185–86.

16. See Aristotle, *Nicomachean Ethics,* 1176a30, and *Politics,* 1324a, in *Basic Works,* 1102, 1279.

17. GW, Address to His Command [August 1756], in WGW, 1:447.

18. GW quoted in Vidal, *Inventing a Nation,* 48.

19. GW to James Warren, March 31, 1779, in WGW, 14:312.

20. GW to Benjamin Harrison, December 18[-30], 1778, in WGW, 13:466.

21. William Ramsay to GW, quoted in Henriques, *Realistic Visionary,* 14.

22. Humphreys, *Life of Washington,* 47.

23. Abigail Adams quoted in Novak and Novak, *Washington's God,* 5.

24. GW, Circular to the States, June 8, 1783, in WGW, 26:485.

25. GW, Circular to the States, June 8, 1783, in GWC, 242.

26. GW to the Secretary of the Treasury, July 29, 1792, in GWC, 572.

27. GW, Farewell Address, September 19, 1796, in WGW, 35:223. For a sustained argument that Washington intended to cultivate a type of Aristotelian civic friendship in America, see Spalding and Garrity, *Sacred Union of Citizens.*

28. GW, Farewell Address, September 19, 1796, in WGW, 35:220.

29. Cicero, *De Officiis,* I, xxv, 87.

30. On the early presidency and the classical notion of the patriot king, see Ketcham, *Presidents Above Party;* on Washington and Bolingbroke, see Brookhiser, *Founding Father,* 170–71.

31. "Stoicism," in *Encyclopedia of Philosophy,* 8:19.

32. "Introduction," in *Marcus Aurelius: Meditations,* 10.

33. Lutz, "Relative Influence of European Writers," 194.

34. Virgil, *Aeneid,* VI, quoted in Grant, *Twelve Caesars,* 57.

35. Sallust quoted in Barrow, *Romans,* 127.

36. GW to James Anderson, December 21, 1797, in WGW, 36:113.

37. Lutz, "Relative Influence of European Writers," 194.

38. On similarities between ancient Rome and early America, see Fears, "Lessons of the Roman Empire," 2.

39. Adcock, *Roman Political Ideas,* 10.

40. Cicero, *Republic,* in Ebenstein and Ebenstein, eds., *Great Political Thinkers,* 137.

41. GW, summary of letter from John Jay, [April?] 1787, in GWC, 366.

42. John Adams, *Thoughts on Government* (1776), in Greene, ed., *Colonies to Nation,* 309.

43. Barrow, *Romans,* 12.

44. Elkins and McKitrick, *Age of Federalism,* 50.

45. George Bennet to his mother, April 15, 1783, in WGW, 26:321n.

46. Cicero, *On Obligations,* I, 8.

47. See Marshall, *Life of Washington,* 2:528–29.

48. Col. William Fairfax to GW, April 26, 1756, in WGW, 1:326n.

49. Abigail Adams quoted in Wiencek, *Imperfect God,* 36.

50. Adcock, *Roman Political Ideas,* 4.

51. Meyer Reinhold quoted in Thornton and Hanson, "'Western Cincinnatus,'" 40.

52. See Thornton and Hanson, "'Western Cincinnatus,'" 40–42.

53. Thomas Jefferson to François D'Invernois, February 6, 1795, in TJW, 1023.

54. Thomas Jefferson to Dr. Benjamin Rush, September 23, 1800, in TJW, 1081.

55. Thomas Jefferson, *Notes on the State of Virginia,* Query XIX, in TJW, 290.

56. Madison quoted in Sheldon, *Political Philosophy of Madison,* 113.

57. GW to Henry Knox, February 3, 1787, in WGW, 29:153.

58. GW to Lafayette, April 28, 1788, in WGW, 29:480.

59. GW to Arthur Young, August 6, 1786, in WGW, 28:510.

60. GW to Arthur Young, December 4, 1788, in WGW, 30:150.

61. GW to the Chiefs and Warriors, Representatives of the Wyandots et al. [November 29, 1796], in WGW, 35:300.

62. GW to Dr. James Anderson, December 24, 1795, in WGW, 34:407.

63. GW, Discarded First Inaugural Address [April 1789], in GWC, 456.

64. GW to Lafayette, July 28, 1791, in WGW, 31:324.

65. GW, Eighth Annual Message to Congress, December 7, 1796, in WGW, 35:315.

66. GW to William Drayton, March 25, 1786, in WGW, 28:394–95.

67. GW to Marquis de Chastellux, April 25[-May 1], 1788, in WGW, 29:485.

68. GW to Alexander Spotswood, February 13, 1788, in WGW, 29:414.

69. GW to the Emperor of Morocco, December 1, 1789, in WGW, 30:475.

70. Barrow, *Romans*, 11.

71. See "Fabius," in Plutarch, *Lives,* 226.

72. GW to the President of Congress, September 8, 1776, in WGW, 6:28.

73. For the best account of this episode, see Fischer, *Washington's Crossing.*

74. George Mason, Virginia Bill of Rights, June 12, 1776, in Greene, ed., *Colonies to Nation,* 334.

75. GW to Henry Laurens, November 14, 1778, in GWC, 113.

76. GW, Conference with the Chevalier de la Luzerne, September 16, 1779, in GWC, 140.

77. GW to John Banister, April 21, 1778, in GWC, 102.

78. Cicero, *On Obligations,* I, 11.

79. GW to John Banister, April 21, 1778, in GWC, 99.

80. Correspondence between Nicola and GW is reproduced in WGW, 24:272–73.

81. GW, Sixth Annual Message to Congress, November 19, 1794, in WGW, 34:34.

82. In the *National Gazette,* "A Farmer" worried that if the public continued to make of Washington an "idol" he might seize the opportunity to make himself another Cromwell; quoted in Flexner, *George Washington,* 4:16. On Washington as Cromwell, see, Randall, *Washington: A Life,* 402.

83. See Carroll and Meacham, *Library at Mount Vernon,* 149, 156.

84. GW to Lafayette, May 28, 1788, in WGW, 29:506.

85. Flexner, *George Washington,* 1:153; see also "Invoice of Sundries to be Sent by Robert Cary and Company for Use of George Washington," in WGW, 2:333, 334n.

86. John Adams to Benjamin Rush, August 22, 1806, in Schutz and Adair, eds., *Spur of Fame,* 63; see also Thomas Jefferson to Benjamin Rush, 1811, quoted in Wills, *Cincinnatus,* 137–38.

87. Thomas Jefferson to George Rogers Clark, December 25, 1780, in Boyd et al., eds., *Papers of Thomas Jefferson* (hereafter PTJ), 4:237–38.

88. Lewis Nicola to GW [May? 1782], in WGW, 24:273n81.

89. GW to Col. Lewis Nicola, May 22, 1782, in WGW, 24:272–73.

90. Wheatley quoted in Flexner, *George Washington,* 2:63; see also GW to Joseph Reed, February 10, 1776, in WGW, 4:323.

91. GW to Joseph Reed, February 10, 1776, in WGW, 4:323.

92. Lord Byron (George Gordon), "Ode to Napoleon Buonaparte" (1814), in More, ed., *Complete Poetical Works,* 182.

93. GW quoted in Flexner, *Washington: The Indispensable Man,* 64.

94. GW quoted in Flexner, *Washington: The Indispensable Man,* 73.

95. GW to the President of Congress, December 20, 1776, in WGW, 6:402.

96. See GW, Proclamation, December 20, 1777, in WGW, 10:175.

97. Flexner, *Washington: The Indispensable Man*, 100, 110.

98. GW, Address to Congress on Resigning his Commission [December 23, 1783], in WGW, 27:284.

99. GW to John Augustine Washington, June 15, 1783, in WGW, 27:12.

100. GW, Discarded First Inaugural, April 1789, in GWC, 447.

101. GW to Catherine Macaulay Graham, January 9, 1790, in GWC, 537.

102. Jefferson quoted in Vidal, *Inventing a Nation*, 29.

103. Randall, *Washington: A Life*, 402.

104. Thornton and Hanson, "'Western Cincinnatus,'" 40.

105. See Randall, *Washington: A Life*, 397.

106. See Johnson, *History of the American People*, 250.

107. See GW to Thomas Jefferson, August 1, 1786, in WGW, 28:504–5.

108. See GW to Rev. Jonathan Boucher, May 13, 1770, in WGW, 3:14; GW to Boucher, June 5, 1771, in WGW, 3:45; and GW to George William Fairfax, November 10, 1785, in WGW, 28:311.

109. See Carroll and Meacham, *Library*, 153.

110. See GW, General Orders, May 24, 1778, in WGW, 11:442; General Orders, December 29, 1778, in WGW, 13:461; and General Orders, September 6, 1780, in WGW, 20:9.

111. GW, Diaries, 5:197.

112. GW to William Pearce, February 21, 1796, in WGW, 34:476.

113. "Invoice of Sundries to be Sent by Robert Cary and Company for Use of George Washington," in WGW, 2:333, 334n.

114. GW to Robert Cary, October 12, 1761, in WGW, 2:371.

115. Kinnaird, *Pictorial Biography*, 220.

116. Brookhiser, *Founding Father*, 153.

117. GW to Lafayette, May 28, 1788, in WGW, 29:506–7.

118. GW to Mrs. George William Fairfax, September 25, 1758, in WGW, 2:293.

119. GW to Comte de Grasse, May 15, 1784, in WGW, 27:401.

120. Addison, *Cato*, Act I, Scene 2, 21.

121. GW to [Rhode Island] Governor Nicholas Cooke, October 29, 1775, in WGW, 4:53.

122. GW to Benedict Arnold, December 5, 1775, in WGW, 4:148.

123. See "Prologue," Alexander Pope, in *Cato*, 14: "Here tears shall flow from a more gen'rous cause,/Such tears as Patriots shed for dying

Laws:/He bids your breasts with ancient ardor rise,/And calls forth *Roman* drops from *British* eyes."

124. GW to Lund Washington, April 30, 1781, in WGW, 22:14.

125. *Cato,* Act IV, Scene 4 (Cato speaking), 67.

126. *Cato,* Act I, Scene 1, 17.

127. GW to Chevalier de Chastellux, February 1, 1784, in WGW, 27: 314–15.

128. GW to Charles Cotesworth Pinckney, June 24, 1797, in WGW, 35:471.

129. See GW to Rufus King, June 25, 1797, in WGW, 35:475; GW to David Humphreys, June 26, 1797, in WGW, 35:481; and GW to the Earl of Buchan, July 4, 1797, in WGW, 35:488.

130. GW, Speech to the Officers of the Army, March 15, 1783, in GWC, 220.

131. *Cato,* Act IV, Scene 4, 69.

132. GW to the Secretary of War, July 27, 1795, in WGW, 34:251.

133. GW to David Humphreys, June 12, 1796, in WGW, 35:91–92.

134. GW to Alexander Hamilton, June 26, 1796, in WGW, 35:103.

135. *Cato,* Act II, Scene 1, 34.

136. *Cato,* Act I, Scene 1, 18.

137. GW to John Robinson, September 1, 1758, in WGW, 2:276.

138. GW to Thaddeus Kosciuszko, August 31, 1797, in WGW, 36:22.

139. See GW to John Robinson, September 1, 1758, in WGW, 2:276; GW to Burwell Bassett, April 25, 1773, in WGW, 3:133; GW to John Augustine Washington, February 24, 1777, in WGW, 7:198; and GW to Reverend Bryan, Lord Fairfax, January 20, 1799, in WGW, 37:92.

140. GW to Thomas Nelson, August 20, 1778, in GWW, 320.

141. GW to Lund Washington, May 29, 1779, in WGW, 15:180.

142. This volume was recorded as "Tullys Offices" in the library inventory made ca. 1764 at Mount Vernon; see PGW, Col. Ser., 7:348.

143. Cicero, *De Officiis,* I, xlii, 153.

144. GW, "Discarded First Inaugural Address" [April 1789], Fragment 34, in GWC, 455.

145. Cicero, *De Officiis,* I, xlii, 155.

146. Cicero, *De Officiis,* I, ix, 31.

147. Cicero, *De Officiis,* I, x, 33.

148. Cicero, *De Officiis,* I, xxi, 73.

149. Cicero, *Republic,* in Ebenstein and Ebenstein, eds., *Great Political Thinkers,* 131.

150. GW to Catherine Macaulay Graham, January 9, 1790, in WGW, 30:495–96.

151. Cicero, *De Officiis,* III, xvii, 339.

152. Cicero, *De Officiis,* I, i, 3.

153. GW to Alexander Hamilton, September 1, 1796, in GWC, 649.

154. Brookhiser, *Founding Father,* 141.

155. For example, see GW to George Washington Parke Custis, December 19, 1796, in WGW, 35:340–42.

156. Cicero, *De Legibus,* I, vi, 317.

157. Cicero, *De Republica,* III, xxii, 211.

158. GW to Bryan Fairfax, August 24, 1774, in WGW, 3:240–42.

159. GW to Bryan Fairfax, July 20, 1774, in GWC, 37.

160. In Allen, "Washington and the Standing Oak," 107.

161. Cicero quoted in Ebenstein and Ebenstein, eds., *Great Political Thinkers,* 131.

162. Cicero, *De Officiis* (Loeb), I, ii, 9.

163. GW to James Warren, October 7, 1785, in GWC, 313.

164. The inventory of the Boston Athenaeum collection of Washington's library books states that a copy with Washington's autograph in his youthful hand puts the acquisition date at about Washington's seventeenth year.

165. *Seneca's Morals,* 108, 119, 150, 200, 227, 249, 266.

166. Smith, *Patriarch,* 6.

167. Seneca, "Of a Happy Life," in *Seneca's Morals,* 100.

168. GW to Dr. James Anderson, December 24, 1795, in WGW, 34:407.

169. William Fairfax to GW, September 5, 1754, in PGW, Col. Ser., 1:201. See also Brookhiser, *Founding Father,* 123; and Flexner, *George Washington,* 1:113.

170. Thomas Jefferson, "The Anas" (1818), in TJW, 661.

171. GW to Rev. Bryan, Lord Fairfax, January 20, 1799, in WGW, 37:94–95.

172. See John Adams to Benjamin Rush, June 12, 1812, in Schutz and Adair, eds., *Spur of Fame,* 225.

173. Seneca, "Of a Happy Life," *Seneca's Morals,* 100.

174. GW, "The Rules of Civility and Decent Behavior in Company and Conversation," 1747, in GWW, 7.

175. See John Adams to Benjamin Rush, September 1807, in Schutz and Adair, eds., *Spur of Fame,* 93–94. Rush emphasized that Washington was "self-taught in all the arts which gave him his immense elevation above all his fellow citizens." See also Rush to Adams, October 31, 1807, 95. For the popularity of Rollin's ancient histories, see Wood, *American Revolution,* 92.

176. John Adams to Benjamin Rush, June 12, 1812, in Schutz and

Adair, eds., *Spur of Fame*, 226. For Jefferson on Adams, see Smith, *Patriarch*, 47.

177. See Flexner, *George Washington*, 4:17.

178. See Thomas Jefferson to Maria Cosway, October 12, 1786, in TJW, 866–77.

179. Seneca, "Of a Happy Life," in *Seneca's Morals*, 99.

180. *Federalist* 55, 342.

181. GW to Henry Knox, March 8, 1787, in PGW, Confed. Ser., 5: 74–75.

182. It is often forgotten that in addition to life and liberty, Locke wrote of the pursuit of happiness; his *Essay concerning Human Understanding*, book II, ch. 21, sec. 50, contains the line: "A constant determination to a pursuit of happiness, no abridgement of liberty." I owe this insight to Walter Berns.

183. Seneca, "Of a Happy Life," in *Seneca's Morals*, 98.

184. Seneca, "Of a Happy Life," in *Seneca's Morals*, 102, 108.

185. GW, First Inaugural Address, April 30, 1789, in GWC, 462.

186. GW to Edmund Pendleton, January 22, 1795, in WGW, 34:99.

187. Jean-Jacques Rousseau, "Discourse on the Sciences and the Arts [First Discourse]," in *Basic Political Writings*, 12.

188. See "Pericles' Funeral Oration," in Thucydides, *History of the Peloponnesian War*, trans. Warner, Book II, 150.

189. Rossiter quoted in Rahe, *Republics Ancient and Modern*, 9.

190. See GW to Annis Boudinot Stockton, August 31, 1788, in WGW, 30:75–76 (quoting Cicero's *On Old Age*).

3. British Liberalism, Revolution, Union, and Foreign Affairs

Epigraph: GW to Bryan Fairfax, August 24, 1774, in WGW, 3:242.

1. Sources for the prologue: Flexner, *Washington: The Indispensable Man*, 57; GW, Address to His Command [August 1756], in WGW, 1: 447; Humphreys, *Life of Washington*, 39–40; Morgan, *Meaning of Independence*, 33; GW to Bryan Fairfax, August 24, 1774, in WGW, 3:242; GW to Gen. Thomas Gage, August 20, 1775, in WGW, 3:431; GW to George William Fairfax, June 10, 1774, in GWC, 31; and Dalzell and Dalzell, *Washington's Mount Vernon*, 47ff.

2. On this interesting and understudied era, the best source is Porter, *British Enlightenment*.

3. David Humphreys, "Outlines for 'The Life of General Washington,'" in *Life of Washington*, 61.

4. GW to Dr. James Anderson, December 24, 1795, in WGW, 34:407.

5. See Curti, "Locke, America's Philosopher."

6. Kloppenberg, "Virtues of Liberalism," 16.

7. Hobbes, *Leviathan,* ch. 21, 165.

8. John Locke, *Two Treatises of Government,* xliii.

9. Banning, "Republican Interpretation," 93.

10. Eisenach, *Two Worlds,* 73.

11. Kloppenberg, *Virtues of Liberalism,* 5.

12. Edmund Burke quoted in Lancaster and Plumb, *Book of the Revolution,* 11. See also Burke, Speech on Conciliation with the Colonies, March 22, 1775, in *Founders' Constitution,* 1:3.

13. GW to George William Fairfax, June 10, 1774, in GWC, 31.

14. "Federal liberty is to the States what civil liberty is to private individuals; and States are not more unwilling to purchase it, by the necessary concession of their political sovereignty, than the savage is to purchase civil liberty by the surrender of the personal sovereignty, which he enjoys in a state of nature." James Wilson, Speech of June 8, 1787, in Madison, *Notes of Debates,* 90.

15. GW, "Discarded First Inaugural Address" [April 1789], Fragment 32, in GWC, 454. See also *Federalist* 48, 308, regarding the insufficiency of "parchment barriers" against the "encroaching spirit of power."

16. Locke, *Two Treatises of Government,* 22.

17. GW to the Roman Catholics in the United States of America, [March 15], 1790, in GWC, 547.

18. GW to John Parke Custis, February 1, 1778, in WGW, 10:414.

19. GW to Thomas Jefferson [January 1, 1788], in WGW, 29:351.

20. GW to Francis Dandridge, September 20, 1765, in GWC, 5.

21. GW to George Mason, April 5, 1769, in WGW, 2:500–502.

22. Flexner, *George Washington,* 1:312.

23. GW to George Mason, April 5, 1769, in WGW, 2:501.

24. See GW, *Diaries,* 2:141–42.

25. See PGW, Col. Ser., 8:177–80.

26. George Mason, "Plan for Non-Importation of British Goods," April 23, 1769, in Rutland, ed., *Papers of George Mason,* 1:103.

27. James Otis, "Rights of the British Colonies Asserted and Proved," 1764, in Greene, ed., *Colonies,* 28.

28. George Mason, Fairfax Resolves, July 18, 1774, in Rutland, ed., *Papers of George Mason,* 1:207.

29. GW to Bryan Fairfax, July 20, 1774, in GWC, 35–37.

30. See GW to Bryan Fairfax, August 20, 1774, in WGW, 3:240–41.

31. In Humphreys, *Life of Washington,* 28.

32. GW to Bryan Fairfax, August 24, 1774, in WGW, 3:240–42.

33. GW to Capt. Robert Mackenzie, October 9, 1774, in WGW, 3:245.

34. Locke, *Two Treatises of Government,* paragraph 87, 163.

35. GW to the Inhabitants of the Island of Bermuda, September 6, 1775, in GWC, 45.

36. GW, Circular to the States, June 8, 1783, in WGW, 26:489; emphasis added.

37. GW to Reformed German Congregation of New York, November 27, 1783, in GWC, 271.

38. GW to James Madison, November 5, 1786, in WGW, 29:52.

39. GW to Henry Knox, December 26, 1786, in WGW, 29:122.

40. GW, Farewell Address, September 19, 1796, in GWW, 963.

41. Edmund Randolph quoted in Bowen, *Miracle,* 258.

42. Shy, "Franklin, Washington, and a New Nation," 321.

43. GW to [Virginia] Governor Robert Hunter Morris, April 9, 1756, in GWC, 21.

44. GW to George William Fairfax, June 10, 1774, in GWC, 31; emphasis added.

45. GW to Bryan Fairfax, August 24, 1774, in GWC, 39.

46. Thomas Jefferson to George Rogers Clark, December 25, 1780, in PTJ, 4:238.

47. GW to Chevalier de Chastellux, October 12, 1783, in WGW, 27:190.

48. GW to John Witherspoon, March 10, 1784, in WGW, 27:352.

49. GW, General Orders, April 18, 1783, in WGW, 26:335–36.

50. GW, "To the Members of the Volunteer Association and Other Inhabitants of the Kingdom of Ireland Who Have Lately Arrived in the City of New York," December 2, 1783, in WGW, 27:254.

51. GW, Circular to the States, June 8, 1783, in WGW, 26:485.

52. Achenbach, *Grand Idea,* 105–6.

53. GW to James Duane, September 7, 1783, in WGW, 27:133–40.

54. GW, Third Annual Address to Congress, October 25, 1791, in WGW, 31:398–99.

55. Johnson, *George Washington,* 44.

56. Sheldon, *Political Philosophy of Madison,* xi.

57. GW, Circular to the States, June 8, 1783, in WGW, 26:489.

58. GW to Lafayette, June 6, 1787, in WGW, 29:229.

59. GW, "Letter of the President of the Federal Convention to the President of Congress, Transmitting the Constitution," September 17, 1787, in Solberg, *Constitutional Convention,* 363.

60. GW to Lafayette, April 28, 1788, in WGW, 29:478.

61. See *Federalist* 84, 515.

62. GW, Discarded First Inaugural Address, April 1789, in GWC, 451–52.

63. GW, Discarded First Inaugural [April?, 1789], in WGW, 30:299.

64. GW to Catherine Macaulay Graham, January 9, 1790, in WGW, 30:495–96.

65. GW to Lafayette, August 15, 1786, in GWC, 325–26.

66. GW to David Humphreys, December 26, 1786, in WGW, 29:126.

67. See Flexner, *George Washington,* 4:28. It is unclear whether Jay's draft proclamation actually made it to GW's desk.

68. See GW to Alexander Spotswood, November 22, 1798, in WGW, 37:23–24.

69. Genet claimed that "Mr. Jefferson gave me some useful hints regarding the men in office, and did not conceal from me that Senator [Robert] Morris and the Secretary of the Treasury Hamilton, attached to the British interest, exerted the greatest influence on the mind of the President, and it was only with the greatest difficulty that he [Jefferson] counteracted their efforts." Quoted in Flexner, *George Washington,* 4:47.

70. John Adams to Benjamin Rush, July 7, 1805, quoted in Schutz and Adair, eds., *Spur of Fame,* 30–31.

71. GW to Lafayette, August 11, 1790, in WGW, 31:87.

72. GW to Alexander Hamilton, May 8, 1796, in GWC, 221.

73. GW to David Humphreys, July 25, 1785, in GWW, 579–80; see also PGW, Confed. Ser., 3:148–51.

74. GW, Last Will and Testament, July 9, 1799, in WGW, 37:279.

75. GW, Farewell Address, September 19, 1796, in WGW, 35:234.

76. GW, Farewell Address, September 19, 1796, in WGW, 35:234.

77. Schwartz, "Whig Conception," 26, 19.

4. Protestant Christianity, Providence, and the Republic

Epigraphs: Washington to the Reformed German Congregation of New York, November 27, 1783, in GWC, 271; and GW to Lafayette, June 10, 1792, in WGW, 32:54.

1. Sources for the prologue: Hay, "American Moses," 780–91; Wills, *Cincinnatus,* 27–37; Franklin, "Proposals Relating to the Education of Youth in Pensilvania," (1749), in Witte, *Experiment,* 34, 39n52; Henriques, *Death of Washington;* GW to Sir Edward Newenham, June 22, 1792, in WGW, 32:73; GW, General Orders, July 4, 1775, in WGW, 3:309; and GW to Rev. John Rodgers, June 11, 1783, in WGW, 27:1. For Marshall's eulogy, see Marshall, "Eulogy on Washington," 288: "Habituated by his care of us to neglect himself, a slight cold, disregarded, became inconvenient on Friday, oppressive on Saturday, and, defying every medical interposition, before the morning of Sunday, put an end to the best of men. An end did I say?—his fame survives!" (In Christian the-

ology, Christ is the good shepherd who cared for and sacrificed himself for his sheep, died on Good Friday, was buried and descended into Hell, and was resurrected on Easter Sunday.) The woodcut is reproduced in Kinnaird, *Pictorial Biography,* 135.

2. Boller, *Washington and Religion,* 24.

3. See Fitzpatrick, *Washington Himself,* 19.

4. Meade, *Old Churches,* 1:191.

5. Fitzpatrick, *Washington Himself,* 130–31.

6. GW to James McHenry, April 23, 1799, quoted in Fitzpatrick, *Washington Himself,* 512. See also Boller, *Washington and Religion,* 29.

7. Boller, *Washington and Religion,* 29.

8. Abercrombie quoted in Boller, *Washington and Religion,* 34.

9. White quoted in Boller, *Washington and Religion,* 33.

10. Boller, *Washington and Religion,* 5.

11. *Book of Common Prayer* (1769), 1.

12. Charles II quoted in Johnson, *History of the American People,* 63.

13. GW to Tench Tilghman, March 24, 1784, in WGW, 27:367.

14. George Mason, Virginia Bill of Rights, June 12, 1776, in Poore, *Federal and State Constitutions,* 2:1909.

15. GW to George Mason, October 3, 1785, in WGW, 28:285.

16. Freeman cited in Flexner, *George Washington,* 1:244.

17. See, for example, "Divine Providence," in Evans, *American Bibliography,* 5:448.

18. "For Deliverance from the Plague or Common Sickness," in "Prayers and Thanksgivings upon Several Occasions," *Book of Common Prayer* (1790), n.p.

19. GW, Answer to the Address of Congress [March 21, 1782], in WGW, 24:83.

20. GW to Rev. John Rodgers, June 11, 1783, in WGW, 27:1.

21. GW to Lafayette, June 10, 1792, in WGW, 32:54.

22. Thomas Jefferson to Maria Cosway, October 12, 1786, in *Portable Jefferson,* 410; emphasis added.

23. GW, Fourth Annual Address to Congress, November 6, 1792, in WGW, 32:212.

24. See *Book of Common Prayer* (1769), 35ff.

25. GW, General Orders for April 15, 1783, in WGW, 26:334–35; cp. Psalm 76:10: "Surely the wrath of man shall praise thee; the remainder of wrath shalt thou restrain."

26. GW to the Hebrew Congregation in Newport, Rhode Island, August 11, 1790, in PGW, Pres. Ser., 6:286.

27. "A General Thanksgiving," *Book of Common Prayer* (1769), 34.

28. GW to Benjamin Lincoln, June 29, 1788, in WGW, 30:11–12.

29. GW, General Orders, May 5, 1778, in WGW, 11:354; GW to the Ministers, Elders, Deacons, and Members of the Reformed German Congregation of New York, November 27, 1783, in WGW, 27:249; and GW to the Inhabitants of Richmond [August 28, 1793], in WGW, 33:72.

30. GW, Sixth Annual Message to Congress, November 19, 1794, in WGW, 34:37.

31. GW, Eighth Annual Message to Congress, December 7, 1796, in WGW, 35:310.

32. "A Prayer for the President of the United States," *Book of Common Prayer* (1790), n.p.

33. GW to Burges Ball, September 22, 1799, in WGW, 37:372.

34. "For a Recovery from Sickness," *Book of Common Prayer* (1769), 39.

35. GW to the Attorney General [Edmund Randolph], August 26, 1792, in WGW, 32:136.

36. John Witherspoon, "Prayer for National Prosperity, and for the Revival of Religion, Inseparably Connected," 1758, in *Works*, 5:58. Witherspoon originally preached this sermon in Scotland in 1758 and quoted from it during the Revolutionary period. See also Morrison, *John Witherspoon*; and Sheldon, *Political Philosophy of Madison*, 10–15.

37. See GW to John Augustine Washington, November 6, 1776, in WGW, 6:247; GW to George Mason, March 27, 1779, in WGW, 14:301; GW to Edmund Randolph, November 7, 1780, in WGW, 20:316; GW to William Fitzhugh, November 8, 1780, in WGW, 20:327; GW to John Sullivan, November 20, 1780, in WGW, 20:371; GW to Bartholomew Dandridge, December 18, 1782, in WGW, 25:446; GW to Charles Thomson, January 22, 1784, in WGW, 27:312; GW to Chevalier de Chastellux, February 1, 1784, in WGW, 27:314; GW to Lafayette, February 1, 1784, in WGW, 27:317; GW to Marchioness de Lafayette, April 4, 1784, in WGW, 27:385; GW to Comte de Rochambeau, September 7, 1785, in WGW, 28:256; GW to Vicomte D'Arrot, September 25, 1785, in WGW, 28:277; GW to John Marsden Pintard, November 18, 1785, in WGW, 28:315; GW to Charles Vaughan, November 18, 1785, in WGW, 28:316; GW to Lafayette, June 19, 1788, in WGW, 29:526; GW to Gouverneur Morris, August 14, 1790, in WGW, 31:93; GW to William Pearce, February 21, 1796, in WGW, 34:476; GW to Landon Carter, October 17, 1796, in WGW, 35:246; GW to George Clinton, February 28, 1797, in WGW, 35:407; GW to Dr. James Anderson, April 7, 1797, in WGW, 35:432; GW to the Secretary of the Treasury, May 15, 1797, in WGW, 35:447; GW to Thomas Pinckney, May 28, 1797, in WGW, 35:452; GW to Charles Cotesworth Pinckney, June 24, 1797, in WGW, 35:471; GW to Louis Philippe, Comte de Ségur, June 24, 1797, in WGW, 35:473; GW to Rufus King, June 25, 1797, in WGW, 35:475; GW to John Quincy

Adams, June 25, 1797, in WGW, 3:476; GW to David Humphreys, June 26, 1797, in WGW, 35:480; GW to the Earl of Buchan, July 4, 1797, in WGW, 35:488; GW to the Earl of Radnor, July 8, 1797, in WGW, 35:493; GW to Sir Edward Newenham, August 6, 1797, in WGW, 36:4; GW to Lafayette, October 8, 1797, in WGW, 36:41; GW to Gov. John Henry, April 3, 1798, in WGW, 36:238; GW to Sarah Cary Fairfax, May 16, 1798, in WGW, 36:263; GW to the President of the United States, June 17, 1798, in WGW, 36:292; GW to Julian Ursyn Niemcewicz, June 18, 1798, in WGW, 36:297; GW to Henry Hill, July 15, 1798, in WGW, 36:343; and GW to Dr. James Anderson, July 25, 1798, in WGW, 36:364.

38. Micah 4:3 (KJV).

39. GW to Catherine Macaulay Graham, July 19, 1791, in WGW, 31:316–17.

40. GW to Marquis de la Luzerne, April 29, 1790, in WGW, 31:40.

41. GW to [Connecticut] Governor Jonathan Trumbull, August 30, 1799, in WGW, 37:349.

42. GW to the President of Congress, December 20, 1776, in WGW, 6:402.

43. GW, General Orders for April 15, 1783, in WGW, 26:334–35.

44. GW to Dr. James Anderson, December 24, 1795, in WGW, 34:407.

45. GW to John Jay, August 1, 1786, in WGW, 28:502.

46. See Henriques, *Realistic Visionary.*

47. GW to John Augustine Washington, May 31, 1776, in WGW, 5:92.

48. GW to Benjamin Lincoln, August 28, 1788, in WGW, 30:63.

49. GW to David Humphreys, March 23, 1793, in WGW, 32:398–99.

50. GW to Lafayette, July 25, 1785, in WGW, 28:206–7.

51. Samuel Eliot Morison, *Young Man Washington,* 37.

52. GW, Farewell Address, September 19, 1796, in WGW, 35:218. See also James Madison, "Madison's Form for an Address as Drafted by Him for Washington," June 20, 1792, in Paltsits, ed., *Washington's Farewell Address,* 163.

53. Allen, GWC, 226.

54. GW, Circular to the States, June 8, 1783, in WGW, 26:486.

55. GW, Circular to the States, in WGW, 26:484, 483. Later in the Circular, Washington restated his determination of "not taking any share in public business hereafter." See 26:486.

56. GW, Circular to the States, in WGW, 26:484.

57. For the references to "Heaven," see WGW, 26:484, 485, 490; to "Providence," see WGW, 26:484, 485; and to "God," see WGW, 26:491, 496.

58. GW, Circular to the States, in WGW, 26:485, 496.

59. GW, Speech to the Delaware Chiefs, May 12, 1779, in WGW, 15:55.

60. See Boller, *Washington and Religion,* 75.

61. GW, Circular to the States, in WGW, 26:496.

62. Thomas Jefferson, by contrast, was more ambiguous when referring to the deity. In his "Bill for Establishing Religious Freedom" (ca. 1777), Jefferson referred to "the holy author of our religion," using a phrase that is very close to Washington's—but it might not be a reference to Christ. See Jefferson, "A [Virginia] Bill for Establishing Religious Freedom," in PTJ, 2:545.

63. Boller, *Washington and Religion,* 71–72. Boller considers that the "allusion to 'the Divine Author of our blessed Religion' was unmistakably a reference to Jesus Christ," although it may have been written by one of Washington's more orthodox aides.

64. GW, Circular to the States, in WGW, 26:496.

65. See Lutz, "Relative Influence," 192.

66. GW, Circular to the States, in WGW, 26:485; emphasis added.

67. GW, "Discarded First Inaugural Address," [April 1789], Fragment 32, in GWC, 454.

68. John Adams quoted in Pangle, *Spirit of Modern Republicanism,* 79.

69. GW, "Farewell Address to the Armies of the United States," November 2, 1783, in GWW, 543.

70. GW to Lafayette, February 7, 1788, in WGW, 29:409–10.

71. GW, Circular to the States, in WGW, 26:487.

72. This section is adapted from Dreisbach and Morrison, "Religion and the Presidency of Washington."

73. Adams quoted in Boorstin, "Washington and American Character," xi. For Jefferson on Washington, see Thomas Jefferson to Dr. Walter Jones, January 2, 1814, in TJW, 1318.

74. See Dreisbach, *Wall of Separation,* 18.

75. "A palpable violation of one of those rights—the freedom of the press . . . may be fatal to the other—the free exercise of religion." James Madison, "Report on the [Virginia] Resolutions" (1799), in Sheldon, *Political Philosophy of Madison,* 97.

76. See Pauley, *President's Constitutional Oath,* 222.

77. Epstein, "Rethinking Ceremonial Deism," 2106, 2110.

78. PGW, Pres. Ser., 2:154, citing congressional sources; *Annals of Congress,* 1:25 (April 25, 1789).

79. PGW, Pres. Ser., 2:154, 156n5–6, citing contemporary accounts.

80. *New York Daily Advertiser,* April 23, 1789.

81. Riccards, *Formation of the Presidency,* 73–74. According to other accounts, the Bible, borrowed from St. John's Masonic Lodge, was opened to Genesis 49; see Bowen, "Inauguration of Washington," 828–30.

82. Brookhiser, *Founding Father,* 146.

83. Brookhiser, *Founding Father,* 146.

84. PGW, Pres. Ser., 2:155.

85. See Freeman, 6:185–98; and Bowen, "The Inauguration of Washington," 803–33.

86. *Annals of Congress,* 1:914–915 (September 25, 1789); Stokes, *Church and State,* 1:486.

87. Thanksgiving Proclamation [October 3, 1789], in PGW, Pres. Ser., 4:131–32.

88. See Medhurst, "Duché to Provoost," 586.

89. See, for example, 5 U.S.C. § 3331 (oath of office required of federal employees); 28 U.S.C. § 453 (oath required of each justice or judge of the United States); 10 U.S.C. § 502 (armed forces enlistment oath); 8 C.F.R. § 337.1 (January 1, 1995) (oath of allegiance for admission to citizenship).

90. Pfander, "Religion and Presidential Oath-Taking," 551.

91. United Baptist Churches of Virginia to GW, May 1789, in PGW, Pres. Ser., 2:424n1.

92. Boller, "Washington and Religious Liberty," 497.

93. GW to the Protestant Episcopal Church [August 19, 1789], in PGW, Pres. Ser., 3:497. See also GW to the Hebrew Congregations of Philadelphia, New York, Charleston, and Richmond [December 13, 1790], in PGW, Pres. Ser., 7:61; and GW to the Clergy of Different Denominations Residing in and near the City of Philadelphia [March 3, 1797], in WGW, 35:416.

94. GW to the Bishops of the Methodist Episcopal Church [May 29], 1789, in PGW, Pres. Ser., 2:411–12.

95. GW to the General Assembly of the Presbyterian Church [May 1789], in PGW, Pres. Ser., 2:420.

96. GW to the United Baptist Churches of Virginia [May 1789], in PGW, Pres. Ser., 2:424.

97. GW to the Society of Quakers [October 1789], in PGW, Pres. Ser., 4:266.

98. GW to the Roman Catholics in America [March 1790], in PGW, Pres. Ser., 5:299

99. GW to the Savannah, Ga., Hebrew Congregation [ca. May 1790], in PGW, Pres. Ser., 5:448–49.

100. GW to the Hebrew Congregation in Newport, Rhode Island, [August 18, 1790], in PGW, Pres. Ser., 6:285.

101. GW to the United Baptist Churches of Virginia [May 1789], in PGW, Pres. Ser., 2:424.

102. GW to the United Baptist Churches of Virginia [May 1789], in PGW, Pres. Ser., 2:424.

103. See Dreisbach, *Jefferson and the Wall of Separation,* 84–85.

104. Presbytery of the Eastward to GW, October 28, 1789, in PGW, Pres. Ser., 4:275.

105. GW to the Presbyterian Ministers of Massachusetts and New Hampshire [November 2, 1789], in PGW, Pres. Ser., 4:274.

106. Boller, *Washington and Religion,* 155.

107. GW to the Hebrew Congregation in Newport, Rhode Island [August 18, 1790], in PGW, Pres. Ser., 6:285. For biblical references to the Hebrew blessing, see Micah 4:4; I Kings 4:25; Zechariah 3:10.

108. See Adair, ed., "Madison's Autobiography," 199.

109. See James, ed., *Documentary History,* 201.

110. See Dreisbach, "Mason's Pursuit of Religious Liberty," 5–44.

111. GW to the Members of the New Church in Baltimore [January 27, 1793], in WGW, 32:315.

112. See PGW, Pres. Ser., 4:129–32.

113. This is true of both the *Book of Common Prayer* of 1662, which was the standard for Anglicans everywhere until it was replaced in America by the 1789–90 version, and the latter edition. For "providence," see, e.g., "The Litany, or General Supplication, to be used after Morning Service . . .," *Book of Common Prayer* (1790), n.p.

114. GW, "Proclamation of Thanksgiving and Prayer," February 17, 1795, in Richardson, ed., *Papers of the Presidents,* 1:171–72.

115. See WGW, 35:215n84.

116. Foster, ed., *Washington's Farewell Address,* 17.

117. For Hamilton's "Original Major Draft for an Address Called 'Copy Considerably Amended,'" see Paltsits, ed., *Washington's Farewell Address,* 179–99.

118. GW, Farewell Address, in WGW, 35:229–30.

119. Jefferson, *Notes on Virginia,* Query XVII, in TJW, 285.

120. [William Loughton Smith], *Pretensions of Jefferson to the Presidency,* 1796, 1:37–38.

121. Green, *Life of Ashbel Green,* ed. Jones, 614–15; and GW to the Clergy of Different Denominations Residing in and near the City of Philadelphia [March 3, 1797], in WGW, 35:416.

122. Abraham Lincoln, General Orders No. 16, February 18, 1862, in *Papers of the Presidents,* 6:3306–8.

123. GW, "Washington's First Draft for an Address," May 15, 1796, in Paltsits, ed., *Washington's Farewell Address,* 170.

124. Hamilton, Major Draft, in Paltsits, ed., *Washington's Farewell Address,* 192.

125. GW, Farewell Address, in WGW, 35:220.

126. Alexander Hamilton, Major Draft, in Paltsits, ed., *Washington's Farewell Address*, 192.

127. GW, Farewell Address, in WGW, 35:229–30.

128. A. Confederation Congress, Ordinance of 1787: The Northwest Territorial Government, Article III, July 13, 1787, in *United States Code* (1995), 1:liii.

129. See, for example, Massachusetts Constitution of 1780, pt. 1, art. III, in Thorpe, ed., *Federal and State Constitutions*, 3:1189–90.

130. GW to David Humphreys, March 8, 1787, in WGW, 29:173.

131. For a discussion of "that veneration which time bestows on everything, and without which perhaps the wisest and freest governments would not possess the requisite stability," see *Federalist* 49, 314.

132. Novak and Novak, *Washington's God*, 15.

133. Novak and Novak, *Washington's God*, 15.

Epilogue

1. Wills, *Cincinnatus*, 3.

2. Thomas Jefferson, Resolution to the Board of Visitors, University of Virginia, March 4, 1825, in TJW, 479.

3. GW, Farewell Address, September 19, 1796, in GWW, 975.

4. GW, Farewell Address, September 19, 1796, in GWC, 519.

5. GW, Farewell Address, September 19, 1796, in GWC, 526.

6. GW, Farewell Address, September 19, 1796, in GWC, 527.

7. GW, Farewell Address, September 19, 1796, in GWC, 527.

8. See Wiencek, *Imperfect God*, 3–4.

9. "The unfortunate condition of the persons, whose labour in part I employed, has been the only unavoidable subject of regret. To make the Adults among them as easy & as comfortable in their circumstances as their actual state of ignorance & improvidence would admit; & to lay a foundation to prepare the rising generation for a destiny different from that in which they were born; afforded some satisfaction to my mind, & could not I hoped be displeasing to the justice of the Creator." GW, "Reflection on Slavery," [ca. 1788–89], in GWW, 701–2.

10. Thomas Jefferson, "Testament," March 16–17, 1826, in Padover, ed., *Complete Jefferson*, 1297.

11. Washington quoted in Kaminski, *Necessary Evil*, 244; see also Wiencek, *Imperfect God*, 362.

12. GW to John Francis Mercer, September 9, 1786, in GWW, 607.

13. See Wills, *Cincinnatus*, 235.

14. The trust fund began paying out when Martha manumitted the

slaves ahead of the schedule in Washington's will; it continued to do so until 1833. See WGW, 37:277n; also Wills, *Cincinnatus,* 234.

15. GW used the phrase "useful knowledge" twenty times in his correspondence between 1771 and 1798.

16. An early instance of this American "spin" on a British custom appeared in the Articles of Confederation (1777), which ended, "Done . . . the ninth day of July, in the Year of our Lord one Thousand seven Hundred and Seventy-eight, and in the third year of the independence of America."

17. GW, Last Will and Testament, July 9, 1799, in WGW, 37:275–94.

BIBLIOGRAPHY

Achenbach, Joel. *The Grand Idea: George Washington's Potomac and the Race to the West.* New York: Simon and Schuster, 2004.

Adcock, F. E. *Roman Political Ideas and Practice.* Ann Arbor: University of Michigan Press, 1959.

Addison, Joseph. *Cato: A Tragedy.* London: The Company of Booksellers, 1730; repr. Elibron Classics, 2003.

Antoninus, Marcus Aurelius. *Marcus Aurelius: Meditations.* Trans. Maxwell Staniforth. London: Penguin, 1964.

Aristotle. *The Basic Works of Aristotle.* Ed. Richard McKeon. New York: Random House, 1941.

Baker, Ray Stannard, ed. *Woodrow Wilson: Life and Letters.* 8 vols. Garden City, NY: Doubleday, Page, 1927–39.

Banning, Lance. "The Republican Interpretation: Retrospect and Prospect." In Milton M. Klein et al., eds., *The Republican Synthesis Revisited: Essays in Honor of George Athan Billias.* Worcester, MA: American Antiquarian Society, 1992.

Barrow, R. H. *The Romans.* Harmondsworth, UK: Penguin, 1951 [1949].

Beard, Charles A. *An Economic Interpretation of the Constitution.* New York: Macmillan, 1913.

Boller, Paul F. *George Washington and Religion.* Dallas: Southern Methodist University Press, 1963.

———. "George Washington and Religious Liberty." *The William and Mary Quarterly.* 3d ser. 17 (1960): 486–506.

The Book of Common Prayer. Oxford: T. Wright and W. Gill, 1769.

The Book of Common Prayer. Philadelphia: Hall and Sellers, 1790.

Boorstin, Daniel J. "George Washington and American Character." In Matthew Spalding and Patrick J. Garrity, *A Sacred Union of Citizens: George Washington's Farewell Address and the American Character,* ix–xviii. Lanham, MD: Rowman and Littlefield, 1999.

Bowen, Catherine Drinker. *Miracle at Philadelphia.* Boston: Little, Brown, 1986.

Bowen, Clarence Winthrop. "The Inauguration of Washington." *Century Magazine* 37 (1889): 803–33.

Bradley, Harold W. "The Political Thinking of George Washington." *Journal of Southern History* 11 (1945): 469–86.

Brookhiser, Richard. *Founding Father: Rediscovering George Washington.* New York: Free Press, 1996.

Carroll, Frances Laverne, and Mary Meacham. *The Library at Mount Vernon.* Pittsburgh: Beta Phi Mu, 1977.

Chernow, Ron. *Alexander Hamilton.* New York: Penguin, 2004.

Cicero Marcus Tullius. *De Re Publica; De Legibus.* Trans. Clinton Walker Keyes. Cambridge, MA: Harvard University Press, 1961 [1928].

———. *De Officiis.* Trans. Walter Miller. Cambridge, MA: Harvard University Press, 1975.

———. *On Obligations.* Trans. P. G. Walsh. Oxford: Oxford University Press, 2000.

Clark, Ellen McAllister, comp. "A Checklist of the Pamphlets in Bound Volumes in George Washington's Library." Unpublished manuscript. Library of the Society of the Cincinnati, Washington, D.C.

Crèvecoeur, J. Hector St. John de. *Letters from an American Farmer, and Sketches of Eighteenth-Century America.* New York: New American Library, 1963.

Curti, Merle. "The Great Mr. Locke, America's Philosopher," *Huntington Library Bulletin* 11 (1939): 107–51.

Cushing, Stanley Ellis. *The George Washington Library Collection.* Boston: Boston Athenaeum, 1997.

Custis, George Washington Parke. *Recollections and Private Memoirs of Washington.* New York: Derby and Jackson, 1860.

Dalzell, Robert F. Jr., and Lee Baldwin Dalzell. *George Washington's Mount Vernon: At Home in Revolutionary America.* New York: Oxford University Press, 1998.

The Debates and Proceedings in the Congress of the United States [*Annals of Congress*]. 18 vols. Washington, D.C.: Gales and Seaton, 1834–56.

Documentary History of the Struggle for Religious Liberty in Virginia. Ed. Charles F. James. Lynchburg, VA.: J. P. Bell Co., 1900.

Dreisbach, Daniel L. "George Mason's Pursuit of Religious Liberty in Revolutionary Virginia." *Virginia Magazine of History and Biography* 108 (2000): 5–44.

———. *Thomas Jefferson and the Wall of Separation between Church and State.* New York: New York University Press, 2002.

Dreisbach, Daniel L., and Jeffry H. Morrison. "Religion and the Presidency of George Washington." In *Religion and the American Presidency,* ed. Gaston Espinosa. New York: Columbia University Press, forthcoming.

Ebenstein, William and Alan Ebenstein, eds. *Great Political Thinkers: Plato to the Present*. 6th ed. Fort Worth, TX: Harcourt College Publishers, 2000.

Eisenach, Eldon J. *Two Worlds of Liberalism: Religion and Politics in Hobbes, Locke, and Mill*. Chicago: University of Chicago Press, 1981.

Elkins, Stanley M., and Eric L. McKitrick. *The Age of Federalism*. New York: Oxford University Press, 1993.

Ellis, Joseph J. *Founding Brothers: The Revolutionary Generation*. New York: Alfred A. Knopf, 2001.

The Encyclopedia of Philosophy. Ed. Paul Edwards. 8 vols. New York: Macmillan / Free Press, 1972.

Epstein, Stephen B. "Rethinking the Constitutionality of Ceremonial Deism." *Columbia Law Review* 96 (1996): 2083–2174.

Espinosa, Gaston, ed. *Religion and the American Presidency*. New York: Columbia University Press, forthcoming.

Evans, Charles. *American Bibliography: A Chronological Dictionary of All Books, Pamphlets and Periodical Publications Printed . . . in 1639 Down to and Including the Year 1820*. 14 vols. New York: P. Smith, 1941–59.

Fahim, Kareem. "Washington Letter Found in Scrapbook." *New York Times*, April 26, 2007.

Farrand, Max, ed. *The Records of the Federal Convention of 1787*. 4 vols. New Haven: Yale University Press, 1911–1937.

Fears, J. Rufus. "The Lessons of the Roman Empire for America Today." Washington, D.C.: Heritage Lecture No. 917, September 26, 2005.

Ferling, John. *Setting the World Ablaze: Washington, Adams, Jefferson, and the American Revolution*. Oxford: Oxford University Press, 2000.

Fischer, David Hackett. *Paul Revere's Ride*. New York: Oxford University Press, 1994.

———. *Washington's Crossing*. New York: Oxford University Press, 2004.

Flexner, James Thomas. *George Washington*. 4 vols. Boston: Little, Brown, 1965–72.

———. *Washington: The Indispensable Man*. Boston: Little, Brown, 1974.

Forbes, Esther. *Paul Revere and the World He Lived In*. Boston: Houghton Mifflin, 1942.

Ford, Worthington Chauncey, comp. *Inventory of the Contents of Mount Vernon*. Portland: Vice Regent from Oregon, 1909.

Franklin, Benjamin. *Benjamin Franklin: Writings*. Ed. J. A. Leo Lemay. New York: Library of America, 1987.

Freeman, Douglas Southall. *Washington: An Abridgement in One Volume by Richard Harwell of the Seven-Volume George Washington by Douglas Southall Freeman*. Ed. Richard Harwell. New York: Collier Books, 1992.

George, Alexander L., and Juliette L. George. *Woodrow Wilson and Colonel House: A Personality Study.* New York: Dover Publications, 1964 [1956].

Gordon, George, Lord Byron. *The Complete Poetical Works of Lord Byron: Cambridge Edition.* Ed. Paul Elmer More. Boston: Houghton Mifflin, 1905.

Grant, Michael. *The Twelve Caesars.* New York: Charles Scribner's Sons, 1975.

Green, Ashbel. *The Life of Ashbel Green, V.D.M., Begun to be Written by Himself in His Eighty-Second Year. . . .* Ed. J. H. Jones. New York: R. Carter and Bros., 1849.

Greene, Jack P., ed. *Colonies to Nation, 1763–1789: A Documentary History of the American Revolution.* New York: W. W. Norton, 1967.

Greenstein, Fred I. *The Hidden-Hand Presidency: Eisenhower as Leader.* Baltimore: Johns Hopkins University Press, 1994 [1982].

Gregg, Gary L. II, and Matthew Spalding, eds. *Patriot Sage: George Washington and the American Political Tradition.* Wilmington, DE: ISI Books, 1999.

Griffin, Appleton P. C., ed. *A Catalogue of the Washington Collection in the Boston Athenaeum.* Boston: Boston Athenaeum, 1897.

Gummere, Richard M. *The American Colonial Mind and the Classical Tradition.* Cambridge, MA: Harvard University Press, 1963.

———. "The Classical Ancestry of the United States Constitution." *American Quarterly* 14 (1962): 3–18.

Hamilton, Alexander, James Madison, and John Jay. *The Federalist Papers.* Ed. Clinton Rossiter. New York: New American Library, 1961.

Hartz, Louis. *The Liberal Tradition in America.* New York: Harcourt, Brace, and World, 1955.

Hay, Robert P. "George Washington: American Moses." *American Quarterly* 21 (1969): 780–91.

Heilbroner, Robert L. *The Worldly Philosophers.* 4th ed. New York: Simon and Schuster, 1972 [1953].

Henriques, Peter R. *The Death of George Washington: He Died as He Lived.* Mount Vernon, VA: Mt. Vernon Ladies' Association, 2000.

———. *Realistic Visionary: A Portrait of George Washington.* Charlottesville: University of Virginia Press, 2006.

Herndon, William H., and Jesse W. Weik. *Herndon's Life of Lincoln.* Greenwich, CT: Fawcett Publications, 1961 [1930].

Higginbotham, Don. *George Washington: Uniting a Nation.* Lanham, MD: Rowman and Littlefield, 2002.

Higginbotham, Don, ed. *George Washington Reconsidered.* Charlottesville: University Press of Virginia, 2001.

Hobbes, Thomas. *Leviathan.* Ed. Michael Oakeshott. New York: Macmillan, 1962.

Humphreys, David. *David Humphreys' "Life of General Washington" with George Washington's "Remarks."* Ed Rosemarie Zagarri. Athens: University of Georgia Press, 1991.

Hunt, George L., and John T. McNeill, eds. *Calvinism and the Political Order.* Philadelphia: Westminster Press, 1965.

Hyneman, Charles S., and Donald S. Lutz, eds. *American Political Writing during the Founding Era, 1760–1805.* 2 vols. Indianapolis: Liberty Press, 1983.

Jefferson, Thomas. *The Complete Jefferson.* Ed. Saul K. Padover. New York: Duell, Sloan, and Pearce, 1934.

————. *The Life and Selected Writings of Thomas Jefferson.* Ed. Adrienne Koch and William Peden. New York: Modern Library, 1993.

————. *The Papers of Thomas Jefferson.* Ed. Julian P. Boyd et al. 33 vols. to date. Princeton: Princeton University Press, 1950–.

————. *The Portable Thomas Jefferson.* Ed. Merrill D. Peterson. New York: Penguin, 1975.

————. *Thomas Jefferson: Writings.* Ed. Merrill D. Peterson. New York: Library of America, 1984.

Johnson, Paul. *George Washington: The Founding Father.* New York: HarperCollins, 2005.

————. *A History of the American People.* New York: HarperCollins, 1997.

Ketcham, Ralph. *Presidents Above Party: The First American Presidency, 1789–1829.* Chapel Hill: University of North Carolina Press, 1984.

Kinnaird, Clark. *George Washington: The Pictorial Biography.* New York: Hastings House, 1967.

Klein, Milton M. et al., eds. *The Republican Synthesis Revisited: Essays in Honor of George Athan Billias.* Worcester, MA: American Antiquarian Society, 1992.

Kloppenberg, James T. "The Virtues of Liberalism: Christianity, Republicanism, and Ethics in Early American Political Discourse." *Journal of American History* 74 (1987): 9–33.

Knott, Stephen F. *Secret and Sanctioned: Covert Operations and the American Presidency.* New York: Oxford University Press, 1996.

Kurland, Philip B., and Ralph Lerner, eds. *The Founders' Constitution.* 5 vols. Chicago: University of Chicago Press, 1987.

Lancaster, Bruce, and J. H. Plumb. *The American Heritage Book of the Revolution.* New York: Dell, 1958.

Locke, John. *Two Treatises of Government.* Ed. Thomas I. Cook. New York: Hafner Press, 1947.

Lombardi, Michael J. "Taking the Measure of Washington . . . Once

More." *Colonial Williamsburg: The Journal of the Colonial Williamsburg Foundation* (Summer 2005): 72–78.

Longmore, Paul K. *The Invention of George Washington.* Berkeley: University of California Press, 1988.

Lossing, Benson J. *The Home of Washington.* Hartford, CT: A. S. Hale, 1870.

Lucas, Stephen E. Review of *A Sacred Union of Citizens: George Washington's Farewell Address and the American Character,* by Matthew Spalding and Patrick J. Garrity. *Journal of American History* 84 (1998): 1492–93.

Lutz, Donald S. "The Relative Influence of European Writers on Late Eighteenth-Century American Political Thought." *American Political Science Review* 78 (1984): 189–97.

Madison, James. *Notes of Debates in the Federal Convention of 1787.* Ed. Adrienne Koch. New York: W. W. Norton, 1987 [1966].

Marshall, John. "Eulogy on Washington" [December 26, 1799]. In Gary L. Gregg II and Matthew Spalding, eds., *Patriot Sage: George Washington and the American Political Tradition,* 287–98. Wilmington, DE: ISI Books, 1999.

———. *The Life of George Washington.* 5 vols. Philadelphia: C. P. Wayne, 1804–07.

Mason, George. *The Papers of George Mason.* Ed. Robert A. Rutland. 3 vols. Chapel Hill: University of North Carolina Press, 1970.

McCullough, David. *John Adams.* New York: Simon and Schuster, 2001.

McDonald, Forrest. *The Presidency of George Washington.* Lawrence: University Press of Kansas, 1994.

McMichael, George et al., eds. *Anthology of American Literature: Colonial through Romantic.* New York: Macmillan, 1974.

Meade, William. *Old Churches, Ministers, and Families of Virginia.* 3 vols. Baltimore: Genealogical Publishing Co., 1966 [1857].

Medhurst, Martin J. "From Duché to Provoost: The Birth of Inaugural Prayer." *Journal of Church and State* 24 (1982): 573–88.

Moehlman, Conrad Henry. *The Wall of Separation between Church and State: An Historical Study of Recent Criticism of the Religious Clause of the First Amendment.* Boston: Beacon Press, 1951.

Morgan, Edmund S. *The Genius of George Washington.* New York: W. W. Norton, 1980.

———. *The Meaning of Independence: John Adams, George Washington, Thomas Jefferson.* New York: W. W. Norton, 1976.

Morison, Samuel Eliot. *The Young Man Washington.* Cambridge, MA: Harvard University Press, 1932.

Morrison, Jeffry H. *John Witherspoon and the Founding of the Ameri-*

can Republic. Notre Dame, IN: University of Notre Dame Press, 2005.

Mount Vernon: A Handbook. Mount Vernon, VA: Mount Vernon Ladies' Association of the Union, 1985.

Novak, Michael, and Jana Novak. *Washington's God: Religion, Liberty, and the Father of Our Country.* New York: Basic Books, 2006.

Paltsits, Victor Hugo, ed. *Washington's Farewell Address.* New York: New York Public Library, 1935.

Pangle, Thomas L. *The Spirit of Modern Republicanism: The Moral Vision of the American Founders and the Philosophy of Locke.* Chicago: University of Chicago Press, 1988.

Pauley, Matthew A. *I Do Solemnly Swear: The President's Constitutional Oath: Its Meaning and Importance in the History of Oaths.* Lanham, MD.: University Press of America, 1999.

Pfander, James E. "So Help Me God: Religion and Presidential Oath-Taking," *Constitutional Commentary* 16 (1999): 549–53.

Phelps, Glenn A. *George Washington and American Constitutionalism.* Lawrence: University Press of Kansas, 1993.

Plato. *The Collected Dialogues of Plato, Including the Letters.* Ed. Edith Hamilton and Huntington Cairns. Princeton: Princeton University Press, 1961.

Plutarch. *The Lives of the Noble Grecians and Romans.* Trans. John Dryden. Rev. Arthur Hugh Clough. New York: Modern Library, n.d.

Poore, Benjamin Perley, ed. *The Federal and State Constitutions, Colonial Charters and Other Organic Laws of the United States.* 2 vols. Washington, D.C.: Government Printing Office, 1877.

Porter, Roy. *The Creation of the Modern World: The Untold Story of the British Enlightenment.* New York: W. W. Norton, 2000.

Randall, Willard Sterne. *George Washington: A Life.* New York: Henry Holt, 1997.

Reinhold, Meyer. *Classica Americana: The Greek and Roman Heritage of the United States.* Detroit: Wayne State University Press, 1984.

Riccards, Michael P. *A Republic, If You Can Keep It: The Formation of the American Presidency: 1700–1800.* New York: Greenwood Press, 1987.

Richardson, James D., ed. *A Compilation of the Messages and Papers of the Presidents, 1789–1902.* 10 vols. Washington, D.C.: Bureau of National Literature and Art, 1905.

Rossiter, Clinton. *The American Presidency.* 2d ed. New York: Harcourt, Brace, and World, 1960.

Rousseau, Jean-Jacques. *The Basic Political Writings of Jean-Jacques Rousseau.* Trans. and ed. Donald A. Cress. Indianapolis: Hackett Publishing, 1987.

Schutz, John A. and Douglass Adair, eds. *The Spur of Fame: Dialogues of John Adams and Benjamin Rush, 1805–1813.* San Marino, CA: Huntington Library, 1966.

Schwartz, Barry. "George Washington and the Whig Conception of Heroic Leadership." *American Sociological Review* 48 (February 1983): 18–33.

Seneca, Lucius Annaeus. *Seneca's Morals by Way of Abstract. To Which is Added a Discourse, under the Title of an After-Thought.* Ed. Sir Roger L'Estrange. 9th ed. London: Jacob Tonson, 1705.

Shalhope, Robert E. "Toward a Republican Synthesis: The Emergence of an Understanding of Republicanism in American Historiography." *Willliam and Mary Quarterly,* 3d ser., 29 (1972): 49–80.

Sheldon, Garrett Ward. *The Political Philosophy of James Madison.* Baltimore: Johns Hopkins University Press, 2001.

———. *The Political Philosophy of Thomas Jefferson.* Baltimore: Johns Hopkins University Press, 1991.

Shy, John. "Franklin, Washington, and a New Nation." *Proceedings of the American Philosophical Society* 131 (1987): 308–24.

Smith, Richard Norton. *Patriarch: George Washington and the New American Nation.* Boston: Houghton Mifflin, 1993.

Solberg, Winton U., ed. *The Constitutional Convention and the Formation of the Union.* 2d ed. Urbana: University of Illinois Press, 1990.

Spalding, Matthew, and Patrick J. Garrity. *A Sacred Union of Citizens: George Washington's Farewell Address and the American Character.* Lanham, MD: Rowman and Littlefield, 1996.

Stevens, Richard G. "George Washington and the Constitution." In *The American Constitution and its Provenance,* 97–106. Lanham, MD: Rowman and Littlefield, 1997.

Stokes, Anson Phelps. *Church and State in the United States.* 3 vols. New York: Harper and Brothers, 1950.

Thomas, Joseph, comp. *Universal Pronouncing Dictionary of Biography and Mythology.* 4th ed. Philadelphia: J. B. Lippincott Co., 1915.

Thornton, Bruce S., and Victor Davis Hanson. "'The Western Cincinnatus': Washington as Farmer and Soldier." In Gary L. Gregg II and Matthew Spalding, eds., *Patriot Sage: George Washington and the American Political Tradition,* 39–60. Wilmington, DE: ISI Books, 1999.

Thorpe, Francis N., ed. *The Federal and State Constitutions, Colonial Charters, and Other Organic Laws of the States, Territories, and Colonies Now or Heretofore Forming the United States of America.* 7 vols. Washington, D.C.: Government Printing Office, 1909.

Thucydides. *History of the Peloponnesian War.* Trans. Rex Warner. Baltimore: Penguin, 1954.

Tocqueville, Alexis de. *Democracy in America*. Trans. George Lawrence. Ed. J. P. Mayer. New York: Harper and Row, 1969.

Toner, J. M. "Some Account of George Washington's Library and Manuscript Records and Their Dispersion from Mount Vernon, with an Excerpt of Three Months from His Diary in 1774 while Attending the First Continental Congress, With Notes." In *Annual Report of the American Historical Association for the Year 1892*, 73–111. Washington, D.C.: Government Printing Office, 1893.

Vidal, Gore. *Inventing a Nation: Washington, Adams, Jefferson*. New Haven: Yale University Press, 2003.

Washington, George. *The Diaries of George Washington*. Ed. Donald Jackson and Dorothy Twohig. 6 vols. Charlottesville: University Press of Virginia, 1976–79.

———. *George Washington: A Collection*. Ed. W. B. Allen. Indianapolis: Liberty Classics, 1988.

———. *George Washington Himself: A Common-Sense Biography Written from His Manuscripts*. Ed. John C. Fitzpatrick. Indianapolis: Bobbs-Merrill, 1933.

———. *George Washington: Writings*. Ed. John Rhodehamel. New York: Library of America, 1997.

———. *Maxims of Washington: Political, Social, Moral, and Religious*. Ed. John Frederick Schroeder. 3d ed. New York: D. Appleton and Co., 1855. Repr. Harrisonburg, VA: Sprinkle Publications, 1995.

———. *The Papers of George Washington*. Ed. W. W. Abbot et al. 50 vols. to date. Charlottesville: University Press of Virginia, 1983–.

———. *The Writings of George Washington, from the Original Manuscript Sources, 1745–1799*. Ed. John C. Fitzpatrick. 39 vols. Washington, D.C.: Government Printing Office, 1931–44.

White, Leonard D. *The Federalists: A Study in Administrative History*. Westport, CT: Greenwood Press, 1978 [1948].

White, Morton. *The Philosophy of the American Revolution*. Oxford: Oxford University Press, 1978.

Wiencek, Henry. *An Imperfect God: George Washington, His Slaves, and the Creation of America*. New York: Farrar, Straus and Giroux, 2003.

Wills, Garry. *Cincinnatus: George Washington and the Enlightenment*. Garden City, NY: Doubleday, 1984.

Witherspoon, John. *The Works of John Witherspoon*. 9 Vols. Edinburgh: Ogle and Aikman et al., 1804–05.

Witte, John Jr. *Religion and the American Constitutional Experiment*. 2d ed. Boulder, CO: Westview Press, 2005.

Wood, Gordon S. *The American Revolution*. New York: Modern Library, 2002.

INDEX